ORGANIZED LABOR
IN LATIN AMERICA

the text of this book is printed
on 100% recycled paper

Crosscurrents in Latin America
Edited by Joseph S. Tulchin

Roberto Cortés Conde	THE FIRST STAGES OF MODERNIZATION IN SPANISH AMERICA
Tulio Halperin-Donghi	THE AFTERMATH OF REVOLUTION IN LATIN AMERICA
Jorge Hardoy	LATIN AMERICAN CITIES
Harmannus Hoetink	SLAVERY AND RACE RELATIONS IN THE AMERICAS
Jay Kinsbruner	CHILE: A HISTORICAL INTERPRETATION
Anthony P. Maingot	PERSONALISM IN LATIN AMERICA
Gilbert Merkx	TWENTIETH-CENTURY LATIN AMERICA
Hobart A. Spalding, Jr.	ORGANIZED LABOR IN LATIN AMERICA
Joseph S. Tulchin	LATIN AMERICA IN WORLD AFFAIRS

ORGANIZED LABOR IN LATIN AMERICA

Historical Case Studies of Workers in Dependent Societies

HOBART A. SPALDING, JR.

HARPER TORCHBOOKS
Harper & Row, Publishers
New York, Hagerstown, San Francisco, London

ORGANIZED LABOR IN LATIN AMERICA. Copyright © 1977 by Hobart A. Spalding, Jr. All rights reserved. Printed in the United States of America. No part of this book may be used or reproduced in any manner whatsoever without written permission except in the case of brief quotations embodied in critical articles and reviews. For information address Harper & Row, Publishers, Inc., 10 East 53rd Street, New York, N.Y. 10022. Published simultaneously in Canada by Fitzhenry & Whiteside Limited, Toronto.

First edition: HARPER TORCHBOOKS, 1977

LIBRARY OF CONGRESS CATALOG CARD NUMBER: 76–55499

ISBN: 0–06–131923–6

77 78 79 80 81 10 9 8 7 6 5 4 3 2 1

CONTENTS

PREFACE

Six years' intermittent research and writing went into this book, which scarcely resembles the initial draft proposal. Its evolution flowed naturally from the material and from comments and criticisms offered by friends, colleagues, and audiences at scholarly gatherings. Bits and pieces of this work formed part of presentations at the American Historical Association, the Columbia University Seminar on Latin America, the Latin American Studies Seminar at the University of Indiana in Bloomington, the Rutgers University Conference on Labor and Social Change in the Americas, the Center for Cuban Studies, the California State University at Los Angeles Conference on Argentina, the Latin American Studies Association, the Yale University Graduate Seminar on Latin America, and the Southwest Labor History Conference.

The research was done on trips to Latin America in 1967, 1970, and 1972 and at the International Institute for Social History in Amsterdam in 1973. Most of the work, however, was done in the Columbia University libraries, the New York Public Library, and the Library of Congress. I would like to thank especially the staff of the Latin American, Portuguese, and Spanish Division of the Library of Congress for their enormous help. For their help in preparing the manuscript, thanks go to Martha Livingston, Marthalena Avendaño, Merriam Ansara, and above all, Martha Salper. In palmier days, the History Department of Brooklyn College of CUNY provided funds for typing.

Many persons criticized parts of the manuscript within their areas of expertise. Valuable suggestions came from Gordon Adams, David Barkin, Alex Georgadis, Mike Hall, Tim Harding, Mike Locker, Paulo Sérgio Pinheiro, and Steve Volk. And to Ken

Erickson and Pat Peppe I owe a great debt. The hours that we spent discussing Latin American labor while writing papers and articles served to sharpen my thinking and added greatly to my knowledge. Their careful readings of the manuscript proved invaluable. Finally, special appreciation and love go to two persons whose constant aid and support allowed me to complete this work: to Bruce Maliver, whose patience and skill helped create the space in which to write, and to my *compañera,* Renate Bridenthal, whose love and understanding are matched only by her critical editorial eye and intellectual companionship.

INTRODUCTION

The working class, along with the peasantry, constitutes the vast majority of Latin American society. Despite this fact, scholars have devoted scant attention to it. That situation has begun to change, but significant gaps in our knowledge still exist. This book seeks to advance the study of one aspect of working-class history: urban organized labor. It synthesizes older and newer scholarship and formulates a series of hypotheses and theories concerning both the national and the global development of labor movements. It also raises research problems and areas for future investigation.[1]

The argument is based on the premise that labor history can be understood best within the larger context of the world economy. Within this framework, three variables have influenced labor's evolution: fluctuations of the international economy and decisions taken by governments in advanced capitalist nations; the composition of, and tensions between, the international and the local ruling classes; and the composition, structure, and historical formation of the working class. The impact of external events and domestic-foreign interrelations determined that broad trends emerged at roughly the same time throughout Latin America. However, national circumstances also influenced the tide of events, and therefore, local labor movements have their own particular histories.[2]

Each chapter explores both national and international dimensions. Chapters 1 and 2 treat the period prior to 1930 across the continent. Chapter 1 examines labor's formative period, during which working-class organizations first appeared and labor movements took on characteristics that shaped later developments. Chapter 2 explores the expansive and explosive period from World War I to the Depression. It specifically analyzes the spread of labor organization to new sectors of the working class and new geographic areas and looks at the series of violent outbursts that marked the 1920s. Chapter 2 also demonstrates the ways in which the introduction of new ideologies and the evolution of older ones shaped the movement.

Chapters 3 to 6 present individual case studies that demonstrate patterns found after 1930 in varied contexts. Their overarching theme is co-optation and repression. During that period, the state, having largely recognized the right to organize, sought to curb labor's power. On one hand, it attempted to co-opt individuals and organizations by legislating economic or social improvements in the hope that workers would remain temporarily satisfied and support the existing system; on the other, it forcefully repressed labor's attempts to change the system or to act independently. The specific means differed in each nation and over time, but ruling-class goals remained the same.

Chapter 3 concentrates on Mexico as a transition between pre- and post-1930 patterns. There, the 1910 Revolution cut short trends that appeared after 1850 and initiated others that emerged elsewhere only after 1930. Chapter 4 examines labor and populism in Argentina under General Juan D. Perón (1943–1955) and in Brazil during the regimes of Getúlio Vargas (1930–1954) and João Goulart (1961–1964). Labor and revolution in Bolivia and Cuba are the topics of Chapter 5. Chapter 6 turns to the international arena by tracing relationships between national labor movements and imperialist agencies.

A number of crucial concepts need definition. The term *North America* refers to the United States, *Latin America* means all the Latin countries to the south. *Communist* or *Socialist* indicates either a specific political party or identifies one of its members. The terms *reformist*, *progressive*, and *revolutionary* correspond to specific political attitudes. Reformists wish to change a given system by using mechanisms sanctioned by that system while retaining its basic features. Under capitalism, that means preserving private property and the corresponding legal system. Progressives call for more substantive changes by means that may or may not involve a restructuring of society. Progressives, however, may sharpen contradictions, thus increasing the potential for change. For example, they may advocate nationalization of specific sectors of the economy, severe restrictions on foreign capital, or significant income redistribution. These measures are not revolutionary in themselves, but they can induce conflict between interest groups such as labor and the national or international ruling class. These conflicts, in turn, can lead to situations that mobilize or radicalize sectors of society or that place radical solutions on the national political agenda. Revolutionaries, in contrast, expressly aim to overthrow the existing system of property and power relationships, using a variety of means, including armed struggle. They may see that overthrow as an immediate or a long-range possibility, but it always constitutes their final goal.

This analysis assumes a two-class schema incorporating the ruling and the working classes. However, neither class is monolithic. The ruling class owns and controls the means of production. It monopolizes power in the industrial, agricultural, and financial spheres. Its members usually run the society's principal institutions, such as the church, the administrative apparatus, the military, and the judiciary. Those who actually hold office may not be members of the ruling class, but they act as its representatives. The ruling class thinks of itself as a group, but its members do not act always in concert. Subgroups based on specific interests, such as industry, agriculture, or ties to international capital, may oppose each other or even forge temporary cross-class alliances to bolster their own position. Thus constant tensions arise between segments of the ruling class. In this context, the term *ruling elite* refers to that fraction of the ruling class or its representatives that holds power at the particular time. The term *bourgeoisie*, national or international, is interchangeable with the term *ruling class*.

Identifiable subgroups also exist within the working class. Industrial and agricultural workers, for example, at times adopt different short-range aims; employed and unemployed people may also perceive divergent goals; white- and blue-collar workers frequently see their interests as contrary; and workers in different sectors of the economy, such as those tied to domestic capital and those linked to foreign investment, may take opposite sides on issues of national or labor policy.

The terms *middle groups* and *middle sectors* mean white-collar and professional workers as distinguished from blue-collar workers. Members of the middle groups include students, government employees, lawyers, doctors, and office workers. Finally, in order to avoid repetition, the term *movement* refers to organized labor as a whole, as does the generic term *labor*.

Any short history of organized labor obviously has limitations. Areas such as Central America, Colombia, Ecuador, and Uruguay are largely neglected here. Their exclusion, due in part to the paucity of available material, does not indicate that their historical experiences lie outside patterns found elsewhere. On the contrary, they fully share a common heritage and present. The original manuscript of this study included the examples of the Chilean Popular Front (1936–1948) in the examination of populism and the Guatemalan experience (1944–1954) as a part of the discussion of labor and revolution. Unfortunately, considerations of space caused their deletion. The chapter on populism might have included studies of labor under Acción Democrática in Venezuela or APRA in Peru as instances of conservative, reformist populism. The recent case of the Chilean Unidad Popular government (1970–1973), which received massive working-class support, might have served as another example of radical populism. Finally, rural labor lies mostly outside this treatment despite its importance in working-class history.

Other major topics are touched on only briefly. For example, the questions of tactics, internal union organization, and working-class culture are not discussed in detail. Instead, this book focuses on labor as an actor upon the national scene and on interactions between the working class and the national and international ruling classes. As in any synthesis, there are exceptions to the generalizations presented. Some of my hypotheses derive from fragmentary sources, and future studies will surely modify them.

A number of general themes and conclusions emerge from this

study. Local conditions hinder the development of underdeveloped areas. Within the world capitalist economy, these areas are conditioned by the development and expansion or contraction of the developed areas. International capitalism limits the range of possibilities open to underdeveloped areas because the ruling class controls vital factors, such as access to export markets, the price and supply of manufactures and technology, the availability of capital for direct and indirect investment, and the conditions under which such capital is or is not forthcoming.[3]

These pages explore one dimension of this dependency by examining relationships between the international economy and ruling class, the domestic ruling classes or elites, and labor. The first two mightily influence labor's evolution. The growth of export economies after 1880, the temporary restoration of prosperity in the 1920s, the Great Depression, World War II, and the postwar recovery after 1945 under U.S. hegemony all shaped national labor movements in similar ways. Each period also conditioned the composition of local ruling classes. By opening opportunities or limiting options available to ruling elites to accomplish their goals, these stages affected the interaction between labor and the ruling class. Local bourgeoisies responded to each circumstance according to their own internal dynamics, in turn a product of their relative cohesion and their sense of threat from external and internal forces. In the nineteenth century, ruling classes almost universally refused to accept the existence of organized labor as a national power factor. Their tolerance, however, depended not only upon labor's ability to oppose them but also upon the degree to which they perceived labor as a threat. In Argentina, agrarian elites felt less threatened by urban labor than did agrarian-industrial elements in Brazil. As a result, the Argentine state pursued a less repressive policy toward labor than did its Brazilian counterpart.

Economic cycles also conditioned labor's evolution by opening or closing opportunities for workers. Dependency both helped and hindered the growth of working-class organizations and affected their ability to act. The existence of economies based on the export of a single product, for example, enhanced labor's possibilities of attacking the system by concentrating efforts in the export sectors. The beginning of industrial development raised the demand for skilled labor, and that demand aided organization because skilled workers were harder to replace.

External factors influenced Latin American labor in other ways. The movement adopted foreign ideologies. Anarchism, syndicalism, communism, and parliamentary socialism, for example, all originated in Europe. Only a local variant of populism, which emerged in the 1930s and 1940s, can be called distinctive. Nevertheless, its appearance also responded to historical events produced by outside happenings, specifically the Depression and World War II. Labor legislation also was modeled on laws passed either in Europe or in North America. Finally, after 1945, imperialist agencies sought to mold those Latin American labor organizations and political parties that appealed to workers in favor of their own policies.

The argument that outside factors played a crucial role in local history does not deny the importance of domestic events. Latin American labor history displays a remarkable unity, but significant national differences also exist. Nor does the historical process unfold at an even pace. Specific configurations determined that particular areas vary from dominant patterns. The Mexican Revolution of 1910 accelerated labor's development by temporarily shattering ruling-class cohesion. As a result, the co-optive–repressive stage began earlier in Mexico than it did in most nations. By the 1930s, however, the others "caught up" on the historical continuum. The Bolivian Revolution also served as an accelerating factor. Events in Bolivia from the 1930s to the 1950s telescoped stages that took other nations longer to pass through. As an area of backward labor development in 1930, Bolivia experienced a rapid growth of working-class activity that was capped by the 1952 Revolution and its aftermath.

Finally, a high degree of disunity characterized the movement at all times. Labor seldom if ever organized or operated independently; its fortunes have always been tied to political parties or power blocs at the national level. Only occasionally has it occupied the center stage. Even in Cuba's Revolution of 1959, it played a supporting rather than a leading role.

However, the working class never abandoned its struggle. The persistence of workers in organizing and fighting to improve their lives remains constant throughout Latin American labor history. These pages record their struggle for a new and more just society. But the impersonality of the written word is painfully clear. Every action, every episode, sometimes recorded in a single line, reference, or footnote, involved real people, each with hopes, angers, and aspirations. They lived that past, and they live this present. It is these anonymous human beings who collectively created the historical events that follow, and it is they who will create the ones to come.

NOTES

1 Existing works surveying Latin American labor are Robert J. Alexander, *Organized Labor in Latin America* (New York, 1965); Moisés Poblete Troncoso and Ben G. Burnett, *The Rise of the Latin American Labor Movement* (New Haven, Conn., 1960); Victor Alba, *Politics and the Labor Movement in Latin America* (Stanford, Calif., 1969); and Carlos Rama, *Mouvements ouvriers et socialistes: L'Amérique Latine: 1492–1936* (Paris, 1959). Each contains valuable information but is mostly descriptive.

2 Earlier formulations of these theses appeared in Hobart A. Spalding, Jr., "The Parameters of Labor in Hispanic America," *Science & Society* 36, no. 2 (Summer 1972): 202–216; and Kenneth Paul Erickson, Patrick V. Peppe, and Hobart A. Spalding, Jr., "Research on the Urban Working Class and Organized Labor in Argentina, Brazil, and Chile: What Is Left to Be Done?" *Latin American Research Review* 9, no. 2 (Summer 1974): 115–142.

3 For a discussion of dependency theory and labor, see Kenneth Paul Erickson and Patrick V. Peppe, "Dependent Capitalist Development, U.S. Foreign Policy, and Repression of the Working Class in Chile and Brazil," *Latin American Perspectives* 3, no. 1 (Winter 1976): 19–44.

1

THE FORMATIVE PERIOD: FROM THE FIRST STEPS TO WORLD WAR I

The years before World War I constitute the formative period for Latin American organized labor. During that period, the continent's first labor organizations were formed and the movement acquired the basic characteristics that shaped its later course. Developments mirrored those in Europe, largely because of the links between Latin America and Europe. Increasing integration into the world capitalist system through the growth of exports and substantial foreign investment consolidated a new stage in Latin American socioeconomic evolution and brought capitalist development based on the Old World model. The resulting growth of large export-import–oriented urban centers, expansion of the service sector, increase in light manufacturing industries, and heightened exploitation of primary products all influenced the formation of an ever larger working class. They also created new conditions that favored the emergence of working-class organizations, just as the initial stages of modern capitalist growth had in Europe and North America.[1]

Within Latin America, the level of organization varied widely, and local circumstances conditioned labor's development. In Argentina, Brazil, and Chile, for example, full-scale movements appeared that included significant pockets of workers. In Ecuador, Venezuela, and Central America, on the other hand, few workers managed to organize on a permanent basis. Objective conditions did lead workers to seek improvement in their lives through collective actions, but with divergent results.

The qualitative advance represented by collective action emerged partly in response to an acceptance of new ideologies of European origin. Anarchism, revolutionary syndicalism, socialism, and reformism emerged as the strongest. Liberal political parties and a

Catholic social movement also competed for worker allegiance. And in some countries, the beginnings of state paternalism further confused the situation.

Starting in the 1840s, a variety of organizations turned their attention to working-class problems, and a modern labor movement gradually emerged. At first, mutual-aid societies, liberal political movements, and utopian experiments were the principal forms of organization. Toward the end of the nineteenth century, faced with the failure to improve their lot and under the influence of European working-class philosophies, workers moved toward more militant expressions of their goals and sought more adequate forms through which to achieve their aims. By World War I, unions, federations, and confederations constituted the predominant working-class organizational vehicles. In addition, political parties representing workers' interests formed in several nations.

Numerically, the movement remained small despite heroic struggles. Although conflicting ideologies and state and employer opposition hindered working-class organization, some groups within the working class succeeded in improving their position. Highly skilled railroad workers and typographers, for example, achieved real economic gains. The Argentine movement, by far the strongest at the time, demonstrated its strength by closing down major urban centers through general strikes, and some of its members won substantial improvements in both living and working conditions. In addition, representatives from worker-oriented political parties won local or congressional office in Argentina, Chile, Cuba, and Uruguay. Although the vast majority of workers remained unorganized, by 1914 an embryonic movement existed throughout the continent, and workers in most large cities had taken collective action.

OBJECTIVE CONDITIONS

Workers throughout Latin America lived and worked under miserable conditions. This fact, more than any other, spurred people to action. The workday averaged twelve, fourteen, even seventeen hours. Employees in commercial establishments often began duty at 5:00 or 6:00 A.M., sometimes serving as watchmen by sleeping on the premises. Peruvian miners, for example, worked thirty-six hours, rested twelve, and then returned for another thirty-six-hour shift. In rural areas, custom dictated that laborers toil from sunup to sundown with only short breaks for meals.[2]

On the job, employers practiced no industrial hygiene, and disease and occupational hazards constantly threatened workers. Owners scarcely took safety precautions and considered accidents the responsibility of the workers. Repressive internal regulations governed most factories. In Buenos Aires, for example, any worker who arrived ten minutes late lost a quarter-day's pay; unacceptable work had to be paid for; protest resulted in dismissal; factories set salaries fifteen days after initial employment; and workers could not talk, smoke, wash, or change clothes before the quitting bell. Infractions resulted in fines, some owners subjected employees to corporal punishments, and male supervisors often sexually exploited women.[3]

Living conditions matched working conditions. Industry tended to locate in large urban areas. The concentration of people and the increasing value of urban real estate drove rents steadily upward. More people crowded into less space, paying higher sums for small accommodations. One source cites that slum rents rose an average of 14 percent annually in downtown Buenos Aires between 1890 and 1912. Dwellings called *cortiços* (literally, "beehives") in São Paulo and *conventillos* in Montevideo and Buenos Aires housed a large proportion of the working class that lived near city centers. Single structures covered entire blocks, and whole families crowded into the small rooms, many of them windowless, that honeycombed these buildings. In São Paulo, four to six persons occupied each room, and the average living space measured ten by eighteen by ten feet; even so, Brazilian workers enjoyed slightly more space than their Argentine counterparts. In most slum housing, a central water supply and bathroom served all inhabitants, and Draconian internal regulations matched those posted in factories. As workers gradually moved to the suburbs, a development greatly facilitated by the advent of the tramway, slums grew around core cities. Shacks made of wattle and daub, often with sheet metal roofing, surrounded many cities. Living conditions in these newer slums often resembled those of downtown areas.[4]

In the countryside, industrial and mining companies sometimes provided housing. At one time considered an obligation, although also attracting workers, company towns became another source of profit. Under the guise of caring for workers, a firm would build houses and then rent them at nominal rates. In the long run, the company secured a return on its capital, promoted a positive image, and assured itself of a docile labor force because workers lost their required down payments if fired. Company housing in isolated areas around mining camps and textile mills also provided management with a lever against workers considered troublesome. In Mexico, for example, fired workers had to vacate their houses on the same day that they were dismissed. As one observer said, in Brazil, "few are the industrialists who concern themselves with the problem of workers' houses. Of these none does so in a humanitarian or altruistic spirit."[5]

The average worker's financial status mirrored his or her living and working situation. Constant inflation marked these years, generally accelerating during the final decades of the nineteenth century as the economic tempo across the continent quickened. Wage levels steadily lagged behind prices. One study concluded that because of the steady inflation in Chile it is "doubtful if real wages rose," while in Brazil there might have been a small rise in money wages during the last half of the nineteenth century. Another study found that real wages in Mexico declined by some 57 percent between 1876 and 1910. Data for Argentina indicate that the average unskilled worker probably received the same real wages in 1914 as in 1890.[6] Available evidence thus suggests little, if any, improvement in the real economic situation of the working class as a whole, although wide variations existed within each country and special groups, such as the highly skilled, improved their financial position over the years.

Workers faced additional difficulties. Often they were paid irregularly and sometimes not at all. In isolated workplaces such as the mines in northern Chile, Mexican textile communities, or sugar estates in Argentina and Peru, company stores monopolized commerce. To conserve cash and enhance profits, companies often paid salaries in scrip that could either be spent at the store or exchanged for real money at a substantial loss. Company stores also extended credit at high interest, thus keeping workers perpetually in debt and binding them to their jobs. A 1912 congressional investigative committee report in Chile cited a mining office that paid 75 percent of its salaries in scrip and noted that the company made about 15 percent on its investment in the store. Companies further exploited workers by deducting from their pay fees for services such as infirmaries or a doctor, even when those services did not exist, and foremen could fine workers arbitrarily for a variety of reasons.[7]

Workers faced still other uncertainties. Contracts, particularly in rural areas, often consisted of verbal agreements, which were easy to break or change. Illiterates signed papers they could not read. When a surplus of labor existed, a company might fire everybody and hire others at lower pay. Many men worked on a day-to-day basis. On the docks, jobs depended upon the amount of cargo to load and unload; in the construction trades, straw bosses selected gangs from a daily shape-up. Seasonal factors complicated the economic cycle. Rural workers often spent several idle months after the harvest, some commuting between city and countryside in search of supplementary employment.[8] The legal system favored employers. Police usually sided automatically with bosses. Under vagrancy laws passed in several areas, unemployed persons could be rounded up and carted off to work. In some areas, virtual slavery still existed. One particularly flagrant case surfaced in Mexico, where rural landowners found it cheaper to starve workers to death and replace them rather than pay the cost of food.[9]

WORKING-CLASS IDEOLOGIES

During the 1870s and 1880s, a growing acceptance of new and more militant ideologies led to the emergence of a modern labor movement. These doctrines, adopted from Europe but at times molded to local circumstances, served as guides for workers seeking to improve their lives. Before 1870, names and labels meant little. But as ideological lines hardened in both Europe and Latin America, workers deepened their knowledge of existing theory and intensified the search for a solution to daily problems. Accordingly, descriptive titles assumed more concrete meaning and reflected increasingly systematic stances on the part of individuals and organizations.

Movement activists and ideologues agreed that the owners of the means of production (the capitalists) exploited workers, but they favored differing solutions to end this relationship. In all, three ideological currents most influenced working-class movements: Socialism, revolutionary syndicalism or anarchosyndicalism, and anarchism or anarchocommunism. At times, exact differences blurred, and both individuals and organizations often combined features from more than one ideology. Their principal tenets, however, can be summarized by examining their attitudes toward the state, labor organization, and tactics.

Throughout Latin America, the predominant position within Socialist groupings closely mirrored that of European Social Democrats, who made up the right wing of the Socialist movement on the Continent. Although this position had not yet abandoned long-range goals, such as the socialization of the means of production, it stressed immediate gains within the framework of the state as it existed. It emphasized changes within the system, holding that legal means could satisfactorily reform prevailing socioeconomic patterns as a first step toward more radical changes. Socialists thus particularly urged electoral organization. They held that all activity should be directed through a legal political party to which unions were subordinate. They believed that peaceful protest could achieve socialism's short-range goals and generally shunned violent confrontation, preferring to use constitutional guarantees, the right of assembly, and petitions. Socialists supported unlawful acts or general strikes only in extreme situations, and then they generally called for limited participation.

Anarchosyndicalists or revolutionary syndicalists saw the industrial proletariat and the bourgeois state and ruling class locked in a perpetual antagonism within which no compromise was possible. Rather than reform the system, they aspired to take over and then transform the state. They held that only coordinated efforts of unions of wage earners working together to undermine and then destroy the economic power of the capitalists, who controlled the state, could achieve this end. They claimed that the general strike constituted the proletariat's principal weapon. Wage earners, organized into a cohesive block operating through a central organization, the Federation of Syndics, would plan joint action. After uniting all workers, this body would proclaim the final general strike to paralyze the economy, bankrupt the capitalists, and take over the means of production. The workers would then control the state, the federation would form the governing body, and the wage-earning population would become the collective ruling and property-owning group. In reality, however, most syndicalists eventually came to recognize the state's immediate power. As a result, they sometimes called short-term strikes for local or limited demands that they believed would build the movement for the future.

Anarchocommunists rejected any concepts of a state and of private property. They, too, agreed that organized groups of workers should band together for self-defense, but they projected a loose federation of unions that would allow both individuals and organizations substantial freedom. The ultimate goals of this brand of anarchism were the destruction of the state and its replacement by a society in which small groups of individuals made basic decisions. Like syndicalists, they believed that only an unlimited, spontaneous general strike could eliminate the state; but they, too, sometimes limited the duration of a particular action. In addition, they believed that the existing state held power by force and therefore illegitimately; thus violence or lawbreaking constituted a just and moral retaliation against repressive mechanisms.

Independent and reformist groups also existed. The former refused to endorse any ideology; the latter sought only immediate improvements for workers.

In daily concrete actions, groups did not always behave consistently with their stated ideologies. Conflicts between differing points of view led to compromises, as did the realities of specific situations. The rank and file did not always grasp the intellectual nuances of a particular doctrine, and so theory sometimes became less important than the workers' immediate perceptions of existing reality.

THE SPREAD OF IDEAS

Several circumstances aided the spread of ideas. Foreign immigrants played a major role in the process. In all, just under 10 million persons emigrated to Latin America before World War I; almost 8 million of them went to Argentina and Brazil, which actively encouraged immigrants. They generally settled in urban zones, although many farmed or worked on the land. Foreign-born men and women made up more than 50 percent of the population over eighteen in Buenos Aires by 1900, and in that city and in São Paulo foreigners constituted two-thirds of the industrial work force. Liberal immigration laws allowed Europeans fleeing political persecution to settle in Latin America. Groups of German Socialists escaping Bismarck's anti-Socialist laws and ex-Communards from France emigrated to Argentina, Brazil, and Chile.[10]

By far the largest number of immigrants came from Italy and Spain, and anarchism's strong roots in both those countries partly account for its strength throughout Latin America. The majority from these two nations settled in the Platine basin and southern Brazil, but they also made notable contributions elsewhere. Between 1895 and 1912, some 30,000 skilled workmen emigrated to Chile from Spain and northern Italy. Spaniards also influenced the development of the Cuban movement along anarchist lines. Even in areas that did not attract massive immigration, foreigners greatly aided working-class organization. They played important roles in both Paraguay and Mexico, while Austro-Hungarians, Jews, Poles, and Russians also took part in the movement, particularly in Argentina.[11] The overall importance of foreigners is hard to measure. A student of Brazilian labor, however, recently calculated that of 119 significant leaders active between 1890 and 1920, 67 percent were foreign-born. A partial listing of workers' groups in Argentina and Brazil at the turn of the century supplies another indication of the breadth and scope of foreign participation; eight distinct nationality groups took part in these organizations.[12]

Latin Americans who traveled to Europe absorbed the ideas and tactics of the European left and thus also contributed to the dissemination of ideology. Camilo Arraga returned to Mexico with a considerable library; Luis Emilio Recabarren, a Chilean, and Juan B. Justo, an Argentine Socialist leader, both sharpened their thinking while on European trips. Foreign residents and visitors also helped build working-class movements and raise workers' consciousness. Enrico Malatesta and Pietro Gori, reknowned Italian anarchists, traveled to Latin America. Malatesta spent four years in Argentina, aiding in the formation of anarchist groups and writing extensively. Gori, as part of a world tour, gave speeches and talked to workers in Argentina, Chile, and Paraguay. Permanent residents such as Rafael Barrett, Bartolomé Victory Suárez, and Germán Ave Lallemant in the Platine basin also contributed to the intellectual formation of the working class and to organizing activities.[13]

But not all influential foreigners came from Europe. A delegate from the American Brotherhood of Railwaymen visited Argentina and Chile in 1887, aiding in the formation of railway unions. Similarly, North Americans employed by Mexican railroads shared their experiences and ideas with fellow workers.

The steady growth of internal communications aided the circulation of people and ideas. Railroads expanded rapidly after 1880, linking urban centers and in some cases crossing national boundaries. At the same time, coastal and river trade increased, adding another means by which workers could travel to propagandize. These developments meant that news reached more people, inspiring some to act by example, and it facilitated the nationwide coordination of workers' actions.

An expanding working-class press also helped ideas and news spread. European Socialist and anarchist newspapers circulated throughout Latin America, and hundreds of local publications printed theoretical articles and accounts of events at home and abroad. A foreign-language press flourished in centers of immigration, and several newspapers published multilingual editions. In 1896, *O Socialista*, a São Paulo Socialist paper, printed articles in German, Italian, Portuguese, and Spanish. The anarchist daily *La Protesta* of Buenos Aires ran articles for a time in both Yiddish and Spanish and published pieces in Italian.[14]

Most radical periodicals had a precarious and often brief existence, but some achieved a circulation of 3,000 to 4,000. The Buenos Aires Socialist daily *La Vanguardia* claimed a press run of 50,000 copies for a special May Day issue.[15] Despite severe handicaps, such as lack of money and government censorship, many periodicals survived. *La Vanguardia* (founded in 1894), *La Protesta* (1897), and *Avanti!* (1900) continued publishing until well after 1914. Most working-class papers ran a wide variety of articles by local participants and extensive translations of articles and books from abroad. A number of European publishing houses distributed books and pamphlets throughout Latin America, often in inexpensive popular editions, and local presses issued books and pamphlets.[16]

Although much of the pamphlet literature has been destroyed or lost, surviving collections give some idea of its scope. In Buenos Aires, the continent's leading publishing center, anarchist literature alone amounted to several hundred titles by Latin Americans and foreigners, often issued in several editions of up to 10,000 copies each. They included theoretical discussions, plays, speeches, almanacs, and translations of classic works. The writings of all leading theoreticians, including Marx and Engels, Bakunin, and Kropotkin, circulated widely, as evidenced by Spanish-language versions published in Buenos Aires.[17]

At the same time, a gradual rise in literacy meant that more workers had access to these publications. Although as much as 80 percent of the Mexican and Brazilian populations could not read or write, urban areas and immigrant centers boasted much higher literacy rates. In São Paulo, for example, literacy in 1887 stood at 45 percent overall, but over half the foreign population could read and write. Literacy rates for all of Argentina reached 63 percent by 1914, but in Buenos Aires, it rose from 60.5 percent in 1887 to 82.2 percent in 1914. Moreover, workers who could not read learned from their comrades during family gatherings, café conversations, social outings, union meetings, or in jail.[18]

GENERAL CONDITIONS FAVORING LABOR ORGANIZATION

A number of factors favored the development of labor organizations. The growth of a large-scale export trade and the influx of foreign investment linked Latin America to the international economy in new ways after 1880. Argentina and Uruguay sent meat, grains, hides, and wool to Europe; Brazil expanded its coffee exports; Chile and Mexico stepped up mineral production for sale abroad; and Cuba emerged as the world's tobacco and cane sugar capital. Modernization of transport systems, ports, and commercial-financial centers accompanied this process. Capital cities and leading provincial centers grew in size, and industry developed along with consumer demand. Imports of manufactured products, technology, and capital from Europe completed Latin America's economic interchange. The quickened pace of economic activity, in turn, generated specific conditions that aided workers once they decided on collective action to improve their lives. Almost without exception, worker militancy and the level of working-class organization reached their highest points in those nations that experienced the greatest jump in economic activity as measured by the growth of export-import indexes and foreign investment.

The slow, steady growth of light industry and the transport sector aided possibilities for organization in a number of ways. The number of industrial workers increased, and larger factories presented a chance to organize more persons at a time. The need for skilled workers as production became more mechanized meant that owners found it harder to recruit and replace key workers. Mechanization also bred an interdependency among workers that could form a basis for collective action. Industrialization placed economic pressures on artisans who manufactured products largely by hand in their own shops. Moreover, these artisans usually could read and write and often possessed a tradition of independent action. Many movement militants, mostly anarchists or anarcho-syndicalists, came from an artisanal background. And last, expanded transportation systems allowed workers to travel across the land to neighboring cities or other countries.

Constant population growth and increasing urbanization reflected in industrial expansion and a rise in the number of white-collar jobs. As previously noted, in several countries immigrants accounted for a proportion of the demographic expansion and played an important role in labor organizing. Foreign workers constituted a majority of the industrial proletariat in Argentina, Brazil, and Uruguay and usually occupied a large percentage of positions requiring higher skills. Although at times vulnerable to deportation, immigrant workers often proved less malleable than nationals because of their prior exposure to collective action and their previous work experiences. Working-class neighborhoods, sometimes based on nationality, provided excellent conditions for building solidarity around personal relationships. In rural areas, closed and isolated communities such as mining camps or villages huddled next to textile mills offered comparable opportunities. There men toiled together, wives met while shopping or washing, and families frequently gathered on social occasions.

Economic dependence on exports that generated money for needed imports also opened possibilities for effective organization and action. Most governments relied heavily on customs taxes. Any stoppage in foreign trade struck a hard blow at ruling groups. In such situations, two courses remained open: either to crush strikes before they gained momentum or to secure labor peace quickly through concessions. Several factors aided labor in this situation. Many export items—wheat, for example—needed relatively quick shipment lest they spoil, and idle ships or empty rail cars cost exporters money every day. Moreover, many workers in the export-import–related industries tended to be highly skilled and hard to replace. Working conditions in this sector also favored organizational growth; dockers and railroad men, for example, worked in teams. The tough, dangerous process of unloading and loading ships, in which loose cargo, a carelessly balanced load, or a poorly tied knot could result in serious accident, led dockers to form affinity groups. Workers on the production end of the export process also depended on one another. In the mines, for example, badly placed explosives or failure to watch for cave-ins or lack of air in tunnels could spell the difference between life and death. As a result, mutual trust among open-pit and underground workers became a necessity.

In general, the economic vulnerability of individual employers helped successful organizing. Marginal workshops or factories could survive only brief closings when struck, and most establishments at the time were marginal. Brazilian construction workers, for example, were among the first to win their demands in that country. Small contractors hired people for jobs with specific termination dates. Therefore, any stoppage threatened quick bankruptcy because contractors paid heavy penalties for delays. Thus they often soon granted improvements in order to get workers back on the job.[19]

Less tangible factors also provided a basis for organization. Notions of national identity occasionally served as grounds for solidarity. Cubans, for example, organized to gain access to the jobs in the tobacco industry that were reserved for Spaniards. Wage differentials and job discrimination in favor of foreigners lay behind several strikes in Mexico in the mining and railroad industries.[20]

Foreign exploitation often served as a rallying point for workers. Chilean miners and Mexican textile workers singled out foreign-owned factories and stores as particular targets for their wrath. Xenophobia on the part of ruling elites sometimes made it easier for workers to act. Strikes against foreign companies at times elicited less immediate and less repressive government actions than those involving local firms. The Argentine government, for example, did not immediately move against the so-called Great Strike of 1912 against British-owned railroads. Popular clamor in the face of the companies' arrogance in defying the law led the government to mediate a settlement by which some workers gained economic concessions and other demands.[21]

GENERAL CONDITIONS RETARDING LABOR ORGANIZATION

Workers faced numerous obstacles in the struggle to organize. Established law and custom often precluded labor organizations. Of necessity, the movement first formed outside existing legal frameworks. As one participant said, "We were not against the law, the law was against us."[22] Backed by the law, states curbed disruptions of social peace or the economy with force, and the workers had few defenses.

Sometimes, low levels of consciousness hindered organizational efforts. With some exceptions, workers knew little about their rights or about ways to better their lives. A strong tradition of paternalism only gradually eroded, even in industrial settings. In some areas (Brazilian textile mills, for example) hard-to-organize groups such as minors and women constituted a substantial proportion of the labor force. Even among the immigrant population, workers remained relatively unmilitant. As a result, a highly vocal minority rather than the mass of workers carried forward the movement.[23]

Furthermore, ideological splits weakened actions by workers. Internal conflicts between anarchists, syndicalists, and socialists doomed many organizations or divided workers in the same factory or trade into smaller and therefore weaker groups. The existence of rival organizations that often refused to support each other or spent energy combating one another further tended to reduce the movement's overall impact.

The workers' precarious economic situation also circumscribed their ability to act. Most people lived on the brink of starvation and could not afford union dues or save for payless days during strikes or lockouts. Thus strikes that were not immediately repressed usually lasted only a few days. In addition, most urban areas had a pool of hungry, able-bodied people, a situation that allowed owners to replace strikers or organizers almost at will except when they required skilled operatives.

Lastly, nationality differences worked against the movement as well as for it. Although ethnic affinity led at times to solidarity, it also served as a wedge that employers could exploit. Newcomers often accepted low wages, and owners used them to replace workers receiving higher pay rates. Persons of a particular nationality tended to form work gangs, and bosses hired their compatriots. At times, tensions between rivals looking for work erupted into pitched battles in which nationals were usually pitted against immigrants. Antagonisms also stemmed from differences in language, customs, and work attitudes and from prevailing social bigotry that assigned inferior status to specific immigrant groups.[24]

ORGANIZATION

The First Steps

The first organized activity by workers took place in mutual-aid societies, liberal political parties, and utopian experiments. All three proved abortive as permanent forms of working-class activity, and by the last decades of the nineteenth century, unions supplanted them as focal points for collective action. Nonetheless, they provided many workers with important organizational experiences and sowed intellectual seeds that later bore fruit under the impact of more militant working-class ideologies.

Mutual-aid societies initially appeared shortly before 1850 and by the end of the century had spread throughout the continent. Artisans composed a majority of their membership, but most admitted owners of artisanal shops, and some even included a substantial representation of factory owners and professionals. In many cases, the societies provided owners with a means to regulate entry into a trade and paternalistic control over workers. The statutes of one mutual-aid society stated that its purpose was to "watch over the conduct, morality, and interests of the trade; [and] establish rules of organization and hierarchy among its members."[25] In general, the aims of the societies remained limited. In return for a monthly payment, members received accident, sickness, and death benefits when needed. At times, societies ran employment centers and schools for workers or their children.

Others offered savings plans, lent money at reasonable rates, and established cooperatives.[26]

The vast majority of societies functioned as isolated entities in determined geographic areas. Often they accepted members from only one work center. Others limited membership to persons of specific nationalities. In Paraguay, for example, 11 societies in 1887 represented seven different nationalities; a similar situation existed in São Paulo; and in Cuba organizations divided along both national and racial lines. The largest mutualities attracted several hundred members, with the most extensive networks developing in Chile and Mexico. In Chile, 269 functioned by 1910, and a loose national confederation of societies was formed.[27]

A scattering of societies took more aggressive positions, usually under the influence of anarchists following in the tradition of the Frenchman Pierre Joseph Proudhon. Before the Mexican Gran Círculo de Obreros was taken over by Juárez Liberals in the 1870s, it pledged itself to the "struggle for the complete emancipation of the working class . . . to be conducted by the workers themselves, using as their ultimate weapon the social revolution." In 1882, this same organization, which endorsed a Liberal program at its 1876 convention, claimed over 50,236 active members in more than a hundred affiliated associations across the nation.[28]

Liberal politicians and intellectuals and, occasionally, Liberal governments aided future organizations by spreading progressive European ideas and by founding a variety of entities that incorporated workers. The general Liberal attack against entrenched Conservatives in the late nineteenth century often included limited acceptance of social movements and social programs. Brazilian abolitionists sometimes advocated measures to improve free-workers' rights. The Chilean Generation of 1842 and its successors formed a series of clubs at which many workers heard lectures and readings on egalitarian concepts. In Mexico, the followers of Benito Juárez actively encouraged artisans' societies and advocated some workers' rights. Similarly, in Bolivia and Paraguay, nineteenth-century Liberal governments subsidized mutual-aid societies.[29]

Workers also experimented with alternative life-styles by founding a variety of utopian communities. Between 1840 and 1870, there were unsuccessful attempts in Brazil, Chile, and Mexico to form colonies on the model proposed by the Frenchman Charles Fourier. A group of European immigrants led by the Italian anarchist Giovanni Rossi established a communistic settlement in Brazil on government-donated land. After struggling for nearly five years, the colony disappeared in 1893, a fate shared by a Cuban experiment based on that of the Rochdale pioneers.[30]

Unions, Federations, and Confederations

Unions, federations, and confederations of unions, political parties, and temporary community-action groups constituted the principal types of working-class organization after 1870. The economic and social changes of the late nineteenth century, easier access to militant working-class ideologies, and the failure of previous forms of organization to improve their lives significantly led more and more workers to seek new forms of struggle. Gradually, the first modern unions formed, and a labor movement appeared that spread over entire nations and, eventually, the whole continent. This process took place unevenly. In Central America and Venezuela, there were only a few signs of workers' activity during these years. But in Argentina, Brazil, Chile, and Uruguay, organization reached a relatively high level of expression.

Unions, federations, and confederations formed in almost every country, but their effectiveness, longevity, and character varied. Most tended to be small, ephemeral groupings confined to a particular trade or workplace. In some areas, however, strong national networks developed; in other areas, unions in similar trades or representing geographic regions formed confederations.

The Federación Obrera Regional Argentina (FORA) developed into the largest and most important federation in all Latin America, but it still could not rally the majority of unions or workers in Argentina. Its history illustrates the problems faced by the movement everywhere. Between 1890 and 1901, four attempts to build a central organization failed. In 1901, yet another effort resulted in a new entity, which soon became the FORA. Anarchists captured a majority at the organization's congress in 1902, and independents and Socialists withdrew and founded a rival federation that combined Socialist and syndicalist unions. This grouping lasted until 1906, when it dissolved following disagreements between the two political positions. Syndicalists then fashioned a separate labor body that convened a series of unification meetings with the FORA. The two organizations momentarily fused on the eve of the Great War, but the unity soon collapsed in the face of renewed factional disputes.[31]

Other attempts to form a single central federation proved less successful. In Uruguay, following a decade of inactivity, the movement revived after 1896. The Federación Obrera Regional Uruguaya (FORU), with anarchosyndicalist tendencies, vied with a Socialist entity. As in Argentina, many unions remained unaffiliated with either federation. The FORU attained less influence than its Argentine counterpart and by 1911 no longer represented an important force within the then flagging movement. Similarly, a Paraguayan federation founded in 1906 lasted only a few years; and the Brazilian Confederação Operária Brasileira (COB), formed in the same year with member unions drawn from the main cities, never achieved a level of effectiveness comparable to that of the FORA. In Chile, despite at least five attempts, no single federation emerged until just before World War I, and sporadic efforts to establish a national federation in Mexico failed to bear fruit.[32]

Uniting workers in a particular trade or on a regional basis proved a simpler task. A number of such groupings operated with mixed results; the strongest appeared among port workers, railroaders, and typographers, trades demanding a relatively high level of skill. As early as 1892, an International Maritime League boasted branches in Chilean and Peruvian Pacific ports. The Argentine dockers' federation, which joined unions along the entire Platine coast, held regional congresses in 1904 and 1906 attended by members from twelve Argentine and Uruguayan ports. The same organization maintained contacts with Brazilian dockers, and union representatives from all three countries signed a solidarity pact pledging reciprocal action during strikes.[33]

Federations of workers in specific trades functioned in other areas, too. In Chile, a league of typographers included unions in five cities; a breadmakers' organization listed affiliates from seven cities; and a shoemakers' group claimed members from Santiago and Valparaíso. On a provincial level, workers from both Santiago and Tarapacá attempted to coordinate activities, and a number of provincial federations formed in Argentina.[34] Finally, confederations of tobacco workers, railroad personnel, textile workers, typographers, and several artisanal groups existed before 1910 in Mexico City and other urban areas of Mexico.

Agrarian organization remained backward, and conditions in rural areas continued to be almost feudal during this period. The best-organized movement in the countryside developed in Argentina, not coincidentally an area of relatively advanced capitalist agriculture. There, tenant farmers' strikes in Santa Fe province in 1912 spread to adjoining areas and, aided by Socialist Party organizers, enjoyed some success. However, the goal of achieving a permanent, militant agrarian movement eluded organizers. Several agrarian leagues formed in Mexico during the 1870s and 1880s but did not survive; in addition, anarchists or peasant leaders educated by them led a series of rebellions, almost all of which quickly succumbed to superior government forces. Coffee workers in Brazil and Colombia and laborers on large Peruvian sugar estates also protested violently against existing conditions, but their actions represented spontaneous outbursts rather than serious attempts to form lasting organizations.[35]

Political Parties and Other Forms of Organization

Anarchosyndicalists and anarchists dominated most unions. Adherents to these positions consistently maintained that workers should not participate in bourgeois politics. Socialists and independents, who endorsed political action within the existing system as a means of changing it, usually found themselves outnumbered in the union movement. Despite this fact, both Socialists and independents formed unions that played an important role in these years. Many Socialists, however, devoted their energies more to building a political party than to unionizing workers. As a result, almost all political parties exclusively espousing workers' causes either hewed to a Socialist position or contained a substantial membership of that persuasion.

These parties achieved limited success. A few elected candidates to office, but most waged futile electoral campaigns, and many did not survive long enough to build an electoral base. In Chile, six attempts to found a working-class party brought meager results. The Partido Socialista, formed in 1900, soon foundered because of ideological conflicts between reformists and revolutionaries. The Partido Obrero Socialista (POS), born at Iquique in 1912, had a more solid worker base. Its statutes stipulated that members must join a union and prohibited electoral alliances with bourgeois parties; moreover, it succeeded in electing one of its representatives to national office. The Cuban experience mirrored the Chilean. Six parties of varying tendencies sprang into existence between 1898 and 1912; most proved short-lived, but the Partido Socialista Obrero successfully ran candidates for town council in Manzanillo in 1908 and 1912.[36]

Socialists convened two congresses in Brazil between 1892 and 1902, endorsing a reformist platform echoing European Social Democratic views at the second gathering. The party included sections from leading urban centers. A number of factors—repressive conditions, the fact that southern European immigrants who made up the majority of the urban proletariat remained more attuned to anarchistic ideologies, and the impossibility of reformist politics within the Brazilian political system, which severely limited the right to vote—combined to blunt the party's effort. As a result, socialism never took firm root in the country. The Uruguayan party, although never large numerically, elected a candidate to the national legislature in 1910 with the help of Liberal votes, and it consistently drew sizable electoral support in Montevideo and other urban areas.[37]

The Argentine Socialist Party proved the strongest, best organized, and most effective in Latin America. Shortly after its formation in 1896, a moderate, reformist leadership composed mostly of intellectuals with university degrees gained a majority position over more radical elements. Initially, the party actively organized among the working class, but after splitting with the syndicalists in 1906, it de-emphasized this activity. The party's strength centered in the city and province of Buenos Aires, but it drew support in other urban areas. In 1904, it succeeded in electing a candidate to the Chamber of Deputies and prior to World War I won several additional victories in provincial and local elections. After the vote was extended and the secret ballot guaranteed in 1912, Socialists regularly elected candidates to both the Senate and the Chamber. The party also continued to win occasional provincial and municipal elections.[38]

In Mexico, a group of anti-Díaz dissident intellectuals founded the Partido Liberal Mexicano (PLM) in 1905. An outgrowth of the network of Liberal clubs that spread across Mexico after 1900, it served as a training ground for future revolutionaries and a focal point for the dissemination of ideas, winning some influence within the embryonic labor movement. The party's Manifesto of 1906 clearly outlined a comprehensive sociopolitical program for workers, and PLM members, most of them anarchists, worked within unions. Persecuted in Mexico by the Díaz regime and in the United States, where many of its members took refuge, it managed to survive, and its newspaper, *Regeneración*, which appeared irregularly as a result of political pressures, became an important forum for movement news and ideas.[39]

Most working-class people did not belong to any group or organization. However, when latent antagonisms between working and ruling classes exploded, they formed temporary organizations to deal with their immediate problems. In Santiago, ad hoc committees demanded a series of measures to lower the steadily rising cost of living in 1905, only to meet with violence when the government tried to prevent mass rallies. The 1907 Buenos Aires rent strikes provide another example of temporary organization. Increases in slum rents led to the formation of strike committees throughout the city; some 10 percent of the population—over 100,000 people—joined the action. Violence erupted here, too, when police harassed meetings and landlords forcefully evicted those withholding payment. Strikers won temporary triumphs in many cases, but because of insufficient housing, rents again spiraled upward shortly thereafter.[40]

THE MOVEMENT'S SIZE AND SCOPE

Organized labor grew numerically and spread to new geographic areas throughout this period. In places where activity lagged, only a few thousand workers participated. In other areas, 10 percent of the urban labor force may have joined some organization. In Argentina, the scene of this period's most intense struggles, as many as one out of every four urban workers took part in some form of collective effort. The movement also spread from larger cities to provincial towns and, to a far lesser extent, penetrated the countryside.

In Chile, labor activity indicates a steady growth in participation by workers. Between 1884 and 1889, some 60 strikes or actions occurred; in the next decade, over 300 strikes erupted. From 1870 to 1890, the number of workers' organizations grew from thirteen to seventy-six, although most incorporated only a few people. In the north, the *mancomunales*, a mixture of mutual-aid society and union, claimed as many as 6,000 members, and a 1902 congress said that it represented 20,000 workers. On the other hand, government statistics for 1908 show an average of only 62 persons per strike, implying a restricted mass base and probably indicating that activity remained confined to local actions in a single trade or workplace. Official figures, however, do not include secondary movements or general strikes. Action in mining areas, ports, or urban centers drew substantial support once started. Spontaneity proved to be one of the Chilean movement's characteristics, and strikes spread like brush fires through whole areas with little or no apparent preplanning.[41]

In Brazil, industrial centers such as São Paulo and Rio de Janeiro and ports such as Santos became movement focal points. By 1914, seventy-four unions had formed in São Paulo state, and at least 143 strikes had been called. Labor's largest actions, such as generalized strikes in São Paulo in 1906, 1907, and 1912 and the Rio textile strike in 1903, mobilized tens of thousands of workers, but individual organizations remained relatively small. The 1906 workers' congress attracted representatives from fewer than fifty unions; a 1912 congress attracted representatives from only sixty-two groups.[42]

Similar patterns appeared in Mexico. The Círculo de Obreros boasted 8,000 members in 1876, and over 250 strikes occurred in the Díaz period (1876–1910) despite the fact that he outlawed them. One contemporary estimated that in 1909 the seven leading organizations had a membership of 16,000 and that the railroad workers' union alone represented 10,000 persons. In specific instances, general strikes paralyzed whole industries across the country. In 1906, textile workers closed ninety-three different establishments. Data from Uruguay suggested the limited scope of the movement there. By 1905, some thirty-eight unions existed; but judging from available information, they probably numbered no more than 50 workers each. In 1912, the FORU counted on about 7,000 members out of over 80,000 urban workers.[43]

In Argentina, new unions formed, and worker activity increased sharply, particularly in Buenos Aires, in response to rising inflation after 1884. By 1895, at least twenty-five organizations functioned in the capital, and activity had spread to most major cities and smaller towns in the populated eastern provinces. Ten years later, the FORA claimed forty-one member unions in addition to five provincial federations that, in turn, represented fifty-three additional organizations. The fusion congress of 1907 attracted delegates representing over 120 organizations.[44]

Argentine unions appear to have been larger than those elsewhere, averaging about 100 members. The railroad engineers' and trainmen's organization, La Fraternidad, founded in 1887, soon grew into one of the largest. Taking a militant but almost always nonviolent position, it won several important strikes and enrolled over 7,000 dues payers. The printing trades federation counted about the same number of members after its consolidation in 1906; and other groups, such as the coachmen, attracted over 1,000 persons.[45] Participation in most unions, however, varied widely, depending upon their level of activity, the workers' economic situation, and immediate circumstances. Table 1 illustrates this

TABLE 1. MONTHLY DUES PAYERS, FEDERACIÓN
OBRERA LOCAL BONAERENSE (FOLB)

	Dues Payers		Dues Payers
October 1906	3,167	January 1907	2,291
November 1906	4,654	February 1907	7,794
December 1906	11,685	March 1907	3,734

SOURCE: Diego Abad de Santillán, *La F.O.R.A.: Ideología y trayectoria del movimiento obrero revolucionario en la Argentina,* 2d ed. (Buenos Aires, 1970), p. 166.

fluctuation. In this instance, membership grew as the FOLB's parent organization, the FORA, prepared for a January strike. After that action, as a result of which many workers lost their jobs or paydays, membership declined drastically, no doubt reflecting the facts that some workers could no longer afford dues and that others became disillusioned.

The number of workers mobilized provides a truer measure of the movement. In the Buenos Aires general strike of 1907, a Socialist newspaper estimated that 93,000 workers in sixteen trades left their jobs (the police calculated 80,000). Of these, 31,000 actively participated in a union, but only 10,000 regularly paid dues. If this example is typical, the labor movement reached far beyond the number of persons who belonged to organizations. Government statistics, kept only after 1907, registered 231 strikes in the capital that year (not including the general strike), in which 169,017 workers participated, or an average of 731.6 workers per strike. Clearly, at times the movement reached considerable proportions.[46]

The data in Table 2 combined with other information suggest further generalizations about the size and scope of the Argentine movement. First, there was a steady growth in the number of strikes after 1880 and then a proliferation as the movement

TABLE 2.   STRIKES IN ARGENTINA, 1880–1913

	Total	Strikes			Causes		% in Buenos Aires
		Won	Lost	Neither	Salary	Other	
1880–1890	48	21	21	6	40	11	94
1891–1896	58	26	24	8	38	38	83
1907–1913[a]	1,081	328	634	119	—	—	—

[a] In Buenos Aires only.

SOURCES: Julio Godio, *El movimiento obrero y la cuestión nacional, Argentina: Inmigrantes asalariados y lucha de clases, 1880–1910* (Buenos Aires, 1972), pp. 58–59, 62–63, 102–104; Hobart A. Spalding, Jr., *La clase trabajadora argentina: Documentos para su historia, 1890–1912* (Buenos Aires, 1970), p. 88.

flowered in the years immediately before World War I. Second, strikes spread to areas outside of Buenos Aires, accelerating after 1896. During 1903–1904, for example, only 56 percent of all actions occurred in the capital. A reversal seems to have set in thereafter. In the final years of the century's first decade, strikes in Buenos Aires outnumbered those in provincial areas by about 7 to 1. This trend probably reflects a second wave of organizational activity that began in the capital and then spread to other areas. Unfortunately, a lack of data for subsequent years do not allow a test of this hypothesis.[47]

Argentine political organizations that appealed to the working class failed to attract a mass following. The Argentine Socialist Party, which grew slowly and steadily, proved to be an exception. By 1912, it listed sixty-two sections, eighteen in the capital and forty-four elsewhere. Membership, however, did not keep pace; as of 1912, it counted no more than 4,000 adherents. The party's voting strength, on the other hand, multiplied. In 1896, it drew 1,700 votes in Buenos Aires; after electoral laws passed in 1912 mandated both a secret ballot and compulsory voting, its strength grew dramatically, reaching almost 50,000 in a local election held in Buenos Aires. The number of union members who voted Socialist cannot be determined, but the party polled well in working-class districts. However, the vast majority of workers still did not support the party, in part because foreigners could not vote, and because rival working-class groups advised electoral abstention.[48]

WORKERS' DEMANDS AND ACTIVITIES IN THEORY AND PRACTICE

Both workers' demands and the types of action undertaken by organizations changed over the years. At the same time, unions, federations, confederations, and political parties clarified their positions and developed more concrete strategies and increasingly militant and sophisticated tactics. In addition to job-related actions, the movement carried on activities designed to improve the quality of the worker's life at home and to promote workers' solidarity at the national and international levels.

The specific demands and goals of labor changed in content over time. The first strikes were generally defensive responses by workers who sought to recover purchasing power lost through inflation, to restore wage cuts, or to protest against a lengthened workday. Local issues such as protests against harsh work rules, demands for regular payment in hard currency, or abolition of the company store also cropped up in lists of grievances presented by workers to employers. After 1900, particularly in those areas where the movement reached its highest stage of development, labor broadened its efforts, demanding recognition of unions, reinstatement of dismissed comrades, accident insurance, and improved hygienic conditions. Workers also struck in solidarity with those already engaged in struggles against employers.

Table 2 suggests the pattern of changing demands in Argentina. From 1881 to 1890, a vast majority of strikes involved primarily economic issues. Between 1891 and 1896, economic grievances motivated only half of the strikes, and this trend probably continued. Government statistics for Buenos Aires, for example, show less than 40 percent of all strikes concerned solely with economic demands between 1907 and 1910.[49] This change reflects a gradual growth in workers' consciousness through the realization that material improvements alone could not create a more desirable life.

Theoretical considerations directly influenced organizational programs and tactics. Anarchists and syndicalists tended to avoid immediate, concrete goals in their platforms, preferring broad principles about the nature of struggle or generalizations concerning society's future. Their position flowed from the belief that circumstances dictated immediate tactics and from the firmly held tenet that the workers should decide each case as it arose and should not become locked into a dogmatic program. As a result, these groups often cited ends such as the socialization of the means of production and liquidation of the bourgeois state, or they endorsed class struggle and the general strike, omitting mention of the concrete means and tactics that might achieve them. The Uruguayan FORU, for example, declared in favor of "the realization of anarchic communism or libertarianism"; its Paraguayan counterpart proclaimed that it sought a "federation of free associations of free producers."[50]

Socialists usually outlined detailed programs that included lists of specific demands and a minimum program, but they also formulated longer-range goals. In general, Socialist programs followed those of European parties and concentrated on economic reforms of the system. An examination of programs put forth in Argentina, Brazil, Chile, and Cuba reveals eleven points in common; three parties endorsed eight other points. The most salient were the eight-hour day, free education, inheritance taxes, direct elections, lower cost of living, and a variety of measures designed to make workplaces safer for men, women, and children. Many Socialist parties tended to adopt reformist positions for the short run, stressing immediate gains rather than class warfare; a Brazilian group, for example, advocated that "exploited and exploiters should work together for social 'readjustment.' "[51]

The strike developed into the most widely used weapon. However, its nature varied from area to area and over time. Before the emergence of national organizations, it usually occurred in a single factory or trade in a given locale. Later, after the development of regional or national labor bodies, general strikes became common. These divided into two types: strikes on a national or local level that embraced, in theory at least, all workers in a trade (e.g., shoemakers) or in related trades (e.g., port or construction workers) and strikes that involved the entire working population of a city or even a country, a goal obviously less attainable during this period.

Ten general strikes of the second type erupted in Argentina during the first decade of the century. Some paralyzed only larger cities like Buenos Aires or Rosario; but others also affected smaller urban areas and mines, quarries, or rural workplaces. In other nations, the general strike was used less extensively and, when called, had limited impact because of labor's weakness. Nevertheless, in individual instances, such as the strikes called by Mexican and Chilean miners, or textile and railroad workers in a half-dozen countries, they proved temporarily effective.

Anarchists and syndicalists in particular used the general strike, but working people of all persuasions called and participated in stoppages. Socialists and independents sometimes joined larger movements. The 1902 Argentine general strike is illustrative not only of the process by which strikes built but also of the frailty of workers' solidarity during this period. In November, Buenos Aires port workers struck after demanding limits on the weight of individual loads, which averaged 220 pounds. The tough, experienced dockers soon won the day. The movement, however, spread to include workers at other ports and at the Buenos Aires central produce market. At this point, the FORA declared a nationwide general strike. The government, faced with a paralysis of the ports at the height of the export season, reacted. It first passed a bill in the National Congress that legalized the deportation of foreign-born "agitators" and then declared a state of seige under which it protected strikebreakers, closed union headquarters, and silenced the working-class press. The Socialists and some independents now joined the movement in protest against those actions, and the FORA called for an unlimited strike to bring down the state. By this time, the strike had closed or severely crippled the country's major maritime centers, but working-class unity shattered when the Socialists opted for a five-day walkout and then ordered their followers to return to work. This split, combined with government repression, seriously weakened the action, and as the economic noose tightened, workers gradually drifted back to their jobs. Many activists permanently lost their employment, others suffered deportation, and capitalists black-listed hundreds of participants and organizers.[52]

Aside from strikes, workers also used boycotts, slowdowns, and more rarely, sabotage. The individualistic brand of anarchism, which sometimes resulted in terrorism, gained few adherents in Latin America, but violence in the face of violence did occur. The most notable example consisted in the blowing up of the Buenos Aires police chief and his secretary in 1909, an act designed to avenge a police massacre of unarmed workers during the general strike earlier that year. Much of the fiery rhetoric of the era came from the advocates of using force against force. One columnist called for anarchists to teach their children to "hate, until the hatred accumulated from generation to generation produces the proud explosion of the final liquidation." This extremist strain, however, represented a minority; and in general, the movement, including the anarchists, showed a high regard for human life. During Argentine general strikes, for example, pickets allowed hospitals and asylums to receive food and fuel.[53]

Working-class organizations engaged in a variety of endeavors to provide services and actively propagandize among the proletariat. Unions and political parties alike ran schools and libraries, edited numerous publications, formed study groups, and sometimes provided free legal services. They also appealed to people off the job. Group outings on weekends and cultural events made low-cost entertainment available and helped spread the word. Lectures, conferences, plays, musical evenings, and similar entertainments appealed to all members of the working-class family. Art and literature by and for the proletariat began to flourish in these years, suggesting the existence of a Latin American working-class culture separate from that of the bourgeoisie. Workers even celebrated their own holidays. The First of May, designated as the international working people's holiday in 1889, became the most important date on the workers' calendar.[54]

Internationalism also came into play. Latin American labor, as a branch of the larger international workers' movement, attempted to organize beyond national boundaries and responded to the call of fellow workers across land and sea. Argentine commercial employees, for example, sponsored a congress in 1903 that drew delegates from neighboring countries. Argentine, Brazilian, and Uruguayan port workers planned a Federation of Maritime and Land Transport, Stevedores, and Related Trades and even hoped to include workers from faraway Mexico. FORA projected a South American federation but never carried out its plans.[55]

All groups within the movement maintained contacts with European organizations, and many sent delegates to international meetings. Workers also organized in response to events in other lands. Demonstrations protested the Spanish government's execution of the anarchist Francisco Ferrer, and gatherings expressed solidarity with Russian workers in the 1905 Revolution. Workers also demonstrated their support for Cuban independence from Spain, the Chinese Republic of 1911, and Morocco's struggle against Spain's colonial ambitions. Other actions called for world peace and condemned the international and continental arms race then under way.[56]

What results did worker actions accomplish? Unions and other organizations formed, and many survived; workers either seized or gained the right or power to strike; and as their collective experience accumulated, workers developed new goals and tactics. Most important, workers demanded and increasingly received recognition as a legitimate part of society.

Some concrete progress was also visible. By World War I, many workers toiled only eight or nine hours daily, rather than twelve, fourteen, or seventeen hours, as they had a few decades earlier. Job conditions also improved as a result of union pressures and government legislation. Nevertheless, many urban workers failed to improve their situation appreciably. Salaries, particularly in highly skilled trades, climbed only slowly. In jobs where a shortage of skilled workers existed, remuneration tended to outstrip the rise in cost of living; but in most trades, it lagged behind or remained just equal in real terms. This pattern initiated a gradual stratification within the working class. Railroad workers, for example, because they could paralyze whole economies by striking won a standard of living equal to that of higher-paid white-collar workers. But in the countryside, where organization remained weakest, conditions stayed much the same during the entire period.

It is possible, however, to sound overoptimistic. Even in Argentina and the movement's center there, Buenos Aires, workers usually failed to win desired results. Table 2 (p. 25) shows that only half the strikes between 1881 and 1906 resulted in victory or even partial gains. After that, results actually deteriorated. Between 1907 and 1913, only 30 percent of the strikes brought victory, and just over 10 percent achieved a partial triumph. In individual terms, workers did worse. Just under 86 percent of all strikes brought no immediate positive results, 10.2 percent won something, and only 4.2 percent emerged fully triumphant.[57] However, viewed as a whole, the outstanding fact is that by 1914 the movement had touched hundreds of thousands of persons and given them at least a glimpse of their potential power when acting collectively.

RULING-CLASS REACTION TO LABOR

Direct Opposition

As noted in the Introduction, Latin American labor movements passed through historical stages conditioned by the ways in which local economies were integrated into the world economy and by the specific nature of national elites. Because the Latin American ruling classes remained dependent upon outside centers, the second usually reflected the first. Fundamental changes in either variable, however, in some cases altered labor's patterns of development. A shift in the economic base of the elites generally changed their attitudes and behavior toward the working class and labor. During labor's formative period, national economies changed with the growth of exports. This change influenced the composition of local ruling classes. The particular formation of each, in turn, led to differing responses toward the labor movement.

In Argentina, agrarian interests held power, leaving industrial investment mostly to foreigners. The agrarian elements did not react harshly to organization by industrial workers so long as it did not threaten them directly. A relatively strong urban movement thus could form without constant harassment from the state. In Brazil, coffee barons controlled the government, but after 1880 they intermingled with a growing industrial bourgeoisie centered in São Paulo. The new ruling class, representing both agricultural and industrial sectors, cracked down hard on all working-class activity. The Brazilian movement, therefore, did not develop as fully as did its Argentine counterpart. Nor could Brazilian workers lay the basis for permanent mass organization. In Mexico, the pattern most resembled that in Brazil. In the 1880s, the nascent bourgeoisie began to form links with landed elements, and state repression severely restricted the movement until 1910. In Chile, agrarian and industrial groups unified during the middle of the nineteenth century, allowing for their consolidation before any significant working-class organization occurred. As a result, despite its industrial component, the relatively secure Chilean ruling class did not perceive the need to repress labor severely when the first working-class organizations appeared; consequently, a relatively strong labor movement eventually emerged.[58]

Despite these variations in long-range attitudes toward labor organization, ruling-class responses showed marked similarities because the elites everywhere recognized the implied threat behind working-class mobilization. When challenged, they quickly turned to force either by using available state agencies or by enacting repressive legislation. Confrontations between troops or police and workers dot this period. Sometimes, these confrontations turned into massacres when law enforcement officers fired on crowds of demonstrators or strikers. In 1907, for example, the Chilean army shot down over 2,000 men, women, and children at Iquique when demonstrators refused to obey an order to disperse within five minutes. Yet, a Chilean aristocrat could coolly say, "Repression by armed force has been good. Each time that strikes occur, energetic repression is advisable for reasons of social order and justice."[59]

Armed confrontations represented only one aspect of the violence unleashed against the working class. Governments or local authorities also regularly closed union headquarters, shut down newspapers and presses, confiscated written materials, denied permits for parades or meetings, and arrested labor organizers, often holding them for long periods without trial. The state's ultimate weapon was to declare a state of siege. Used in case of serious agitation, it sanctioned the use of troops or police against demonstrators, the closing of workers' centers, the seizure of persons without evidence or right of habeas corpus, and even the summary execution of persons charged with curfew violations or alleged resistance to authorities. Finally, the ruling class sometimes repressed working-class organizations even when they did nothing. During the 1905 Revolution by the Radical Party, for example, the Argentine government closed union headquarters and labor publications despite the fact that the movement did not participate in the attempt to overthrow the government.[60]

Increasing workers' discontent also brought a series of laws designed to contain unrest. In the first decade of the twentieth century, Argentina, Brazil, Cuba, and Uruguay enacted legislation allowing the deportation of persons considered foreign agitators. These laws stipulated that authorities could hold those arrested incommunicado or expel them speedily. The ruling class justified ousting foreigners by consistently denying the existence of any home-grown cause for workers' protests. Official and public political statements nearly always blamed "foreign elements and professional agitators" or "outside agitators" for working-class protest, leading to the conclusion that without these particular "subversive" elements no problems would exist. Under this type of legislation, Brazil deported 342 persons between 1907 and 1916.[61]

Workers faced other legal obstacles. Governments often refused legal recognition to unions, thus denying the force of law to contracts negotiated and signed by them. Authorities also supplied strikebreakers or protected workers who wished to continue to work in establishments embroiled in labor conflicts. In addition, judges regularly denied workers the legal right to organize. Some governments screened immigrants to prevent known labor organizers from entering the country, and Argentina, Brazil, and Uruguay signed a pact to exchange information on anarchists. At times, government representatives even violated their own laws. In Chile, the Chamber of Deputies voted to exclude a labor representative after he had fairly won election to it.[62]

The movement also encountered determined opposition from employers. Owners banded together against both potential and real workers' actions and instituted measures to ensure tranquillity in their establishments. Coordinating through organizations such as Unión Industrial Argentina, the Argentine Maritime Shippers and Owners Association, the São Paulo Commercial Association, or the Centro Industrial Mexicano, they exchanged black lists of militants, plotted common strategy against all forms of workers' associations, and coordinated lockouts. Capitalists cooperated with labor only when it clearly redounded to their benefit. After a Buenos Aires graphic arts union showed that it could successfully challenge proprietors, for example, a joint commission of owners and workers in the printing trades hammered out a series of collective industry contracts starting in 1906.[63]

Social Legislation and Liberal and Catholic Reform Movements

These years also produced Latin America's first social legislation. Sometimes such legislation aimed at mollifying the working class after violent demonstrations or strikes, and sometimes liberal or Catholic reformers championed minimal legislation. Everywhere, social legislation was piecemeal; and despite occasional proposals in several countries, no nation hammered out a comprehensive labor code.

Conservatives almost always opposed social laws, denying their validity for Latin America, and most projects favoring such legislation failed. Before World War I, however, accident compensation laws, although partial and covering only scattered groups of workers, were passed in Guatemala, El Salvador, Peru, and in two Mexican states. Argentina, Chile, and Peru approved laws protecting women and children and providing for a weekly rest period. Numerous countries enacted laws that encouraged or financed workers' housing. Argentina, Chile, and the Brazilian state of São Paulo created government labor bureaus, and several countries named official commissions to investigate working conditions as a possible basis for future laws.[64]

Liberal political parties backed workers' causes in an effort to capture their votes and, often, to pre-empt the appeal of progressive ideologies. In São Paulo, the Civilistas included social legislation in their electoral program for 1910; the Chilean Radical and Liberal parties took similar stands at other times. In Argentina, the Radical Party and the Partido Demócrata Progresista both sought votes by voicing approval of measures favoring white- and blue-collar groups. As so often happened, once in power, the Radicals pursued an antilabor policy with regard to the majority of workers (see Chapter 2). In Uruguay, José Batlle y Ordóñez passed substantial social legislation during his first presidency (1903–1907) assuring the right to strike, creating the continent's first ministry of labor, and including such measures as the eight-hour day.[65]

A Catholic social reform movement also tried to gain working-class support. At first a response to the liberal attack on church prerogatives in the last decades of the nineteenth century, it developed into a full-fledged movement after the promulgation of the papal encyclical *Rerum Novarum* in 1891. This document urged the creation of Catholic workingmen's societies and other measures to combat the rising tide of godless doctrines such as socialism or anarchism, and Catholic reformers in a half-dozen Latin American countries responded to the call. Catholics conceived of their organizations as joining workers and owners in a common cause and held that labor and management could peaceably settle any differences between them. However, most Catholic groups did not truly test this proposition. Employers rather than workers occupied positions of authority within these organizations, and Catholic groups operated on a strictly hierarchical basis.

In Mexico, the National Catholic Congress of 1903 proposed a series of measures to aid workers and encourage them to organize under Catholic auspices. Later congresses approved similar motions, made concerted efforts to educate Catholics on social questions, and endorsed reformist legislation. The 1908 congress reported the existence of fifteen workers' circles; by 1911, these numbered forty-six, with 12,320 members. Chilean Catholic efforts took a frankly conservative position and strongly identified with the Conservative Party. Church representatives specifically denounced "Socialist manifestations that reveal the existence of unhealthy germs," "tumultuous attacks on private property," and "Socialist doctrines" that employed "the people's antagonism against the rich and democracy against aristocracy." Catholic conservatives formed the Federación Obrera de Chile, the nation's first national workers' organization, and controlled it until driven out by socialist workers. Catholic reform movements also functioned in Brazil and Bolivia, but had minimal impact.[66]

The strongest Catholic drive developed in Argentina. By 1895, a Federation of Catholic Workingmen's Circles existed; and by 1912, it boasted seventy-seven groups with a total membership of 22,930. The federation held congresses that discussed legislative projects and social topics. The circles constantly petitioned the National Congress and the executive, seeking a Sunday rest law, among other measures. At the same time, Catholics initiated a voluntary Sunday business closing in Buenos Aires, and Catholic reformists in Congress eventually pushed through laws that guaranteed a weekly day of rest and regulated working conditions for women and minors.

Other Catholic efforts brought them into contact with the working class. The Liga Demócrata Cristiana, founded in 1902, started a workers' academy and sponsored a series of conferences to propagate the faith and publicize its social activities. Other programs included a women's employment bureau and institutions designed to protect female workers. Catholics also founded and financed antisocialist clubs in universities, and their active press campaigned against all philosophies that denied the existence of God or opposed capitalism.

Catholics also formed a few unions. The most important of these enrolled Buenos Aires port workers. Its regulations stated that no member could espouse anarchist causes, hold socialist ideas, or deny the right of property and the Constitution. In 1906, after supplying workers to break an anarchist-led strike, the Catholics called a work stoppage. The owners, more interested in continuing work than in the beliefs of strikers, rehired the anarchist workers, which led to the Catholic union's demise.[67]

On the whole, social legislation probably benefited capitalists more than it harmed them. Shorter hours, better working conditions, minimal rights on the job, and even higher salaries often increased productivity, and increased productivity translated into larger profits. Limited state protection and the promise of more led some workers to abandon the movement and settle for small but immediate improvements rather than join struggles that involved risking both job and personal security. It should not be overlooked, however, that these laws also helped protect some workers from the worst abuses by their employers.

CONCLUSION

Labor's formative period in Latin America has many similarities to its European counterpart. Common ideologies, tactics, strategies, and forms of organization and activity appeared in both areas. However, significant differences also emerged. The Latin American movement passed through its formative years in less time. That development probably both aided and hindered labor organization. On one hand, workers had existing sets of ideologies, strategies, and tactics available to them; they did not need to discover them, as European workers had done. On the other hand, the collective learning experience of the working class may consequently have been cut short. Consciousness evolves from long-term struggle, and the brevity of the formative period may have impeded such growth.

Another difference lies in the relative strength of anarchism in Latin America. Even in Argentina and Uruguay, where the strongest Socialist parties developed, anarchist variants eclipsed them. The reasons are complex. The nature of the Latin American state worked to discourage reformist political participation. Any attempt to secure reforms through electoral pressure must have appeared utopian in the face of rigged elections and the frequent use of force by the ruling classes. Prevailing legal systems and intransigent ruling-class opposition forced workers to organize outside the law and led them to adopt ideologies proposing alternative forms to existing institutions. Anarchism also attracted immigrants who sought to escape the hierarchical structures of their home countries and who were prohibited from voting by Latin American laws. As in Europe, anarchism appealed particularly to southern Europeans and to artisans, who constituted a substantial segment of the working class.

Effective Socialist mobilization depended on concessions from the ruling class in the form of economic benefits or limited political input. In Argentina and Uruguay, and to a lesser degree in Chile, a special set of circumstances existed that made the Socialists' tactics, including electoral politics, appear to be a viable alternative: A secure ruling class controlled the state, a relatively prosperous economy existed, and within a context of liberal traditions, electoral politics were generally recognized as a legitimate activity. The first circumstance indirectly aided organization because secure elites did not feel immediately threatened by industrial organization. The second allowed for limited concessions without undue pressure on capital accumulation, thus providing a measure of upward mobility for select groups of workers. The third protected working-class organizations from state repression so long as they stayed within the system. At the same time, the existence of groups pledged to overthrowing the system probably made the Socialists seem less menacing.

By 1914, Latin American labor had passed through its formative stage in almost every country. Although vast sectors of the urban and rural proletariat remained unorganized, workers as a class had forced their way into the national scene as an emerging power factor and had laid the groundwork for future advances. The character and intensity of the movement varied from area to area, but broad similarities in the historical experience of the working class clearly emerge.

NOTES

1 See Celso Furtado, *Economic Development of Latin America: A Survey from the Colonial Times to the Cuban Revolution* (Cambridge, 1970), pt. 2; North American Congress on Latin America (hereafter NACLA), *Yanqui Dollar: The Contribution of U.S. Private Investment to Underdevelopment in Latin America* (New York and Berkeley, Calif., 1971), pp. 3–8. For individual country studies, see Ronald H. Chilcote and Joel C. Edelstein, eds., *Latin America: The Struggle with Dependency and Beyond* (Cambridge, Mass., 1974). Also in this series is Roberto Cortés Conde, *The First Stages of Modernization in Latin America* (New York, 1975).

2 For descriptions of working conditions, see Warren Dean, *The Industrialization of São Paulo. 1880–1945* (Austin, Tex., 1969); Elías Lafertte, *Vida de un comunista: Páginas autobiográficas* (Santiago, 1961); Hobart A. Spalding, Jr., *La clase trabajadora argentina: Documentos para su historia, 1890–1912* (Buenos Aires, 1970). For conditions in Argentine commercial establishments, see Pablo Storni, "La situación de las clases obreras en la Capital de la República" (Doctoral diss., Faculty of Law, University of Buenos Aires, 1909); on Peruvian conditions, see Dora Mayer de Zulen, *The Conduct of the Cerro de Pasco Company* (Lima, 1913), p. 6; and for Peru and Chile, see Moisés Poblete Troncoso, *Condiciones de vida y de trabajo de la población indígena del Perú* (Geneva, 1938).

3 Spalding, *La clase trabajadora argentina*, pp. 188–189, 213–221; and on Mexico, for example, see Rodney D. Anderson, "The Mexican Textile Labor Movement, 1906–1907: An Analysis of a Labor Crisis" (Ph.D. diss., History, The American University, 1968), pp. 82, 118–120.

4 Richard M. Morse, *From Community to Metropolis: A Biography of São Paulo* (Gainesville, Fla., 1958), pp. 193–194; Francisco R. Pintos, *Historia del movimiento obrero del Uruguay* (Montevideo, 1960), pp. 28–46; Spalding, *La clase trabajadora argentina*, pp. 447–495, rent calculation from p. 40. On Buenos Aires in general, see James R. Scobie, *Buenos Aires: Plaza to Suburb, 1870–1900* (New York, 1974).

5 Morse, *From Community to Metropolis*, p. 223, quoting the *São Paulo Department of Labor Boletim*; Dean, *Industrialization of São Paulo*, pp.

156–157; Anderson, "Mexican Textile Labor Movement," pp. 81, 162, 171.

6 James O. Morris, *Elites, Intellectuals, and Consensus: A Study of the Social Question and the Industrial Relations System in Chile* (Ithaca, N.Y., 1966), p. 87; Stanley Stein, *The Brazilian Cotton Manufacture* (Cambridge, Mass., 1957), p. 63; James D. Cockcroft, *Intellectual Precursors of the Mexican Revolution: 1900–1913* (Austin, Tex., 1970), pp. 41, 108; Seminario de historia moderna de México, *Estadísticas económicas del porfiriato: Fuerza de trabajo y actividad económica por sectores* (Mexico City, 1964). My work on Argentine wages is not published.

7 Jorge I. Barría Serón, *Los movimientos sociales de Chile desde 1910 hasta 1926* (Santiago, 1960), p. 43; Anderson, "Mexican Textile Labor Movement," pp. 174–175.

8 See, for example, Adrián Patroni, *Los trabajadores en la Argentina: Datos acerca de salarios, horarios, habitaciones obreras, costo de la vida, etc.* (Buenos Aires, 1898). Patroni estimates the average working month at twenty-four or twenty-five days, including Sundays.

9 Spalding, *La clase trabajadora argentina*, pp. 191–192, 242–245; Nathan Whetten, *Guatemala: The Land and the People* (New Haven, Conn., 1961), Poblete Troncoso, *Condiciones de vida y de trabajo*, continuously cites the ineffectiveness of laws prohibiting the *enganche* of Indians; Mayer de Zulen, *Conduct of the Cerro de Pasco Company*, pp. 7–11; John K. Turner, *Barbarous Mexico* (Austin, Tex., 1969), p. 68; Friedrich Katz, "Labor Conditions on Haciendas in Porfirian Mexico: Some Trends and Tendencies," *Hispanic American Historical Review* 54, no. 1 (February 1974): 1–47.

10 Everardo Dias, *História das lutas sociais no Brasil* (São Paulo, 1962), p. 65; Sebastián Marotta, *El movimiento sindical argentino: Su génesis y desarrollo*, 2 vols. (Buenos Aires, 1960–1961), vol. 1, chap. 2; Hernán Ramírez Necochea, *Origen y formación del partido comunista de Chile* (Santiago, 1965), p. 28; Hermínio Linhares, *Contribução à história das lutas operárias no Brasil* (Rio de Janeiro, 1955), p. 38.

11 An increasing number of works treat immigration and the labor movement. For Brazil, see Michael Hall, "Emigrazione italiana a San Paulo tra 1880 e 1920," *Cuaderni Storici* 25 (January–April 1974): 138–159, and "Immigration and the Early São Paulo Working Class," *Jahrbuch für Geschichte von Statt, Wirtschaft un Gesellschaft Lateinamerikas* 12 (1975): 393–407; Sheldon L. Maram, "Anarchists, Immigrants, and the Brazilian Labor Movement: 1890–1920" (Ph.D. diss., History, University of California at Santa Barbara, 1972). The data on Chile are from Morris, *Elites, Intellectuals, and Consensus*, p. 85. Also see Francisco Gaona, *Introducción a la historia gremial y social del Paraguay* (Asunción and Buenos Aires, 1967), p. 93; Luis Araiza, *Historia del*

movimiento obrero mexicano, 4 vols. (Mexico City, 1964), 3:10; Marjorie Clark, *Organized Labor in Mexico* (Chapel Hill, N.C., 1934), p. 23; Manuel Díaz Ramírez, *Apuntes históricos del movimiento obrero y campesino de México, 1844–1880* (Mexico City, 1938), esp. p. 29; Alfonso López Aparicio, *El movimiento obrero en México: Antecedentes, desarrollo y tendencias* (Mexico City, 1952), p. 149; John Mason Hart, "Anarchist Thought in Nineteenth Century Mexico" (Ph.D. diss., History, University of California at Los Angeles, 1970), and esp. pp. 20–21.

12 Statistics from Maram, "Anarchists, Immigrants, and the Brazilian Labor Movement," p. 16. Lists of organizations from Jacinto Oddone, *El gremialismo proletario argentino* (Buenos Aires, 1949), esp. p. 49; Marotta, *El movimiento sindical argentino,* vol. 1, esp. chaps. 3 and 4; Linhares, *Contribução à história;* Dias, *História das lutas sociais no Brasil;* and Jover Telles, *O movimento sindical no Brasil* (Rio de Janeiro, 1962). The immigrant factor can be overemphasized even in countries such as Argentina; Ofelia Pianetto, "Industria y formación de la clase obrera en la ciudad de Córdoba: 1880–1906," *Homenaje al Doctor Ceferino Garzón Maceda* (Instituto de Estudios Americanistas, Córdoba, 1973), pp. 335–354, shows that nationals, not immigrants, founded the vast majority of unions in Córdoba.

13 Cockcroft, *Intellectual Precursors of the Mexican Revolution,* esp. chaps. 3 and 4; Julio César Jobet, *Recabarren: Los orígenes del movimiento obrero y del socialismo chileno* (Santiago, 1955); Dardo Cúneo, *Juan B. Justo y las luchas sociales en la Argentina* (Buenos Aires, 1956). On Malatesta, see Max Nettlau, *Enrico Malatesta: Vita e pensieri* (New York, 1936), pp. 207–233; and Gonzalo Zaragoza Ruvira, "Enrico Malatesta y el anarquismo argentino," *Historiografía y Bibliografía Americanista* 16, no. 3 (1972): 401–424, which also examines the impact of immigrants on anarchism and disagreements between those who favored less and more organization. On Gori, see Oddone, *El gremialismo proletario Argentino,* p. 23; Gaona, *Introducción a la historia,* pp. 199–200; and Lafertte, *Vida de un comunista,* p. 108 Rafael Barrett, *Obras completas,* 2d ed., 3 vols. (Buenos Aires, 1954); José Ratzer, *Los marxistas argentinos del 90* (Córdoba, 1969), pp. 27, 33, and chaps. 4 and 5. On rail unions, see Francisco Agnelli and Juan B. Chiti, *La Fraternidad: Fundación, desarrollo, obra: 1887–20 de junio —1937* (Buenos Aires, 1937), chap. 1; Marcelo N. Rodea, *Historia del movimiento obrero ferrocarrilero en México, 1890–1943* (Mexico City, 1944), chap. 1.

14 Lafertte, *Vida de un comunista,* p. 90; Abguar Bastos, *Prestes e a revolução social* (Rio de Janeiro, 1946), p. 42.

15 Telles, *O movimento sindical no Brasil,* p. 22; Linda Mascona Davidoff, *Orígenes del socialismo en México: 1867–1876* (Mexico City, 1963), pp. 118, 130; *La Vanguardia,* no. 103 (Mar. 29, 1906) 1; the figure of

50,000 is from Jean Longuet, "Le mouvement socialiste internationale," *Encyclopédie socialiste et cooperative de l'internationale ouvrière* (Paris, 1912), 4:621, quoting the Socialist Party's official report.

[16] The weekly *La Vanguardia* in 1894 published Engels, Tolstoy, and Vandervelde (three times); Plekhanov and Marx (twice); and Bebel, Ferri, Lombroso, Unamuno, and H. G. Wells, according to research data in my possession compiled by Maria M. Arruñada and summarized by me. *La Protesta* and *La Vanguardia* regularly announced available European book and pamphlet titles. Additional information may be found in Cockcroft, *Intellectual Precursors of the Mexican Revolution,* pp. 55, 70–72, 84; Dias, *História das lutas sociais no Brasil,* p. 41; Vamireh Chacon, *História das idéias socialistas no Brasil* (Rio de Janeiro, 1965), pp. 293, 299–300, 306; Hernán Ramírez Necochea, *Historia del movimiento obrero en Chile, siglo XIX* (Santiago, 1957), pp. 146–147; Oscar Alvarez Andrews, *El desarrollo industrial de Chile* (Santiago, 1936), p. 165.

[17] On Argentine and Brazilian publications, see Eric Gordon, Michael M. Hall, and Hobart A. Spalding, Jr., "A Survey of Brazilian and Argentine Materials at the Internationaal Instituut Voor Sociale Geschiedenis in Amsterdam," *Latin American Research Review* 8, no. 3 (Fall 1973): 27–77; Felix Weinberg, "Movimiento obrero y literatura utópica en la Argentina," *Caravelle,* no. 25 (1975), pp. 7–29.

[18] On literacy, see Morse, *From Community to Metropolis,* pp. 156–174; Hobart A. Spalding, Jr., "Education in Argentina, 1890–1914: The Limits of Oligarchical Reform," *Journal of Interdisciplinary History* 3, no. 1 (Summer 1972): 45–46. On recruitment, see one example in Enrique Dickmann, "Como me hice socialista," in *Memorias de un militante socialista* (Buenos Aires, 1936).

[19] Maram, "Anarchists, Immigrants, and the Brazilian Labor Movement," p. 49.

[20] On Cuba, see Aleida Plasencia Moro, ed., "Introducción," in *Documentos de Carlos Baliño* (Havana, 1964), pp. 9–20; José Rivero Muñiz, *El movimiento obrero durante la primera intervención: Apuntes para la historia del proletariado en Cuba* (Las Villas, 1961); Philip S. Foner, *A History of Cuba and Its Relationship with the United States,* 2 vols. (New York, 1963), 2:300–304; Charles A. Page, "The Development of Organized Labor in Cuba" (Ph.D. diss., Latin American Studies, University of California at Los Angeles, 1952), chap. 1. On Chile, see Tulio Lagos Valenzuela, *Bosquejo histórico del movimiento obrero en Chile* (Santiago, 1941), pp. 18–23; Jobet, *Recabarren,* has many details, as does Ramírez Necochea, *Historia del movimiento obrero en Chile.* On Mexico, see Araiza, *Historia del movimiento obrero mexicano,* vol. 2; Cockcroft, *Intellectual Precursors of the Mexican Revolution,* chap. 6; Leon Díaz Cárdenas, *Cananea: Primer brote del sindicalismo en México*

(Mexico City, 1936); Rodea, *Historia del movimiento obrero ferro-carrilero*, pp. 81–83, 132–135; Anderson, "Mexican Textile Labor Movement," pp. 6, 230, 238, 258.

21 Spalding, *La clase trabajadora argentina*, pp. 559–560, 609–621.

22 Linhares, *Contribução à história*, pp. 58–59.

23 Stein, *Brazilian Cotton Manufacture*, p. 57; Telles, *O movimento sindical no Brasil*, pp. 21–22; Jorge N. Solomonoff, *Ideologías del movimiento obrero y conflicto social* (Buenos Aires, 1971).

24 Spalding, *La clase trabajadora argentina*, p. 187; Maram, "Anarchists, Immigrants, and the Brazilian Labor Movement," pp. 3–4, 21–22.

25 Agustín Barcelli S., *Medio siglo de luchas sindicales revolucionarias en Bolivia: 1905–1955* (La Paz, 1956), pp. 49–50.

26 Page, "Development of Organized Labor in Cuba," p. 14; Ramírez Necochea, *Historia del movimiento obrero en Chile*, p. 147; Erasmo Barrios Villa, *Historia sindical de Bolivia* (Oruro, Bolivia, 1966), p. 26; Morse, *From Community to Metropolis*, p. 132; Miguel Urrutia, *The Development of the Colombian Labor Movement* (New Haven, Conn., 1969), pp. 51–54; James L. Payne, *Labor and Politics in Peru: The System of Political Bargaining* (New Haven, Conn., 1965), p. 37; Hilda Iparraguirre and Ofelia Pianetto, *La organización de la clase obrera en Córdoba: 1870–1895* (Córdoba, 1968), p. 27. On Mexico, see Hart, "Anarchist Thought in Nineteenth Century Mexico," pp. 6, 21, 35, 53; and Díaz Ramírez, *Apuntes históricos*.

27 Gaona, *Introducción a la historia*, pp. 34–35; Morse *From Community to Metropolis*, p. 132; Foner, *History of Cuba*, 2:138–139; Iparraguirre and Pianetto, *La organización de la clase obrera*, p. 16, cite a Córdoba society with over 800 members; Jobet, *Recabarren*, p. 112.

28 Quote from *El Socialista*, no. 16 (Sept. 29, 1872), in Hart, "Anarchist Thought in Nineteenth Century Mexico," p. 77; Luis Chávez Orozco, *Historia económica y social de México* (Mexico City, 1938), p. 32.

29 Linhares, *Contribução à história*, esp. p. 36; Lagos Valenzuela, *Bosquejo histórico*, pp. 12–13; Ramírez Necochea, *Historia del movimiento obrero en Chile*, pp. 82–83; López Aparicio, *El movimiento obrero en México*, p. 108; Hart, "Anarchist Thought in Nineteenth Century Mexico," pp. 80, 90, 97–98, 105; Barcelli, *Medio siglo de luchas*, pp. 49–50; Guillermo Lora, *Historia del movimiento obrero boliviano, 1848–1900* (La Paz, 1967), pp. 295–301; Gaona, *Introducción a la historia*, p. 88.

30 On these experiments, see Linhares, *Contribução à história*, p. 28; and Franyo Zapatta Alvarado, *Apuntes sobre el movimiento obrero chileno* (Concepción, Chile, 1958), p. 36; Hart, "Anarchist Thought in Nineteenth Century Mexico," p. 33. On Rossi's colony, see Newton Stadler de Souza, *O anarquismo da colônia Cecilia* (Rio de Janeiro, 1970). For the Cuban case, see Foner, *History of Cuba*, 2:143.

31 On the FORA and the movement, see Marotta, *El movimiento sindical*

Argentino, vols. 1 and 2; Oddone, *El gremialismo proletario argentino*; Spalding, *La clase trabajadora argentina*; and especially Diego Abad de Santillán, *La F.O.R.A.: Ideología y trayectoria del movimiento obrero revolucionario en la Argentina*, 2d ed., (Buenos Aires, 1970).

32 On the FORU, see Pintos, *Historia del movimiento obrero del Uruguay*; on Paraguay, see Gaona, *Introducción a la historia*. On Brazil, see Astrogildo Pereira, *A formação do PCB, 1922–1928* (Rio de Janeiro, 1962); and Leôncio Martins Rodrigues, *Conflito industrial e sindicalismo no Brasil* (São Paulo, 1966), p. 153; Edgard Carone, *A primeira república, 1889–1930* (São Paulo, 1973), pp. 233–239. On Chile, see Ramírez Necochea, *Historia de la clase obrera en Chile*, pt. 2, on attempts to federate; Moisés Poblete Troncoso, "Labor Organizations in Chile," U.S. Department of Labor, Bureau of Labor Statistics, *Bulletin of the United States Bureau of Labor Statistics*, no. 461 (October 1928), pp. 17–19.

33 Ramírez Necochea, *Historia de la clase obrera en Chile*, chap. 3; Spalding, *La clase trabajadora argentina*, pp. 82, 438–442.

34 Ramírez Necochea, *Historia de la clase obrera en Chile*, chap. 3.

35 On agrarian and other organizations in Mexico, see José Mancisidor, *Historia de la revolución mexicana* (Mexico City, 1958), esp. p. 71; Díaz Ramírez, *Apuntes históricos*, pp. 35, 48, 53; Hart, "Anarchist Thought in Nineteenth Century Mexico," pp. 21–22, 61–65. On Brazil, see Dean, *Industrialization of São Paulo*, p. 6. On Peru, see Antonio Ulloa Sotomayor, *La organización social y legal del trabajo en el Perú* (Lima, 1916), p. 163; and Peter F. Klarén, *Modernization, Dislocation and Aprismo: Origins of the Peruvian Aprista Party, 1870–1932* (Austin, Tex., 1973), chap. 2. On Argentina, see Plácido Grela, *El Grito de Alcorta* (Rosario, 1958). On Colombia, see Pierre Gilhodés, "Agrarian Struggles in Colombia," in Rodolfo Stavenhagen, ed., *Agrarian Problems and Peasant Movements in Latin America* (Garden City, N.Y., 1970), p. 411.

36 Ramírez Necochea, *Historia de la clase obrera en Chile*, pp. 224–246; Jobet, *Recabarren*, pp. 17–20, 27–33; Moro, ed., *Documentos de Baliño*.

37 Chacon, *História das idéias socialistas no Brasil*, pp. 283–286; John W. F. Dulles, *Anarchists and Communists in Brazil, 1900–1935* (Austin, Tex., 1973), pp. 11–12; Dias, *História das lutas sociais no Brasil*, pp. 244–245; Bastos, *Prestes e a revolução social*, p. 75 n.l; Carone, *A primeira república*, pp. 222–232; Eduardo Jaurena, *Frugoni* (Montevideo, 1950), pp. 23–24.

38 Jacinto Oddone, *Historia del socialismo argentino*, 2 vols. (Buenos Aires, 1934), is a detailed description of the party's early years and activities; Cúneo, *Juan B. Justo*; Spalding, *La clase trabajadora argentina*, esp. pp. 65–76.

39 Cockcroft, *Intellectual Precursors of the Mexican Revolution*, has con-

siderable material on the PLM; Anderson, in "Mexican Textile Labor Movement," and "Mexican Workers and the Politics of Revolution, 1906–1911," *Hispanic American Historical Review* 54, no. 1 (February 1974): 94–113, challenges Cockcroft's view on PLM influence among workers.

40 Lagos Valenzuela, *Bosquejo histórico*, pp. 24–25; Spalding, *La clase trabajadora argentina*, pp. 449–496; Hobart A. Spalding, Jr., "Cuando los inquilinos hacen huelga . . . ," *Extra*, no. 4 (September 1966), pp. 32–38.

41 Information from Ramírez Necochea, *Historia de la clase obrera en Chile*, pp. 283–285, and *Origen y formación del partido comunista en Chile*, p. 54; República de Chile, Ministerio de Industria y Obras Públicas, *La estadística del trabajo: Su historia, su naturaleza, y sus límites por Simón B. Rodríguez* (Santiago, 1908), pp. 53–54; Moisés Poblete Troncoso and Ben G. Burnett, *The Rise of the Latin American Labor Movement* (New Haven, Conn., 1960), p. 58; Jobet, *Recabarren*, pp. 12, 105; Ricardo Donoso, *Alessandri, agitador y demolador: Cincuenta años de historia política de Chile*, 2 vols., 2d ed. (Mexico City, 1953), 1:153; Alvarez Andrews, *El desarrollo industrial de Chile*, p. 188.

42 Dean, *Industrialization of São Paulo*, p. 161; Telles, *O movimiento sindical no Brasil*, p. 19; Michael Hall, letter to the author, January 1975.

43 On Mexico, see López Aparicio, *El movimiento obrero en México*, p. 108; Cockcroft, *Intellectual Precursors of the Mexican Revolution*, p. 48; John K. Turner, *Barbarous Mexico* (Chicago, 1910), pp. 206–207. On Uruguay, see Pintos, *Historia del movimiento obrero*, pp. 67–68, 89, 93; Héctor Rodríguez, *Nuestros Sindicatos* (Montevideo, 1965), p. 11.

44 Details in Spalding, *La clase trabajadora argentina*, esp. pp. 92–94; Santillán, *La F.O.R.A.*, chaps. 1–12.

45 Julio Godio, *El movimiento obrero y la cuestión nacional, Argentina: Inmigrantes asalariados y lucha de clases, 1880–1910* (Buenos Aires, 1972), p. 165; Spalding, *La clase trabajadora argentina*, pp. 92–94; Agnelli and Chiti, *La Fraternidad*, p. 465.

46 Santillán, *La F.O.R.A.*, p. 150; *La Vanguardia*, no. 640 (Dec. 20, 1907): 1.

47 Data from Godio, *El movimiento obrero y la cuestión nacional, Argentina*, pp. 182–183, 216–219.

48 Spalding, *La clase trabajadora argentina*, pp. 165–174.

49 Summarized from material in Godio, *El movimiento obrero y la cuestión nacional, Argentina*, pp. 58–59, 62–63, 102–104, 182–183, 216–219.

50 Gaona, *Introducción a la historia*, p. 171.

51 Compare programs in Spalding, *La clase trabajadora*, pp. 268–271; Linhares, *Contribução à história*, pp. 48–49; Jobet, *Recabarren*, pp. 97–99; Moro, ed., "Introducción," pp. 71–72; quote from Dulles, *Anarchists and Communists in Brazil*, p. 12.

52 Details in Marotta, *El movimiento sindical argentino*, 1:145–151; Oddone, *Historia del socialismo argentino*, 2:9–22.

53 Quoted from the anarchist newspaper *La Campana* in Ramírez Necochea, *Historia de la clase obrera en Chile*, p. 240; also see Spalding, *La clase trabajadora argentina*, pp. 399, 428–429.

54 On working-class culture, see, for example, Boris Fausto, *Trabalho urbano e conflito social (1890–1920)* (São Paulo and Rio de Janeiro, 1976), pp. 80–91. On May 1, see Rubens Iscaro, *Breve historia del l de Mayo* (Buenos Aires, 1961). On anarchism, see the personal testimony in Eduardo G. Gilimón, *Un anarquista en Buenos Aires (1890–1910)* (Buenos Aires, 1971).

55 Gaona, *Introducción a la historia*, pp. 117–118; Spalding, *La clase trabajadora argentina*, pp. 442–445.

56 Carlos M. Rama, *Mouvements ouvriers et socialistes: L'Amérique Latine, 1492–1936* (Paris, 1959), chaps. 1–3, has information on the Internationals in Latin America. On internationalism and protests, see Pereira, *A formação do PCB*, p. 17; Spalding, *La clase trabajadora argentina*, pp. 400–401, 436–445; Bastos, *Prestes e a revolução social*, p. 85; Linhares, *Contribução à história*, p. 54; Ramírez Necochea, *Origen y formación del partido comunista en Chile*, pp. 8, 55 n.l.

57 Summarized from material in Godio, *El movimiento obrero y la cuestión nacional, Argentina*, pp. 58–59, 62–63, 102–104, 182–183, 216–219.

58 On the relationship between elites and labor, see Kenneth Paul Erickson, Patrick V. Peppe, and Hobart A. Spalding, Jr., "Research on the Urban Working Class and Organized Labor in Argentina, Brazil, and Chile: What Is Left to Be Done?" *Latin American Research Review* 9, no. 2 (Summer 1974): 123–125; Hart, "Anarchist Thought in Nineteenth Century Mexico," pp. 17–18.

59 On the massacre, see Frederick B. Pike, *Chile and the United States, 1880–1962* (South Bend, Ind., 1963), p. 109; aristocrat quoted in Ramírez Necochea, *Historia de la clase obrera en Chile*, p. 205.

60 On 1905, see Spalding, *La clase trabajadora argentina*, pp. 398–399, 422–423.

61 Brazilian figures from Dulles, *Anarchists and Communists in Brazil*, p. 22 n.10. Typical examples of rhetoric blaming outsiders can be found in the Report of the Comisión Consultiva de Tarapacá y Antofagasta sent by congress to investigate labor unrest cited in Donoso, *Alessandri*, 1:152; Spalding, *La clase trabajadora argentina*, pp. 555–557, 577–584; Anderson, "The Mexican Textile Labor Movement," p. 139.

62 Dias, *História das lutas sociais no Brasil*, 250, 257–258; Rivero Muñiz, *El movimiento obrero durante la primera intervención*, p. 104; Spalding, *La clase trabajadora argentina*, p. 52; Morris, *Elites, Intellectuals, and Consensus*, p. 102.

63 See, for example, Spalding, *La clase trabajadora argentina*, pp. 375–393.

64 On ruling-class attitudes and legislation, for example, see Luis Miro Quesada, *Albores de la reforma social en el Perú* (Lima, 1965); Donoso, *Alessandri*, 1:151.

65 Dean, *Industrialization of São Paulo*, p. 158; Sergio Guiliasti Tagle, *Partidos políticos chilenos* (Santiago, 1964), pp. 133–135; Milton I. Vanger, *José Batlle y Ordóñez of Uruguay: The Creator of His Times, 1902–1907* (Cambridge, Mass., 1963).

66 On Mexico, see Genaro María González, *Catolicismo y revolución* (Mexico City, 1961), pp. 76, 314; on Chile, Morris, *Elites, Intellectuals, and Consensus*, pp. 104–106; on Brazil, Diva Benavides Pinho, *Sindicalismo e cooperativismo* (São Paulo, 1967), p. 98.

67 Néstor R. Auza, *Los católicos argentinos: Su experiencia política y social* (Buenos Aires, 1962); Spalding, *La clase trabajadora argentina*, pp. 499–549.

2

FROM WORLD WAR I TO THE DEPRESSION: EXPLOSIONS AND EXPANSION

Explosions of labor activity and a quantitative and qualitative expansion of the movement mark the period from the outbreak of World War I in 1914 through the initial stages of the Great Depression, which began in 1929. On one level, the entire period represents an explosion, a time of intense labor agitation, when compared with the formative years or the years immediately after 1930. On another level, a continental explosion occurred, sparked by the impact of the war between 1914 and 1919, and explosions took place within national boundaries throughout the period. The movement expanded in several ways. It spread into new geographic areas. Working-class activity was still concentrated in urban environments, but these no longer constituted the only focal points for organization. A rapidly growing white-collar sector and rural workers mobilized en masse for the first time. Finally, existing ideologies changed, and Communism challenged established lines of thought among workers.

The ruling class continued to respond with violent repression when faced with determined working-class actions, but as elsewhere in the capitalist world, governments also passed labor legislation. Such legislation aimed to defuse the movement by softening the worst abuses suffered by workers and to erect mechanisms through which the state could either control labor or induce workers to support the existing system or a particular regime. After 1914, a variety of political parties increased their efforts to win labor backing in order to bolster their position in office or to increase their chances of winning power.

WAR AND LABOR'S EXPLOSION

As in the formative period, outside forces helped shape internal events. The outbreak of war in Europe created sharp dislocations in the export-oriented Latin American economies, but after a brief interruption in the transatlantic flow of products, demand for raw materials and foodstuffs increased dramatically. However, manufactured goods imported from Europe, primarily from Great Britain, could not be secured, giving national industry a chance to expand and sell on the local market unhindered by foreign competition. War thus brought good times for both agrarian interests and a nascent industrial bourgeoisie. Postwar readjustment brought another economic dip when demand for exports slackened and European goods and capital once more flooded Latin America, but a general prosperity followed in the 1920s until the Depression.[1]

By contrast, the war years only heightened the problems confronting the working class. The scarcity of many items that had previously been imported and local industry's new monopoly position sparked a rapid jump in the cost of living, characterized by particularly sharp increases in the price of basic commodities. High world prices and, in some areas, a shift to export crops from those grown for domestic consumption fueled the rise. Substantial unemployment compounded the situation. Trade fluctuations, even of a temporary nature, threw thousands of persons out of work. Nor did industrial expansion provide greatly increased job opportunities. An oversupply of labor already existed in most urban areas, and this reserve army grew during the brief agricultural export crisis of 1914. Moreover, factory owners often used speed-up techniques, lengthened working hours, or demanded overtime from those already employed rather than hiring new workers.

Rapid economic fluctuations and deteriorating conditions galvanized workers into action across the continent. The impetus gained after 1914 carried over into the next years, culminating in the period from 1917 to 1920. Table 3 shows cost-of-living and wage

TABLE 3. COST OF LIVING AND WAGES, SELECTED NATIONS, 1913–1921
(By Index Numbers)

| | Brazil | | Peru | | Argentina | | Uruguay | |
	Cost of Living	Wages	Cost of Living	Wages	Cost of Living	Wages	Cost of Living	Wages
1913	—	—	100	100	—	—	100	100
1914	100	100	104	—	100	100	—	—
1915	108	100	112	—	107	—	—	—
1916	116	101	123	120	115	—	116	—
1917	128	107	142	—	135	—	119	—
1918	144	117	164	—	169	62	126	—
1919	148	123	183	—	186	87	170	—
1920	163	146	210	200	166	106	—	98
1921	167	158	—	—	—	—	—	—

SOURCES: Brazilian data from Octavio Ianni, *Crisis in Brazil* (New York, 1970), p. 56. Peruvian cost of living from *Monthly Labor Review* (Washington, D.C.) 29, no. 4 (1929): 256; Peruvian wage data from Ricardo Martínez de la Torre, *Apuntes para una interpretación marxista de la historia social del Perú* (Lima, 1949), vol. 4, p. 316, and Arturo Sabroso Montoya, *Réplicas proletarias* (Lima, 1934), p. 130. Argentine data from *Monthly Labor Review* (Washington, D.C.) 29, no. 2 (1929): 232–233. Uruguayan figures from Francisco R. Pintos, *Historia del movimiento obrero del Uruguay* (Montevideo, 1960), pp. 146, 206.

data for four countries. Other figures, although more fragmentary, indicate similar trends. In Chile, salaries rose about 30 percent between 1912 and 1923, but the cost of living soared 148 percent. In Cuba, real per capita income dropped from $233 in 1913, to $214 in 1917, and to $198 in 1918.[2]

Working-class unrest occurred in countries where a strong movement had existed before the war, but it also took place in areas where organization remained embryonic. In Ecuador, that nation's first significant strike erupted in 1917. Two years later, miners staged a local general strike, and Guayaquil port workers demonstrated against the high cost of living. Port workers also led the first large-scale unrest in Colombia: during widespread actions in 1918, workers called for salary increases ranging up to 50 percent; demonstrations, strikes, and rallies in several cities resulted in violence and many deaths.[3]

Protest also raged in countries with small but vibrant labor organizations. Bolivian miners demanded better living conditions, higher salaries, and shorter hours. In Cuba, port workers, railroad men, and construction workers, as well as workers in several other trades, struck during 1918 and 1919. Action in Peru coalesced around the cost of living. In early 1919, a brief general strike in metropolitan Lima forced the Conservative president to grant some urban workers an eight-hour day. Shortly thereafter, students and workers formed a committee to fight rising prices, and it soon won widespread support. It first petitioned the government to lower the cost of living and threatened a general strike if no action followed. The ensuing strike lasted over a month, but despite support from over fifty labor organizations, the committee lost control of the movement when authorities jailed its leaders. After clashes marked by army intervention and widespread looting, the strike drifted to an unsuccessful conclusion. The government did set up market stands that undersold local stores by about 40 percent, but when popular pressure faded, it closed them. Labor and working-class protests also broke out in several other cities during 1919.[4]

Actions by workers also rocked Chile, Uruguay, Brazil, and Argentina, where the continent's strongest labor organizations existed. In Chile, the combination of a severe depression in the mining industry and rising prices produced agitation. School-teachers called the nation's first white-collar strike in 1918; the following year, strikers briefly occupied the port of Puerto Natales, until the government called the army in to stop them. An eighty-three-day work stoppage crippled the southern coal mining regions in 1920, and a general strike paralyzed Magallanes in the Antarctic region that same year. The largest protest took place in Santiago. There the national labor federation (Federación Obrera de Chile —FOCh), the Partido Obrero Socialista, and two liberal political parties formed a coalition that agitated for a reduction in the cost of staple foods. In 1919, an estimated 100,000 persons called for government measures to ease the economic situation of the working class.[5]

In Uruguay, the impact of war revived the labor movement. Under the leadership of the anarchosyndicalist FORU and the powerful maritime workers union (Federación Obrera Marítima—FOM), workers went on the offensive during and after the war. The number of strike days, for example, rose from 67,193 in 1916 to a peak of 645,864 in 1920. Meat packers, women garment-workers, waterfront workers, and people in numerous other urban trades across the nation all protested through demonstrations and strikes. The FOM periodically paralyzed the port of Montevideo, winning important concessions for its member unions and supporting actions initiated by other workers.[6]

In Brazil, the movement gathered strength after 1914, peaking in 1917 and 1919. A strike of 2,000 textile operatives in São Paulo during 1917 rapidly spread until it involved an estimated 75,000 workers. Similar actions occurred in Rio de Janeiro, where a workers' committee formulated a series of demands, including higher salaries, a shorter working day, and lower prices. Activity continued for about a month, but government repression, ideological divisions, and the difficulty of coordinating such an action weakened the workers' position. A negotiated settlement by which workers won some temporary improvements ended the strikes, but employers repeatedly violated the terms of the agreement. Agitation did not stop, and the following years brought strikes by maritime and metalworkers, in the construction trades, and in the textile industry. A second set of general strikes shook both Rio and São Paulo in 1919, and that year May Day demonstrations attracted the largest number of workers ever. These strikes, too, quickly collapsed in the face of forceful government measures, poor planning, and internal divisions among workers.[7]

As in previous years, the Argentine movement remained the most vigorous on the continent. Labor slowly recovered from the massive repression unleashed during and after the 1910 general strike. By 1913, it had regained most of the ground lost. During the war years, activity lagged at first; but it picked up in 1917, reaching its peak in 1919 (see Table 4). Before that time, labor,

TABLE 4.   WORKER ACTIVITY IN BUENOS AIRES, 1914–1922

	Number of Strikes	Number of Strikers
1914	64	14,137
1915	65	12,077
1916	80	24,321
1917	138	136,062
1918	196	133,042
1919	367	308,967
1920	206	134,015
1921	86	139,751
1922	116	41,737

SOURCE: Sergio Bagú, *Evolución histórica de la estratificación social en la Argentina* (Caracas, 1969), p. 96.

led by the railroad workers and the militant FOM, called numerous strikes protesting the economic hardships brought on by the war and seeking to strengthen organization and improve the workers' status in general.

The largest and most violent upheaval took place in January 1919. This event, subsequently known as the *Semana Trágica* ("Tragic Week"), began with an isolated strike by metalworkers in Buenos Aires. The stoppage had entered its second month when a clash between picketers and armed guards protecting strikebreakers resulted in several deaths. At this point, the leading labor organizations called solidarity actions, although they could not unite on a common course. The authorities moved forcefully against this new threat. Violent clashes ensued, culminating in a police massacre of workers at the funeral of the slain metalworkers. This escalation triggered a general strike that paralyzed Buenos Aires, and the movement spread to other urban centers. The government then called in troops, and a state of war existed as the army, police, firemen, and vigilante groups battled workers in the streets. By week's end, well over a hundred persons had died, several hundred had been injured, and thousands languished in jail. After protracted negotiations, the government and the leading labor organizations finally settled the issue. The metalworkers won most of their demands, and the government promised to release all prisoners on condition that the workers return to their jobs. Only the anarchocommunists refused to sign the pact, calling for a continued strike, but they could not sustain the movement.[8]

WORKERS' IDEOLOGIES

Communism

The Russian Communist victory in 1917 reverberated throughout Latin America, as it did elsewhere. The Bolshevik triumph demonstrated that an organized working-class movement could seize state power. Its Marxist-Leninist basis introduced new concepts and a fresh vision of the workers' role in the historical process. Communist theory held that a militant, vanguard working-class political party should organize and lead the workers' struggle. The party would operate on two levels: first, to secure short-range goals such as higher salaries and better working conditions; and second, to build a long-range movement that would topple the bourgeois state. Once victorious, Communists envisioned a temporary dictatorship of the proletariat—that is, a period in which the working class held state power to initiate a transition to socialism —and, eventually, the creation of a Communist society. Electoral politics represented an interim means to a final goal rather than an end in itself.

Communists believed in the formation of a single, centralized labor organization that would include all progressive elements within the working class. They wished to organize workers along industrial rather than craft lines so that the workers in an entire industry would join a single union or federation. Such organization would unite people in individual factories and lead to larger groupings for more effective action. Communists believed that all sectors should organize, and they recruited actively among white-collar and rural workers. They also gave special attention to minorities by forming women's and youth sections and taking pains to incorporate Blacks and Indians into their organizations.

Communists emphasized the international dimension of proletarian struggle. They pointed to imperialism as a principal obstacle against which the working class must fight, thus linking progressive movements at home and abroad. Their analysis held that workers could take advantage of rivalries between sectors of the local and the international bourgeoisie through temporary alliances that would advance the long-range revolutionary movement. Communists thus at times supported nationalist governments that sought to curb foreign penetration of local economies.

Communist emphasis upon party discipline and thorough training created a militant rank and file that won a reputation for honesty and dedication seldom enjoyed by other labor organizations. By presenting a united front and using superior tactical skills, Communists often gained influence within individual organizations that far exceeded their numerical strength. When necessary, they clandestinely formed small groups or cells of hard-core militants before attempting mass organization. They never insisted that a worker join the party. Instead, they built a movement at several levels that included party members, those in unions, and persons wishing to participate only in support groups. They also displayed an ability to work with others, infrequently indulging in the squabbles that so often split the working class. Because Communists planned for the long run and also for immediate results, their ability to survive repression and temporary defeats was enhanced. Official Communist parties grew rapidly throughout Latin America after 1917. By 1931, seventeen were functioning, and Communists had won a following within the labor movement in almost all areas. Communists also ran for office and won in several countries.[9]

The Brazilian case illustrates both the progress made by Communists and the obstacles they faced. The general strikes of 1917 and 1919 represented the high-water mark of anarchist and revolutionary syndicalist influence. The tactic of calling repeated general strikes that always met government repression eroded support for those positions. Anarchist-oriented federations and unions steadily disappeared or else came under more moderate influence, the last major bastion to fall being the São Paulo federation in 1927. Five years earlier, disillusioned anarchists and syndicalists founded a Communist Party; and despite the fact that it enjoyed only two short periods of legality (from 1922 to the middle of 1924 and briefly in 1927), it achieved notable success. By 1927, it claimed thirty-six unions, twenty-three workers' committees operating inside non-Communist unions, and a base of 80,000 persons. In 1929, it founded the General Confederation of Labor of Brazil, the first central labor organization since the long-defunct COB. It also elected two candidates to the Rio de Janeiro Municipal Council and attempted the first systematic organization of non-urban workers through the Worker-Peasant Bloc, formed in 1927. The bloc, however, brought only meager results because of staunch opposition by landowners and the state.

Still, the labor movement remained weak. After the 1919 general strike, organization continued to be largely decentralized because of ideological divisions, the country's size, and steady and effective state harassment. In 1920, the Third National Labor Congress called for unity, but the plea foundered on a bedrock of partisanship. Five different ideological tendencies all sought working-class support, and rival organizations operated in the same locale or competed in May Day demonstrations. Although Communists and anarchists arranged a temporary truce during the early 1920s, it quickly broke down, largely because of anarchist intransigency.

Three forces in addition to the Communists and anarchists struggled for control of the labor movement. A small Catholic group actively fought atheism and secularism while striving to confine workers to peaceful protest. During the 1919 general strike, for example, the Catholic Workers' Center in São Paulo pledged "unrestricted support to all conservative classes in the present emergency and declared themselves at the side of the government for the repression of anarchism."[10] The 1920s also saw a resurgence of reformism within the movement. *Yellow* unionists, who denied the wisdom of militant strategies, opted for immediate economic gains rather than fundamental social change. These workers advocated cooperation with local or national authorities rather than confrontation as the best way to improve conditions. This approach appealed to the many workers who tired of constant strife and living on the edge of total poverty. Brazilian Socialists also attempted to revive their moribund movement in the 1920s and refounded a political party that unsuccessfully competed with the Communists at the polls.

Efforts to organize workers into militant groups often foundered against reality. Many proletarians did not wish to participate in a long-range struggle; they wanted only immediate improvements. As a labor delegate said to the Rio de Janeiro police chief during a 1918 strike, "Positively, sir, we workers do not want a revolution; we want to work, with our rights respected."[11] Such attitudes combined with fears about job security and employer opposition to hinder mobilization. For example, when a group of carpenters tried to organize a strike for higher wages after a pay cut, only twenty out of sixty workers agreed to participate, and the action failed. Furthermore, existing organizations did not coordinate their efforts. When Communists formed a central labor group in Rio, they found that four similar entities already existed, each operating without contact with the others. In all, probably less than 10 percent of salaried workers joined a union. The situation in Santos was probably typical: there only 6,000 out of 40,000 industrial workers belonged to an organization.[12]

Continuing Divisions, Changing Tactics, and Relative Strength

A brief look at organized labor in several countries indicates the existence of two common patterns across the continent: continued internal divisions and a relative weakness. In Bolivia, workers formed unions in most urban trades but remained divided over ideological issues. Three separate federations organized, but none survived because of disagreements between Communists, anarchists, Socialists, and Trotskyites. The majority of workers belonged to no organization, and the movement remained vulnerable to government pressures. A similar situation existed in Uruguay. After the failure of the 1919 general strike, the anarcho-syndicalist FORU lost ground, and Socialists made advances, particularly in maritime unions. In the early 1920s, syndicalists and Communists formed a central labor body; but near the end of the decade, it claimed only 3,500 persons in twenty-three organizations. The FORU included only 2,250 members in fourteen unions. In 1929, Communists tried unsuccessfully to gain control over the organization they shared with the syndicalists. They then left to form yet another federation.[13]

In Peru, workers founded an anarchosyndicalist federation in the wake of the 1919 strikes; but it never functioned as an efficient body, although it claimed 30,000 members drawn from greater Lima. Gradually, two new forces, Communism and Aprismo, eclipsed the older ideologies and competed with each other.* Communists formed a general labor confederation in 1930. The Apristas, who espoused a reformist ideology based on a redistribution of wealth without class struggle or an end to private property, created many unions. They appealed particularly to white-collar groups that found their thesis of painless redistribution attractive. In 1932, Communists and Apristas supported a mass movement against foreign bus companies in Lima, finally forcing the government to break the monopoly those companies held. Both Communists and Apristas claimed a great victory, but as a whole, the Peruvian movement reached only a small percentage of the total labor force.[14]

In Ecuador, anarchosyndicalists dominated the embryonic labor movement until 1925. At that time, a Socialist Party appeared, but it soon divided between Socialists and Communists and between rival groups in Guayaquil and Quito, the country's two major cities. Communists gradually gained control over the organization, and by 1929, it became the Ecuadorian Communist Party. Socialists then formed a separate group.[15]

The first Colombian workers' congresses met during 1924 and 1925, but divisions between Communists and non-Communists prevented unity. Federations also appeared in Guatemala, the Dominican Republic, and throughout Central America.

---

* *Aprismo* is the name given to the movement formed around the Alianza Popular Revolucionaria Americana, APRA, founded by Víctor Raúl Haya de la Torre in 1924.

Until the repressive Ibáñez government cracked down on it in 1924, the Chilean movement enjoyed relatively more cohesion than its counterparts in most countries, perhaps because neither strong Socialist nor strong anarchist groups existed. In 1919, members from the POS gained control over the pro-Catholic and conservative-leaning FOCh. Within two years, this federation affiliated with the Communist Third International and worked closely with the POS, which became the Chilean Communist Party in 1921. The FOCh reorganized its structure, opting for industry-wide rather than craft unions and including in its statutes the demand that the workers should run the economy. It quickly became the nation's leading labor organization, and it may have reached a membership of 100,000 persons during the decade.

Other organizations also attempted to gain the allegiance of Chilean workers. In 1919, a Chilean branch of the Industrial Workers of the World (IWW) was formed. A radical anarcho-syndicalist group, it gained sympathizers among maritime workers, printers, and artisanal groups in Santiago and the port of Valparaíso, although it never built a mass base. Independent organizations also existed. Railway workers formed a confederation in 1926 that remained unaffiliated with any central labor organization. The Catholic movement dwindled after 1919, ceasing to be an important current within the labor movement. In all, some 2,000 strikes occurred between 1919 and 1926, but in the latter half of the 1920s, the movement declined under government repression. Even at its height, less than 20 percent of all salaried workers, or about 200,000 persons, belonged to an organization.[16]

The Argentine movement displayed nearly all the characteristics found in other countries: It, too, underwent ideological divisions, the appeal of anarchism waned, Communism challenged more established positions, and labor activity declined during the late 1920s. A veritable kaleidescope of organizations came and went during this period. The unity achieved in 1915–1916 resulted in the creation of the FORA IX, so named because it adopted the revolutionary syndicalist position first proposed at its Ninth Congress. It boasted over 350 affiliated groups by 1918 and 734 by 1920. At its apex in 1921, the FORA IX enlisted more than

100,000 dues payers. Its most important member, the FOM, representing maritime workers, virtually controlled the ports. Opposed to the FORA IX stood the anarchocommunist FORA V, a group that split away soon after the fusion, returning to the position endorsed at the federation's Fifth Congress. It contained mostly craft unions at first but later expanded to include industrial and rural workers and even temporarily allied with small rural property holders. By the end of the decade, its proponents claimed a membership of just under 100,000, but the number seems exaggerated.[17]

Independent labor groups also existed, notably among railroad workers, most of whom belonged to either La Fraternidad or the Federación Obrera Ferrocarrilera, founded in 1912. In the mid-1920s, the two joined to form a confederation under Socialist influence. That entity increasingly used peaceful bargaining to secure gains for its members. A continual realignment among organizations further complicated the labor scene. In 1922, the FORA IX incorporated the Communists and changed its name to the Unión Sindical Argentina. Although the Communists gained strength within the new group, it remained under syndicalist control. In 1926, yet another organization emerged, the Confederación Obrera Argentina, composed mostly of railroad workers. Thus, by 1930, three central labor organizations functioned in addition to independent unions. The following year, all major groups except the FORA V again merged to form the Confederación General de Trabajo (CGT). However, it could not function freely because the military government that seized power in 1930 cracked down on labor.

Behind these shifts lay varied ideological positions. In addition to two minority lines, a majority within the anarchist camp backed the FORA V. As anarchocommunists they viewed unions as one arm in a generalized campaign toward a revolutionary seizure of power. They therefore placed less emphasis on union activities than did either the Communists or the syndicalists. The anarchocommunists continued to preach that only violence could topple the state, that total revolution constituted the workers' single legitimate goal, that the revolutionary general strike was the most effective tactic, and that workers should not negotiate with their enemies or accept reformist measures. One new element appeared in their analysis. They now saw international cartels as crucial to maintaining world capitalism. Consequently, they began to emphasize an internationalist position that assigned secondary importance to national factors inside the movement.[18]

Syndicalists developed what they called *workers' politics* (*política obrera*), a formulation which held that unions or federations should adopt no set ideology because their very existence constituted a revolutionary political act and the imposition of a particular set of ideas would only prove divisive. They postulated that the revolutionary general strike could not succeed until a higher level of organization emerged and that therefore actions should seek limited goals within the existing framework. Translated into practical terms, syndicalists now negotiated with the government or local authorities to settle disputes. On several occasions, particularly when the FOM either threatened or called a strike, they mediated conflict through political bargaining. Thus, although in theory they had not abandoned revolutionary goals, in reality they became increasingly narrow unionists.[19]

In Argentina, as elsewhere, political parties also tried to organize workers. The Communist Party, formed in 1920 by dissident Socialists, elected candidates to municipal office in Buenos Aires, Córdoba, and Rosario during the 1920s. The Socialists increasingly turned their backs on the labor movement, concentrating on electoral politics. In 1917, for example, the party dissolved its internal committee for labor, saying that "the union movement is an autonomous movement that has its own ends and tactics and for that reason the party that fights exclusively for political goals should not maintain direct nor intimate relations with it."[20] Socialists often took stands that alienated specific groups of workers. For example, they denounced President Hipólito Yrigoyen's "soft policy" toward railroad strikes (led by syndicalists), which allowed wage increases, because many companies then raised freight rates, thus leading to higher consumer costs. Similarly, their policy of treating working-class issues exclusively within a parliamentary context gained little union support. It totally excluded immigrant workers, who could not vote. Socialism increasingly appealed to the higher-paid members of the working class, such as the elite among railroad workers, who could afford to accept parliamentary gradualism as a valid strategy. Socialists thus consciously courted middle groups over blue-collar workers.[21]

Before 1924, the movement maintained a high level of activity, and constant strikes marked the years after 1916. Maritime workers, meat packers, women cigarette workers, and urban tenants all engaged in protracted struggles in the face of opposition from employers and the state. The first industry-wide organizations also emerged in the 1920s, a factor that aided railroaders in winning the first industry-wide collective contract in the country and that forced the companies to recognize their unions as legitimate bargaining agents. Despite divisions, attempts to unify all workers into one central organization persisted; and at times such as the Semana Trágica labor groups temporarily acted in concert. Specific organizations displayed signs of reaching higher levels of struggle. The FOM called over 90 percent of its strikes during this period in solidarity with other workers, using its powerful position to aid those with less chance of successfully defending their rights.[22]

After 1924, workers' activity declined for several reasons. The burst of activity from 1916 to 1924 and the cost of facing constant government opposition seemed to drain collective energies. After a time, continual calls for general strikes turned workers away from collective action. The sterile ideological debates between rival leaders that often dominated workers' assemblies alienated those who wanted concrete solutions. Repression eliminated many militants and convinced others that safety lay in tolerating existing conditions. Some workers adopted reformists positions and bargained within the established system, occasionally encouraged by the Radical governments (1916–1930), which hoped to enlist working-class voters. At times, the rank and file resisted this trend, but the ability of leadership to win concrete benefits tipped the balance against those backing militant action. As the data in Table 5 suggest, the economic situation influenced the slump in

TABLE 5. REAL SALARY, COST OF LIVING, NUMBER OF STRIKES, AND
NUMBER OF STRIKERS IN BUENOS AIRES, 1924–1929

Year	Real Salary (Index Nos., 1929 = 100)	Cost of Living (Index Nos., 1914 = 100)	Number of Strikes	Number of Strikers
1924	85	128.9	77	277,071
1925	89	125.6	89	39,142
1926	90	122.4	67	15,880
1927	95	120.8	58	38,236
1928	101	119.1	135	22,170
1929	100	120.8	113	28,271

SOURCE: Rubens Iscaro, *Origen y desarrollo del movimiento sindical argentino* (Buenos Aires, 1958), pp. 137 n. 94, 140 n. 98.

workers' activity. After 1924, real salaries rose and the cost of living declined. From a peak in 1924, the total number of strikers fell, as did the average number of participants per strike. Two hypotheses are appropriate here: First, a greater number of workers were at least temporarily content with their situation, a phenomenon not uncommon in periods of rising real wages. Second, after 1924, most activity occurred in smaller enterprises, in which workers got lower wages and in which the worst working conditions prevailed. That explains the increase in activity and the simultaneous decline in the average number of strikers. As real wages of industrial workers rose, those employed in small establishments attempted to equalize the gains made by workers in larger workplaces. On a more general level, the lessened labor activity suggests that when significant segments of the working class can improve their situation by bargaining, the level of militancy may temporarily fall. In other words, given the lack of unity on revolutionary aims and the level of employer and government opposition to violent action, ameliorative solutions proved momentarily effective.

LABOR EXPANSION

White-Collar Groups

The war period and the 1920s accelerated long-term economic trends already in evidence before 1914. The industrial sector continued to grow; consequently, industry hired greater numbers of workers and employed more nonindustrial (i.e., white-collar) workers. At the same time, bureaucracies expanded rapidly as the state administered ever more complex economies. By 1930, for example, public employees and teachers already composed a significant white-collar group. During the 1920s, foreign investment poured into Latin America, and U.S. capital supplanted British as the single most important source of outside monies. In 1914, U.S. investment totaled 17 percent of all foreign capital; by 1930, it reached some $3.6 billion, or 40 percent of the total. Foreign capital invested in the industrial sector, but it also gained control over raw materials such as oil and set up large agricultural enterprises that produced primarily for export. On these huge estates a rural proletariat emerged, forming a separate stratum within the working class. These trends unfolded unevenly across the continent, but in almost every nation, white-collar workers and rural proletarians actively engaged in bettering their lives during the 1920s.[23]

White-collar workers suffered the same economic hardships during the war as blue-collar workers. Communist and reformist socialist parties particularly attracted white-collar groups. Unlike most other parties, neither preached immediate, violent revolution, and both promised a better future. Persons embracing either could participate in a movement against the system while remaining inside it. Aided by the objective reality of vast inequality of wealth and privilege, Communists and reformists pitched their appeals to both white- and blue-collar workers, and their campaigns in unions and in elections helped rouse white-collar workers to action for the first time. Workers who wished to link the international struggle to their own and who desired far-reaching changes within society generally opted for a Communist position; those who viewed the struggle as limited primarily to short-range solutions more often chose reformism.

White-collar organization developed slowly. In Brazil, employees participated in the protests against the high cost of living and often sympathized (passively or actively) with industrial workers' demands. Their first solid organization, the São Paulo Association of Employees in Commerce, counted 30,000 members; but as of 1930, it had attempted no major actions of its own. Bolivian bank workers organized in 1930; Colombian white-collar groups organized in 1932. In most countries, the same legal impediments that faced blue-collar workers also faced white-collar groups. Bolivian law expressly prohibited teachers' strikes, and when telegraph workers attempted to unionize, the government banned all such activities.[24]

White-collar organizations advanced furthest in Chile and Argentina. In Chile, primary school teachers founded a federation in 1915. Three years later, they called a strike; in 1922, they called a second. That same year, primary and secondary school teachers formed an organization that the dictatorship of Carlos Ibáñez deemed strong enough and sufficiently "subversive" to dissolve in 1929. Employees of industrial firms mobilized in this period, too. In 1919, employees in the coal zone of Lota called a strike, and related movements broke out in at least two other areas. In 1920, the Federation of Coal Employees initiated a general strike; three years later, bank workers did the same. In 1925, employees attempted to form a national organization on the basis of existing federations in five cities and incorporating other white-collar groups. In that same year, a national white-collar political association emerged, and its candidate won 80,000 votes in the presidential election. Middle-group agitation reached such a point that, as one contemporary observed, "the real class struggle broke out between the petit bourgeoisie educated in the secondary schools and the traditional society."[25]

A weak federation of employees in commerce formed in Argentina before the war. In 1919, however, militants took control and called a strike against the leading department store in Buenos

Aires, demanding an eight-hour day. When management resisted, the struggle broadened. The printers' union supported the action by refusing to set any advertising for the store. At that point, the employers staged a lockout and got the Liga Patriótica, a strike-breaking association, to supply people to occupy posts in the store and in print shops. The countermove worked, and the federation, hampered by the fact that most employees had little union experience or preparation for a lengthy strike, admitted defeat. Teachers, newspapermen, bank employees, and communications workers also formed unions and waged struggles for their rights. Teachers in Mendoza fought a particularly bitter campaign centering on academic freedom and economic issues. Women led the way in that local movement, which included two general strikes against both provincial and national authorities. Despite repressive tactics, including firings and harassment of union members, the teachers' association survived.[26]

Rural Workers

Workers in the countryside also mobilized during these years. Communists, although by no means the only ones to help organize rural workers, played an important role in the expansion of the labor movement. For several reasons, most large-scale rural actions involved foreign companies. The largest number of wage earners outside urban centers worked for foreign-owned mines, oil fields, large plantations, or cattle ranches. Working and living conditions on these foreign enclaves (as on native-owned rural estates) were dismal. Furthermore, the Communist anti-imperialist campaign called for concrete action against foreign corporations, and large rural holdings presented ideal targets.

The United Fruit Company's vast estates throughout the Caribbean basin and Central America became a major scene of turmoil. In Colombia, workers on the corporation's Santa Marta banana plantations presented a series of demands in 1928 that included improvements in living conditions and economic benefits. The company refused to negotiate. The workers then walked out, and the government sent troops at the manager's request. While the soldiers protected strikebreakers, the military commander tried to impose a solution favorable to the company. Clashes between the military and the strikers ensued, during which at least one hundred workers died. In the aftermath, the government jailed numerous activists, particularly persecuting the Communists who had helped to organize the movement. Banana workers in Honduras called a stoppage in 1930, but the government quickly crushed the action. A second strike, in 1932, ended with similar results, and authorities deported its leaders. Unrest on United Fruit Company lands in Guatemala and Costa Rica ended in the same way. In the latter country, the foreign management successfully defied a government-negotiated settlement.[27]

Workers also struggled against foreign-owned oil, mining, and land development enterprises. In 1922, a strike stopped production at the Colombian subsidiary of the Tropical Oil Company (in turn controlled by Standard Oil of New Jersey, a Rockefeller company—now Exxon), but the protest came to naught. Two years later, workers demonstrated against higher pay scales awarded foreign workers and miserable work conditions, under which as much as 40 percent of the labor force required some hospitalization annually. The company, like other foreign corporations, refused to meet with the workers. Finally, the government dictated a solution that included improved health measures but no wage increases. The workers, exhausted by the lengthy struggle, accepted the pact. But once the movement subsided, the company fired 1,200 persons associated with the strike, and the government jailed some of its leaders. Four years later, when the company refused to consider even a token raise, workers again struck. After twenty days, during which 20,000 to 30,000 persons remained idle, the company won. Government troops again played a decisive role, and the authorities arrested and deported the strike leaders.[28]

Labor unrest at the joint U.S.–British-owned South American Oil and Development Company in Ecuador further illustrates difficulties encountered by organizers in rural areas. In 1919, only the intervention of government forces foiled a strike against the concern's gold and diamond mining operations. Ten years later, despite constant attempts, the workers still had no union because the company dismissed anyone suspected of sympathizing with the idea. In 1934, workers finally formed an organization, but it could not function effectively because of continued company hostility. Peruvian petroleum workers and miners and Colombian coffee workers organized between 1916 and 1930, but government repression, company intransigence, and the workers' vulnerability to both limited efforts to sporadic actions and infrequent successes.[29]

A limited amount of organization among peasants also occurred in the 1920s, and as in earlier years, occasional peasant uprisings swept across the usually placid landscape. In Ica, Peru, a peasants' federation called work stoppages against various large estates but met with brutal repression. In 1932, a *campesino* uprising at Izalco, El Salvador, ended in the massacre of over 10,000 persons. Communists played a leading role in organizing peasants in several countries. At the Peruvian Communist Party's 1930 plenum, for example, delegates representing some 30,000 Indians belonging to peasant federations addressed the meeting in Quechua, their native language. A peasants' convention in 1921 sponsored by the Chilean FOCh united eleven delegations that claimed 2,600 members, and by 1925, it had organized over 5,000 peasants.[30]

In addition to the Communists, urban organizers of other persuasions moved into the countryside, where they met with similar opposition. Bitter strikes erupted in the territories of Chaco, Formosa, and Misiones in the Argentine northeast and in the sugar mills and mines of Cuyo, Jujuy, and Salta provinces. Aided by militants of both the FORA and the FOM, workers for La Forestal, the foreign-controlled tannin and quebracho monopoly, struck in 1919, 1920, and 1921. The corporation finally responded by taking matters totally into its own hands, locking out the workers, and using its private army to hunt down strikers. These measures succeeded in crushing widespread unrest on company lands.[31]

Another important rural movement with urban connections occurred in Patagonia. Helped by the anarchosyndicalist Workers' Federation of Río Gallegos, workers in that city and on nearby estates slowly organized against ranchers and local businessmen, many of them foreigners. After a series of negotiations on demands for better living and working conditions, the situation reached an impasse in 1921. At that point, the workers laid down their tools, paralyzing production in the whole area. The Radical government reacted to the employers' pleas for help and to highly exaggerated reports of burning, looting, and rapine by sending the national army. The troops quickly "normalized" the situation by massacring thousands of unarmed persons, most of them after they had surrendered peacefully. The slaughter reverberated among urban workers, and the FORA IX called a brief general strike in protest. The Patagonian drama did not end there. In 1923, a worker killed the officer who had commanded the military expedition and was, in turn, assassinated in jail. His summary execution triggered another short general strike by the country's leading labor organizations. By that time, however, most Patagonian organizations had been destroyed.[32]

RULING-CLASS REACTION

Repression

Although the vast majority of workers remained outside any organization or political party, labor's real, untapped power could no longer be ignored after World War I. Its potential to mobilize increasing numbers did not escape unnoticed within the ruling class. Accordingly, local governments moved to protect privilege and property in two ways: repression aimed at all forms of workers' organizations and meliorative socialist legislation. At the same time, private citizens formed organizations designed to combat workers' protests.

Four specific factors motivated official action against workers. First, although organized labor seldom threatened long-range political stability or even toppled governments, massive stoppages in larger metropolitan centers indicated its growing power and a willingness to use that power. Moreover, individual strikes temporarily weakened the national economy and hurt profits. Second, unionization, collective bargaining, or picket lines restricted "free" competition on the labor market by impeding workers from competing against one another for jobs or by preventing others from working. Liberals, in particular, argued that all collective combinations violated individual rights and that for this reason alone workers' organizations should be controlled if allowed to exist at all. Third, strikes or demonstrations often boiled over into rioting or other expressions of class rage. Such occurrences disrupted social peace and resulted in extensive property damage and public expense. Fourth, any workers' agitation raised the specter of the Soviet Revolution. Communism as an international, anti-imperialist movement represented an unparalleled challenge. Whereas anarchists or syndicalists had relied primarily on local resources, Communists enjoyed the actual or potential backing of a foreign power and a base from which to operate. Ideologies that espoused immediate violent revolution could be countered by force, but Communism's blueprint for long-term struggle combined with immediate action made it harder to combat. As a result, in almost every country, governments singled out Communists as prime targets for repression.

Additional working-class actions suffered armed violence. Chilean troops killed over a thousand striking miners. In Bolivia, untold numbers of miners fell victim to government repression in 1914, 1919, and 1923, and those incidents merely represent leading examples of force directed against miners. Peruvian agrarian protests nearly always met harsh treatment, resulting in countless casualties.[33]

Authorities constantly harassed meetings, denied permission for demonstrations, arrested organizers and labor leaders, employed paid agitators to provoke workers into illegal acts that then gave police an opportunity to beat or detain people, used informers, and closed unions or working-class cultural organizations. The law sanctioned many of these actions. In Peru, the dictator Sánchez Cerro summarily dissolved the Confederación Regional de Trabajadores Peruanos in 1930, terming it "subversive of public order." The working-class press also suffered. Police closed or suspended, among many others, the Brazilian Communist paper, *A Voz do Povo; Amauta,* organ of the Peruvian left in the 1920s; and the Chilean anarchist publishing house, Numen. Governments also collaborated in tracking suspicious persons. In 1922, for example, Argentina, Brazil, Chile, and Uruguay sent delegations to an international police conference in order to co-ordinate the activities of their respective "red squads."[34]

Most governments encountered little difficulty passing laws legalizing police action against workers. A 1927 Brazilian law allowed police to close union meeting places at will. The Argentine Law of Residence and Law of Social Defense gave authorities ample leeway to arrest almost anyone and to deport foreign-born workers. In Colombia, a law, ostensibly drawn up to protect workers, stipulated that they could stop work but not engage in any further action. As a result, strikes proved virtually untenable in all but those trades involving highly skilled workers (a small percentage of the total). Employers could freely replace those who refused to work, and strikers could not act without risking confrontation with the police.[35]

State authorities also encouraged nationalism, at times an effective weapon against labor. They attributed most labor problems to foreign influence and equated patriotism with a tranquil, law-abiding working class. Ruling-class propaganda and representatives particularly singled out Communists as foreign agents. During the Semana Trágica, rumors abounded that Russian undercover agents plotted strikes throughout the Platine basin; foreign agitators in direct communication with Moscow supposedly organized the 1932 Central American disturbances.[36]

Union opposition to World War I calling on workers not to participate in an imperialist conflict, working-class support for the Russian Revolution, and the attendance of proletarian delegates at peace conferences calling for labor co-operation to end all wars served as "proof" for local governments that many workers' organizations represented antipatriotic elements. In areas where substantial numbers of Jews participated in actions, anti-Semitism often showed itself. So-called patriotic vigilante groups marked Jews for special persecution in Argentina. Uruguayan officials closed a Jewish cultural center and deported several of its members in the early 1920s. In addition, governments of several nations deported numerous workers of foreign origin.[37]

Industrialists and private citizens often supplemented state efforts against labor. The São Paulo Industrialists' Association circulated black lists, kept tabs on workers it deemed undesirable, and co-operated closely with the police. A similar Chilean organization, founded in 1922 with 78 member firms, expanded to include 1,075 establishments the next year. Many companies, even if not members of a business association, employed both spies to ferret out organizers and company police to maintain control over workers. In some factories, owners divided workers into competing ethnic groups to prevent workers' solidarity. Industry-wide lockouts, often instituted in response to a strike in one factory, could throw thousands of innocent people out of work. Employers thus hoped to pit workers against each other and provoke government intervention. When workers protested mass firings or wage cuts during economic recessions, owners used lockouts to double advantage: They reduced excessive inventory and eliminated worker resistance. The actions of a Santos owner exemplify yet another strategy: He fired all 1,200 of his workers after a strike and then, taking advantage of the existing oversupply of labor, replaced them in the next six weeks.[38]

Private organizations such as the Argentine Asociación de Libre Trabajo, the Uruguayan Liga del Trabajo Libre, and the Chilean Liga Patriótica represent another type of antilabor, procapitalist force. They provided and protected strikebreakers, sometimes smashing strikes even when they had not been asked to do so by employers. The Liga Patriótica Argentina, composed of youth from elite families and hired gunmen, forcefully broke strikes, systematically hunted persons suspected of subversive ideas, and supplied thugs (many of them convicts serving long jail terms and especially paroled for this service) to staff private company police forces. All these associations styled themselves as patriotic defenders of law and order against foreignism and subversion.[39]

Legislation

Governments passed additional social legislation during this period. These laws, which formed the second prong of the ruling-class counteroffensive against labor, had two general aims: They placed labor under state control to help assure that it would pursue a docile, nonviolent course, and they projected the image of a state that cared for workers by protecting them from the worst abuses of employers. Legislators hoped that that image would lead workers to support the existing system. Accordingly, parties in power and those out of office at times pushed for social legislation. Catholics also supported such laws as an integral part of the social program outlined in papal pronouncements. External factors aided, too. The peace agreements ending the European War, signed by most Latin American nations, included a basic charter of labor rights and committed the signatories to implement them. Although few Latin American countries fulfilled these provisions, their existence strengthened the cause of those favoring social legislation. Still, laws only grudgingly won approval. Most conservatives believed that armed force provided the best response to working-class demands.

The workers' drive for social legislation derived directly from objective conditions. During the 1920s, these had changed little from the conditions that had prevailed before the war. Hours remained long, companies installed few safety measures or none at all, and arbitrary disciplinary rules regulated job conditions. Few employers recognized unions as legitimate bargaining agents, and insecurity of employment and wages characterized almost every work situation. Furthermore, owners often ignored protective laws, preferring to pay the paltry fines when caught for doing so.

A brief look at prevailing working and living conditions shows why workers demanded immediate and substantial improvements. A Bolivian congressional commission in 1919, for example, learned that miners had to endure twenty-four-hour shifts. Brazilian workers, including women and children (who in some areas made up as much as one-third of the industrial labor force), labored an average of ten hours daily, six days a week. A government survey in that same country calculated that minimum food requirements for an average family cost four times the average wage in 1919. A Cuban study estimated that food alone required 60 percent of a worker's pay, and a similar survey in Chile concluded that the figure stood between 80 and 90 percent. Such circumstances made it mandatory for women and older children to work in order to support their families. Most workers also lived in substandard housing. The Peruvian census of 1920 listed 28 percent of Lima's occupied housing as uninhabitable and found that 25 percent of all families lived in one room. In Santiago, fewer than one in five slum dwellings was classified as livable.[40]

Governments or enlightened legislators in some countries responded to workers' demands. Between 1919 and 1926, Brazil adopted compensation for victims of some industrial accidents, required factory inspections, and passed a series of laws protecting workers under eighteen years of age. Later, railroad pensions and Sunday rest laws complemented these, as did an official commission created to oversee existing legislation and draft additional measures. Other countries passed similar laws, but enforcement everywhere remained scanty at best, and large sectors of the proletariat remained outside their scope.[41]

In areas where a large proportion of the working class could and did vote, a number of political parties and politicians backed social legislation. They thus hoped both to rally workers' support and to protect the system from substantial or violent social change. The second administration of José Batlle y Ordóñez in Uruguay (1911–1915), for example, marked a high tide of labor and social legislation. By the end of his term, laws guaranteed the right to strike, an eight-hour day, minimum wages, old-age pensions, compensation for industrial accidents, a state-run insurance system, and better working conditions for urban workers.[42]

Two other presidents, Arturo Alessandri of Chile (1920–1924) and Hipólito Yrigoyen in Argentina (1916–1922, 1928–1930), attempted to win labor support and keep labor peace. Alessandri bid for working-class votes in his 1920 presidential campaign. He promised a series of reforms that included labor legislation, and his election indicated that the strategy may have worked. In addition, widespread discontent had swept the country in previous years, and the appeal aimed to prevent more violence. However, once Alessandri took office, his proposals met little success. Conservatives, most of them from rural areas and therefore less attuned to urban problems, blocked his legislative program, and he did not even attempt to implement many of his campaign promises concerning social issues.[43]

The Argentine Radical Party, which elected Yrigoyen president in 1916, competed with the Socialists for urban votes. Once in power, it continued to voice approval for reformist labor causes. The Radicals sponsored some social legislation between 1916 and 1930, most of it aimed either at courting elite working-class groups, such as railroaders, or at enhancing the government's image by mandating stricter enforcement of existing laws.

Yrigoyen, and to a lesser extent his successor, Marcelo T. Alvear (1922–1928), built a close relationship with reformist elements among the labor movement. On several occasions, Yrigoyen used his office to mediate labor disputes by talking to syndicalists and Socialists; and at times, he succeeded in settling or preventing strikes. The Radicals worked most closely with the railway unions. Delegates from these bodies frequently met with the president and appointed representatives to a government agency that ruled on conditions governing railroad workers. These unusual procedures were mutually advantageous. Reformist leaders strengthened their positions by delivering concrete economic benefits and by avoiding what could have been long and costly strikes. The Radicals hoped to combat Socialist influence within the unions, which totaled over 100,000 members, many of them voters. The Radicals also helped to prevent labor unity in this vital sector by encouraging a split between reformists and militants. Labor peace, moreover, increased the Radical government's prestige in office and reduced the possibility of criticism from the Conservative opposition or the armed forces. The Radical strategy paid some dividends in that the principal rail union renounced its "revolutionary aims with the hope of furthering the implementation of workers' benefits and wages with the government," thus ultimately dedicating itself to securing "a better standard of living within the capitalist system."[44] Furthermore, there is some evidence that the Radicals garnered working-class votes. And the Radicals enhanced their nationalist image by supporting railroad workers, because most of them toiled for foreign companies.[45]

Although some credit for the Argentine movement's decline after 1924 belongs to the Radicals, their labor policies had strict limits. In 1919, the government used massive force to crush workers' protests throughout the country, as it later did in Patagonia. In the final analysis, the Radical posture toward the working class resembled that of most liberal parties: Co-opt when possible, and repress those elements advocating radical change.

Three nations—Argentina, Brazil, and Chile—all contemplated passing comprehensive labor codes during these years, but the results differed according to local circumstances. A pair of variables conditioned this process: the composition of local ruling classes and the strength of national labor movements. In Brazil, a national labor code never materialized. The conservative and relatively unified ruling class did not need to approve comprehensive labor legislation because the working class posed no real threat. Nor did any liberal middle groups appear to champion labor's cause in the government or the National Congress.

In Argentina, the attempt to pass a labor code in the 1920s also failed, but for different reasons than in Brazil. Although a strong and relatively unified ruling class existed there, a liberal segment of it, represented by the Radicals, controlled the presidency at the time, and furthermore, the Argentine labor movement possessed substantial clout. But because the proposed code endowed the government with extensive powers over labor, nearly all organizations and ideological tendencies violently opposed it. When Radicals first presented the legislation in the National Congress, a quickly mounted protest campaign, culminating in a mass rally of over 100,000 workers in Buenos Aires, convinced the government to drop its plans. The retreat was an immediate response to fears of a mass uprising similar to the one that occurred in 1919. It also stemmed from the fact that rural-based Conservatives, who controlled the Senate, threatened to block the bill. They feared that the code's powers would allow the Radicals to manipulate labor and stay in office. Furthermore, some still argued that there was no need for this type of legislation because the police or armed forces could control worker unrest.[46]

In Chile, a unified ruling class split on the issue of labor legislation. Rural representatives opposed a labor code, whereas urban elements favored it as a means to prevent unrest and extend state control over labor. Liberals, as in other areas, supported it, giving the measure a chance of passing the National Congress. Workers opposed the code as an outright instrument of state control, but they did not have the strength to force the government to withdraw it. Conservatives, however, blocked the legislation. The situation changed when the military overthrew Alessandri in 1924. The ruling junta passed a series of labor laws by decree, and the Conservative Ibáñez, who followed in office, further extended the legislation.[47]

The Chilean code prefigured laws that other Latin American governments instituted after 1930 in the effort to co-opt and control labor by guaranteeing basic rights while placing stringent controls over the exercise of them. Specifically, the code legalized working-class organizations but subjected them to a series of restrictions both in their formation and in their functioning. All unions had to register with the National Labor Department to receive legal recognition, a provision that allowed the government to approve only those unions considered safe and ensured that all legal organizations adhere to the regulations. The law also stipulated that government inspectors could attend union meetings, thus formalizing the gathering of intelligence for state use. By making the process of unionization relatively difficult for urban workers (and impossible for rural ones) and by splitting white- and blue-collar workers into separate legal categories, these laws encouraged a divided and relatively unorganized working class. The code also gave workers increased accident benefits and coverage, created labor tribunals on which the state held a deciding vote for conciliation and arbitration of labor conflicts, instituted obligatory sickness and old-age insurance, regularized the functioning of cooperatives, and strictly regimented collective contracts.[48]

The Depression as Catalyst: The Cuban Case

The first years of the Great Depression brought a sharp decline in labor activity across the continent. Repressive regimes, economic hardships including massive unemployment, and the general fall in militancy during the late 1920s all contributed to that decline. In Cuba, however, the opposite proved true: The Depression served as a catalyst that generated one of the period's major explosions of labor activity.

The world economic disaster of 1929 reverberated throughout Latin America and produced a sharp decline in economic activity. The resulting general dislocations and social tensions led to a series of military coups that toppled constitutional governments. The new regimes took conservative positions and, in most cases, forcefully repressed the labor movement as a potentially disruptive force in a time of crisis. Where the movement had weak roots, governments easily curtailed almost all forms of working-class expression. In some areas, however, a limited resistance occurred, usually led by Communists. In Argentina, for example, the Communists' organizational skills and party discipline allowed them to mobilize workers against the right-wing military government despite unfavorable conditions. Two outstanding struggles of the early 1930s involved the meat-packing industry in greater Buenos Aires and petroleum workers in Comodoro Rivadavia. In both cases, workers, supported by Communists, fought back against wage cuts and dismissals and continued to ask for better working conditions among other demands.[49]

In Cuba, however, the Depression produced a very different effect. The Revolution of 1933 and its aftermath, in which the urban and rural proletariats played major roles, represents one of the most important periods of working-class activity in Latin America. In addition, practically all the long-term trends found throughout the continent between World War I and the Depression manifested themselves in Cuba. The island's labor history is thus a study in microcosm of the period.[50]

Strikes erupted in Cuba, as elsewhere, during the war period and for much the same reasons. After that time, conflicting ideologies rent the ranks of labor, although the majority of organizations remained in the hands of anarchosyndicalists. In the province of Camagüey, to cite an extreme case, railroad workers split along several lines: Socialists and non-Socialists, employees and workers,

Cubans and Spaniards. The collapse of the sugar boom in 1920 brought economic chaos but also led to organizational and ideological advances. That year, a congress attempted to found a national organization capable of channeling all workers' demands. For the first time in Cuba, delegates took clear-cut class positions, calling for a revolutionary working-class movement. The planned federation did not materialize, but the idea prepared the ground for the future. At the same time, the movement gathered strength. As workers banded together to fight the erosion of their wages caused by inflation, they eventually realized that economic improvements alone could not change their situation. More often than not, they included the rights to organize and to strike in their demands. Protest, however, drew only repression. The impact of the Russian Revolution also proved important as students, intellectuals, and workers grasped its implication for the working class, leading to the gradual formation of Communist groups.[51]

The year 1925 produced three key events. First, Gerardo Machado became president, a post he occupied until driven from office in 1933. As the representative of foreign interests and the Cuban bourgeoisie, he promised a law-and-order administration, boasting publicly that "no strike would last more than 24 hours." Second, a national labor organization, the Confederación Nacional Obrera de Cuba (CNOC) emerged. It formulated a set of economic demands and dedicated itself to class struggle and direct action. At first, anarchosyndicalists controlled CNOC, but by 1927 a Communist majority existed. Third, shortly after CNOC's formation, several Communist groups founded the Cuban Communist Party. Its program outlined a series of working-class aspirations that included the interests of agricultural workers, marking the first time a Cuban working-class organization had given such attention to nonurban sectors.

The labor movement remained divided, however. Anarchosyndicalists preached class warfare but avoided direct political action by operating totally outside an electoral or legal union framework. Reformists held that workers should seek economic and social improvements within the legal system. Government-sponsored unions, headed by corrupt leaders who took their orders directly from

Machado, further weakened the ranks of labor after 1925. And the Communists maintained yet a different position. Following the party's general analysis, they held that economic demands formed an important part of any working-class program, but as a means toward the overthrow of capitalism, not as an end in themselves.

The struggle between workers and the government intensified after 1925. The Communists, in particular, pushed to extend working-class organization. Workers slowly learned from the day-to-day struggle that strength lay in organization and solidarity among themselves. They also increasingly put their new knowledge to the test. At first, those in one factory would strike or initiate a job action; then, those in several factories in the same trade would take action; and finally, those in a given region or series of related trades would act together. The Machado government reacted forcefully against this growing threat, unleashing armed violence against strikes and murdering as many as 150 labor leaders.[52]

The Communist Party and other labor groups continued to organize in the face of repression. In 1930, Machado outlawed the CNOC and closed the national university. In response, the confederation, aided by progressive student groups, called a general strike to regain its legality and restore all civil liberties. Approximately 200,000 persons participated in the twenty-four-hour protest, but they faced severe police repression. The action represented the first mass mobilization called by the party and CNOC. Both learned from it that urban protest alone could not topple Machado. After 1930, they concentrated on organizing the agricultural sector.[53]

That new strategy flowed from objective conditions within Cuba and from its dependency on the United States. Agricultural workers, above all those in the sugar industry, formed the largest segment of the working class, numbering about 400,000 out of a population of 3 million. They lacked organization, and primitive working and living conditions prevailed throughout the industry. Foreigners, mostly North Americans, controlled a major portion of the sugar industry, the banking sector, railroads, most public utilities, and other assorted businesses. U.S. investment had grown from $50 million in 1896 to $265 million in 1915 and $1.5 billion in 1928, giving North American capitalism the dominant position within the Cuban economy. Furthermore, Cuba depended on the U.S. market to sell its sugar, and any rise in tariffs on sugar would severely damage the nation's economic health. Under the Platt Amendment (ratified in 1903), the United States could legally intervene in Cuba, even to the extent of using military force. By the 1930s, however, the mere threat of U.S. action usually proved sufficient to produce internal changes, because the Cuban bourgeoisie recognized the impact of the pressures that could be applied.

Under these circumstances, the Communists' anti-imperialist analysis appealed to a broad spectrum within Cuban society. Middle groups resented their nation's relative impotence in determining its own affairs. Workers for foreign companies, although perhaps not understanding the party's sophisticated analysis, clearly understood, through their everyday experience on the job, that foreigners exploited them. For these reasons, foreign companies, particularly those in the sugar sector, presented ideal targets for labor organization.[54]

Despite government and company pressures, Communists, CNOC members, and progressive student organizers fanned out into the countryside during 1931 and 1932. These excerpts from two personal accounts of the organizing effort illustrate its nature:

> The Confederation [CNOC] did not need much money, as its organizers could travel free on buses, many of which were driven by comrades; and upon arriving at a village or mill, they gave organizers food and found them a place to sleep and often offered them clothing. Organizers often arrived without a cent in their pockets.

> I was at a mill for three days during a strike. By day I hid in an abandoned hut and drank sugar cane juice, and only went out at night to walk through many miles of cane to distribute propaganda among the comrades. [55]

The recruiting drive soon paid dividends. In December 1932, a sugar workers' conference founded the Sindicato Nacional de Obreros de la Industria Azucarera (SNOIA), one of the country's first industrial groupings. The organization grew quickly and, under strong Communist influence, soon included a substantial proportion of those toiling in the *centrales* (mills).

The world economic depression hit Cuba hard, further aggravating a bad situation. Unemployment swelled, throwing 250,000 heads of families out of work. In Havana province, workers earned less in 1931 than they had in the period from 1909 to 1910; between 1929 and 1933, wages fell to 50 to 70 percent of 1923 levels. At the height of the crisis, cane cutters earned 20 to 30 cents daily, a sum that "barely provided them with food and clothing, leaving no surplus for the dead season." (The harvest lasted three to four months; the rest of the year was the "dead season.") By 1933, one report stated that approximately 60 percent of the population occupied a position outside the mainstream of the economy.[56]

As in all crises, owners protected themselves by reducing salaries, laying off workers, and generally increasing the level of exploitation. Sharp conflicts between capital and labor ensued as workers fought to preserve their economic position and jobs. Gradually, however, workers stopped trying to just keep from losing ground and began to take active stands by demanding improvements. Simultaneously, their goals became more directly political, and they called for Machado's ouster.

Growing resentment among workers, students, and middle-sector liberals eventually brought matters to a head. In August 1933, a bus drivers' strike quickly spread to almost all industry and commerce. On August 12, under popular pressure and having lost the support of the army and the United States because of his inability to keep social order, Machado resigned. Many persons then returned to work, but the countryside still seethed with discontent. On August 21, workers in Camagüey seized a local sugar mill; and by the end of September, thirty-six *centrales,* representing 30 percent of Cuba's cane production, had been occupied. In some cases, strikers also took over mill towns and nearby ports. At certain locations, workers created a labor-peasant militia and spread their control to whole zones. Tobacco workers in Pinar del Río, coffee pickers in Oriente, and people working for the Bethlehem Steel

Company at Daiquirí led similar actions. The claim that some mills set up soviets in imitation of Russian workers is probably exaggerated, but a worker, a peasant, and a soldier occasionally headed the local government committees that often distributed land, food, and vital supplies to the local population.[57]

The uprising in the countryside and continued urban unrest had immediate repercussions in Havana. On September 3, a coup led by an army sergeant, Fulgencio Batista, deposed the Provisional Government that had replaced Machado. Ramón Grau San Martín, a liberal nationalist law professor, then became provisional president. Grau feared U.S. intervention if the situation deteriorated. He therefore quickly dispatched troops to dislodge workers from occupied areas. Thus Cuban soldiers fought Cuban workers in order to protect U.S.-owned property. Although this act temporarily crushed the movement, many workers did get collective contracts for the first time, and others improved their work situation and economic position.

Once the threat subsided, Grau attempted to defuse the movement by granting a number of the workers' immediate demands. For example, he decreed an across-the-board 50 percent wage increase and the eight-hour day. He then passed legislation designed to bring labor under control and prevent future outbursts. One decree prohibited government employees, army personnel, and police from organizing. It further ruled that all unions must register with the Ministry of Labor and that they must submit their demands to the government before calling a strike. The decree also created machinery for binding arbitration in labor conflicts and gave government officials the right to attend union meetings, thus placing labor under constant surveillance.

Nevertheless, agitation continued on a national scale. CNOC's national congress in 1934 showed labor's potential. The organization claimed 403,000 members in over 200 unions. Although that figure is probably exaggerated, the confederation did have a large-enough membership to pull considerable weight. At the gathering, Communists called for working-class unity around an anti-imperialist, nationalist, and revolutionary program. However, divisions among Communists, Grau's followers, independents, and others prevented any substantial agreement. SNOIA's third congress that same year reflected its progress as representatives from 103 mills endorsed a comprehensive industry-wide program.[58]

Continued domestic unrest, combined with U.S. pressure for the installation of a more reliable regime, resulted in Grau's ouster early in 1934. His successor, Carlos Mendieta—in reality a front man for Batista, whose control over the army made him the real power —strengthened Grau's hard-line labor policy. The government soon prohibited strikes against public services, protecting among others the Havana Electric Company, an American Foreign Power Corporation subsidiary, which was then engaged in a protracted struggle with its workers. The law also outlined a series of measures ostensibly "to protect the right to work" but actually intended to break organized labor's power by facilitating the use of strike-breakers and making it easier to fire union militants.

In response, labor immediately called a general strike. Threatened with the potential loss of the sugar crop, Mendieta promulgated the Law of National Defense. It set up special tribunals to try anyone advocating violent change and ruled that foreigners guilty of this offense could be deported. When the strike continued despite these measures, the government resorted to even harsher acts. It dissolved all unions that refused to order their members back to work in twenty-four hours. Further, it suspended the collective contracts of those organizations that did not observe that proviso, opening the way for mass firings of strikers. Although up to 200,000 workers participated in the general strike, the government, armed with the law and military hardware, proved too strong, and the strike ground to a halt.

A 1935 general strike capped working-class unrest in Cuba during this period. Although the strike ostensibly aimed to oust Mendieta, in fact the workers hoped to eliminate Batista and his antilabor policies. As usual, the government reacted forcefully. It created Emergency Tribunals to try strikers and even empowered them to mete out death sentences in certain cases. It also mobilized the army and gave orders to shoot agitators on sight. These harsh measures, combined with a lack of labor unity stemming from personal and political rivalries, proved sufficient to break the strike.

Its failure, in conjunction with the strict application of antiworker legislation, momentarily reduced the movement to inactivity.[59]

Cuban events thus combined many features found throughout Latin America. First, ideological splits rent labor ranks. Second, anarchosyndicalism lost ground, and communism emerged as the most dynamic ideology within the movement. Third, these years also saw a growing class consciousness marked by attempts to build a unified movement and the growth of new organizations, such as industry-wide federations. Fourth, the ruling class repressed labor by force and restrictive legislation. Fifth, some governments used co-optive measures to pacify labor. Sixth, the movement expanded into new sectors, most notably agricultural workers. Seventh, the period produced a labor explosion that reached its peak with the 1933 revolution. Finally, a relationship existed between the development of Cuban labor and the country's economic situation. An obvious foreign presence and outside control over the economy facilitated the task of building a revolutionary movement and aided the Communists' recruitment process in particular. Unlike other areas in Latin America, the Cuban working class suffered through three economic downturns (the initial years of the war, the crash of 1920, and then the Depression) without the interval of relative prosperity that had retarded the movement elsewhere. The prolonged crisis apparently allowed the impetus generated during the war to continue. As a result, reformism played a minimal role, and militant forces within the working class emerged as the strongest element.

CONCLUSION

The labor movement managed substantial progress during the expansive and explosive period despite serious obstacles. Workers everywhere waged massive struggles, and some won partial victories. The Argentine movement still proved the strongest, but those in a half-dozen other countries also grew. In less-developed areas, organization remained at a low level, and the ease with which governments crushed unions or strikes speaks for labor's precarious condition at the local and national levels.

External phenomena shaped many patterns. Crises within world capitalism led to war and then later to the Depression. War produced economic dislocation and then a growth of exports and local industry. The 1920s brought relative prosperity marked by continued industrial and urban expansion and by a steady stream of foreign investment. These trends led to changes within the working class by increasing the number of industrial workers, enlarging white-collar sectors, and creating pockets of rural proletarians working mostly on foreign-owned land. These new members of the working class joined with industrial groups to carry forward the tradition of struggle born in the formative period.

Latin American communism echoed its European counterpart, challenging the ruling class and competing with other ideologies for the allegiance of the working class. At the same time, the more violent philosophies lost ground, and reformists and Communists emerged as the leading influences within the labor movement. Ruling-class response to labor also mirrored foreign events in its two-pronged counteroffensive of repression and expanded controls over existing labor organizations. Thus, as of the 1930s, the Latin American movement remained to a large degree conditioned by the continent's dependent status.

NOTES

[1] On foreign investment, see United Nations, Economic Commission for Latin America, Department of Economic and Social Affairs, *External Financing in Latin America* (New York, 1965), pp. 7–22; North American Congress on Latin America (hereafter NACLA), *Yanqui Dollar: The Contribution of U.S. Private Investment to Underdevelopment in Latin America* (New York and Berkeley, Calif., 1971), pp. 3–8. The degree of industrial growth during the war has recently been questioned in Warren Dean, *The Industrialization of São Paulo, 1880–1945* (Austin, Tex., 1969) and Carlos F. Díaz Alejandro, *Essays on the Economic History of the Argentine Republic* (New Haven, Conn., 1970).

[2] Oscar Alvarez Andrews, *El desarrollo industrial de Chile* (Santiago, 1936), p. 221; Grupo Cubano de Investigaciones Económicas, *Estudio sobre Cuba* (Miami, 1963), p. 548.

[3] Juan Arcos, *El sindicalismo en América Latina* (Fribourg, Switz., and Bogotá, 1964), pp. 105–106; Ricardo A. Paredes, *El imperialismo en el*

Ecuador (Quito, 1938), p. 43; Jorge Crespo Toral, *El comunismo en el Ecuador* (Quito, 1958), pp. 8, 15; Miguel Urrutia Montoya, *The Development of the Colombian Labor Movement* (New Haven, Conn., 1969), pp. 55–59.

4 Jaime Ponce G., Thomas J. Shanley, and Antonio J. Cisneros, *Breve historia del sindicalismo boliviano y legislación social vigente*, 2d ed. (La Paz, 1968), pp. 13–15; Agustín Barcelli S., *Medio siglo de luchas sindicales revolucionarias en Bolivia, 1905–1955* (La Paz, 1956), pp. 76–80; República Cubana, *Historia de Cuba* (La Havana, 1964), 2:178–180; Jorge Basadre, *Chile, Perú, y Bolivia independientes* (Barcelona–Buenos Aires, 1948), p. 573; Eugenio Chang-Rodríguez, *La literatura política de González Prada, Mariátegui y Haya de la Torre* (Mexico City, 1957), pp. 7–33.

5 Julio César Jobet, "Movimiento Social-Obrero," *Desarrollo de Chile en la primera mitad del siglo XX* (Santiago, 1953), pp. 74–78.

6 Alfredo Errández y Daniel Contabile, *Sindicato y sociedad en el Uruguay* (Montevideo, 1961), p. 135; República Oriental del Uruguay, Ministerio de Industria, Oficina Nacional del Trabajo, *Estadísticas del trabajo y de las subsistencias: Anuario correspondiente a 1919* (Montevideo, 1920), pp. 75, 85; Héctor Rodríguez, *Nuestros sindicatos (1865–1965)* (Montevideo, 1965), pp. 14–18.

7 Astrojildo Pereira, *A formação do PCB, 1922/1928* (Rio de Janeiro, 1962), pp. 20–33; Jover Telles, *O movimento sindical no Brasil* (Rio de Janeiro, 1962), pp. 75–80; Dean, *Industrialization of São Paulo*, p. 161.

8 General background in Sebastián Marotta, *El movimiento sindical argentino: Su génesis y desarrollo*, 2 vols. (Buenos Aires, 1960–1961), vol. 2, chaps. 9–21. On 1919 see Nicolás Babini, *Enero de 1919* (Buenos Aires, 1956); Octavio A. Piñero, *Los orígenes de la trágica semana de enero 1919* (Buenos Aires, 1956); and especially Julio Godio, *Le semana trágica de enero 1919* (Buenos Aires, 1972). Conservatives estimate 141 dead, 400 seriously wounded, a like number injured, and 3,000 jailed; worker sources say over 700 deaths, 2,000 injuries, and over 5,000 arrests.

9 Details on first Communist parties in Rollie Poppino, *International Communism in Latin America, 1917–1963* (London, 1964), p. 58.

10 Quoted in John W. F. Dulles, *Anarchists and Communists in Brazil, 1900–1935* (Austin, Tex., 1973), p. 115.

11 Ibid., p. 75.

12 Information on Brazil from Robert J. Alexander, *Communism in Latin America* (New Brunswick, N.J., 1957), p. 96; Edgard Carone, *A república velha: instituições e classes sociais* (São Paulo, 1970); Dulles, *Anarchists and Communists in Brazil*, books 2–10; Boris Fausto, *Trabalho urbano e conflito social (1890–1920)* (São Paulo and Rio de Janeiro, 1976), pp. 41–61; and Paulo Sérgio Pinheiro, *Política e trabalho no Brasil* (Rio de Janeiro, 1975), chaps. 5–7.

[13] Bolivian information from Raúl Federico Abadie-Aicardi, *Economía y sociedad de Bolivia en el siglo XX* (Montevideo, 1966); Erasmo Barrios Villa, *Historia sindical de Bolivia* (Oruro, Bolivia, 1966); Barcelli, *Medio siglo de luchas*; Guillermo Lora, *Historia del movimiento obrero boliviano, 1923–1933* (La Paz, 1970); and Ponce, *Breve historia del sindicalismo boliviano*. Uruguayan information in Francisco R. Pintos, *Historia del movimiento obrero del Uruguay* (Montevideo, 1960); and Rodríguez, *Nuestros sindicatos*.

[14] On APRA origins, see Peter F. Klarén, *Modernization, Dislocation, and Aprismo: Origins of the Peruvian Aprista Party, 1870–1932* (Austin, Tex., 1973), chaps. 6–7; on APRA ideology, see Harry Kantor, *Program and Ideology of the Peruvian Aprista Party*, 2d rev. ed. (Washington, D.C., 1966). On workers and the Communist Party as well as its principal spokesperson, José Carlos Mariátegui, see José Carlos Mariátegui, *Seven Interpretive Essays on Peruvian Reality* (Austin, Tex., 1971); John M. Baines, *Revolution in Peru: Mariátegui and the Myth* (University, Ala., 1972), an anti-Marxist life and times; Ricardo Martínez de la Torre, *Apuntes para una interpretación marxista de la historia social del Perú*, 4 vols. (Lima, 1949), 1:17ff.; and Chang-Rodríguez, *La literatura política*.

[15] Crespo Toral, *El comunismo en el Ecuador*; Luis E. Maldonado, *Bases del partido socialista ecuatoriano* (Quito, 1938), and *Conferencia sustentada por el Sr. Luis E. Maldonado a nombre de la concentración socialista, integrada por los grupos Acción, Germinal y Revolución Social en el salón máximo de la Universidad de Guayaquil, la noche del 31 de julio de 1935* (Guayaquil, 1935).

[16] See Hernán Ramírez Necochea, *Origen y formación del Partido Comunista de Chile* (Santiago, 1965); Jobet, "Movimiento Social-Obrero"; Jorge I. Barría, Serón, *Los movimientos sociales de Chile desde 1910 hasta 1926* (Santiago, 1960).

[17] Marotta, *El movimiento sindical argentino*, vol. 2, covers this period. Figures from Alfredo López, *Historia del movimiento social y la clase obrera argentina* (Buenos Aíres, 1971), p. 213. The best source on the FORA is Diego Abad de Santillán, *La F.O.R.A. ideología y trayectoria del movimiento obrero revolucionario en la argentina*, 2d ed. (Buenos Aires, 1971), figures from p. 275.

[18] On divisions, see Santillán, *La F.O.R.A.*; Godio, *La semana trágica*, pp. 17–21; and López, *Historia del movimiento social*, p. 207. Those publishing *La Protesta* held one minority anarchist position; the other followed Benvenuto Durruty, a Spanish anarchist, who believed in and practiced violence. On the latter aspect, see Osvaldo Bayer, *Severino Di Giovanni, El idealista de la violencia* (Buenos Aires, 1970), a biography of one Argentine participant. Internationalism, for example, led to wide-scale protests in Argentina and elsewhere against the execution of the two

North American anarchists Sacco and Vanzetti. Anarchists also mounted a concentrated campaign to free Simón Radowitsky, the man who had killed the Buenos Aires Police Chief in 1909. (He was finally released in 1930 and banished, whereupon he went to Spain and fought in the Civil War.) See Santillán, *La F.O.R.A.*, pp. 269–272; Dulles, *Anarchists and Communists in Brazil*, p. 338; and Benito Marianetti, *Las luchas sociales en Mendoza* (Mendoza, 1970), p. 94.

19 Godio, *La semana trágica*, pp. 9, 17–21, 69, 120–122; López, *Historia del movimiento social*, p. 230.

20 Quoted in Rubens Iscaro, *Origen y desarrollo del movimiento sindical argentino* (Buenos Aires, 1958), p. 100.

21 On the Communist Party specifically, I have found only three works: Jorge Abelardo Ramos, *El partido comunista en la política argentina* (Buenos Aires, 1962); Rodolfo Puiggrós, *Las izquierdas y el problema nacional* (Buenos Aires, 1965); and Carlos M. Silveyra, *El comunismo en la Argentina* (Buenos Aires, 1937). On socialism in this period, see Dardo Cúneo, *Juan B. Justo y las luchas sociales en la Argentina* (Buenos Aires, 1965); Godio, *La semana trágica*, pp. 77, 85–98; and Jacinto Oddone, *Gremialismo proletario argentino* (Buenos Aires, 1949), p. 250ff.

22 Martín S. Casaretto, *Historia del movimiento obrero argentino* (Buenos Aires, 1947), p. 26.

23 United Nations, *External Financing in Latin America*, pp. 7–22.

24 On Brazil, see Victor Alba, *Politics and the Labor Movement in Latin America* (Palo Alto, Calif., 1969), p. 256. Information on Colombia, Justiniano Espinosa S., *El sindicalismo* (Bogota, 1962), p. 14. On Bolivia, see Ponce, *Breve historia del sindicalismo boliviano*, pp. 16–19; the authors claim that a commerce employees' union existed as early as 1921 but fail to mention the exact nature of the organization.

25 Quote by Alberto Edwards in 1920, cited in Julio César Jobet, *Ensayo crítico del desarrollo económico-social de Chile* (Santiago, 1951), p. 143. Other material from Julio César Jobet, *Recabarren: Los orígenes del movimiento obrero y del socialismo chileno* (Santiago, 1955), pp. 143–147; Tulio Lagos Valenzuela, *Bosquejo histórico del movimiento obrero en Chile* (Santiago, 1941), chap. 4; Barría Serón, *Los movimientos sociales de Chile*, p. 191ff.; Ramírez Necochea, *Origen y formación del Partido Comunista de Chile*, pp. 94–111.

26 Marotta, *El movimiento sindical argentino*, 2:235–258; Marianetti, *Las luchas sociales en Mendoza*, pp. 69–76.

27 Charles David Kepner and Jan Henry Soothill, *The Banana Empire* (New York, 1935), chap. 12, "Labor Throws Down the Gauntlet," discusses strikes throughout the Caribbean Basin, also pp. 324–325; Urrutia Montoya, *Development of the Colombian Labor Movement*, pp. 100–

104. The strike indirectly influenced future Colombian politics in that it radicalized the leftist leader Jorge Elicier Gaitán, who was a member of the Congressional Committee named to investigate the events.

[28] Urrutia Montoya, *Development of the Colombian Labor Movement*, pp. 93–97, 124–125, notes that Colombia's three largest strikes all involved foreign companies. On foreign oil companies, see J. Fred Rippy, *The Capitalists and Colombia* (New York, 1931), pp. 123–151, 180–191, 249–250.

[29] On Ecuador, see Paredes, *El imperialismo en el Ecuador*, pp. 42, 97–99; for Peru, Martínez de la Torre, *Apuntes para una interpretación marxista*, vols. 3 and 4, abounds with documents on miners, regional federations, and rural movements in general. On Colombia, see Pierre Gilhodés, "Agrarian Struggles in Colombia," in *Agrarian Problems and Peasant Movements in Latin America*, Rodolfo Stavenhagen, ed. (Garden City, N.Y., 1970), pp. 411–413.

[30] On Peru, Martínez de la Torre, *Apuntes para una interpretación marxista*, 3:110–111. On El Salvador, William Krehm, *Democracia y tiranías en el caribe* (Mexico City, 1949), pp. 43–63; and Thomas P. Anderson, *Matanza: El Salvador's Communist Revolt of 1932* (Lincoln, Neb., 1971). For Chile, Ramírez Necochea, *Origen y formación del Partido Comunista de Chile*, p. 92.

[31] On rural movements, see Marotta, *El movimiento sindical argentino*, 2: 259–260; and Iscaro, *Origen y desarrollo del movimiento sindical argentino*, pp. 129–132. On La Forestal, see Gastón Gori, *La Forestal*, rev. ed. (Buenos Aires, 1974), pp. 161–174, 241–260.

[32] On Patagonia, see Osvaldo Bayer, *Los vengadores de la Patagonia trágica*, 2 vols. (Buenos Aires, 1972–1973).

[33] Frederick B. Pike, *Chile and the United States, 1880–1962* (South Bend, Ind., 1963), p. 208; Alejandro Chelén Rojas, *Trayectoria del socialismo* (Buenos Aires, 1969), pp. 34–47. These three Bolivian massacres occurred in the Catavi, Huanchaca, and Patiño mines, which became centers of agitation. See Barrios Villa, *Historia sindical de Bolivia*, pp. 44, 53–54; Barcelli, *Medio siglo de luchas*, p. 74. Peruvian agrarian movements took place in the Cuzco valley, Huacho, Huanca, Huaráz, Ica, and Sayán. See Martínez de la Torre, *Apuntes para una interpretación marxista*, 1:22 n.1, 4:399–404.

[34] Decree Law No. 6926 of Nov. 12, 1930, reproduced in Moisés Poblete Troncoso, *Condiciones de vida y de trabajo de la población indígena del Perú* (Geneva, 1938), p. 132; Pintos, *Historia del movimiento obrero del Uruguay*, p. 175; Dulles, *Anarchists and Communists in Brazil*, p. 125.

[35] See Dulles, *Anarchists and Communists in Brazil*, pp. 107, 121–123, 139, 279, 334, on Brazil; Marotta, *El movimiento sindical argentino*, vols. 1 and 2, and Santillán, *La F.O.R.A.*, contain material on Argentina; for

Colombia, see Urrutia Montoya, *Development of the Colombian Labor Movement,* pp. 57, 65–66.

36 Dulles, *Anarchists and Communists in Brazil,* p. 54; Babini, *Enero de 1919,* pp. 23–25, on the Semana Trágica; Anderson, *Matanza,* pp. 83–86.

37 Marotta, *El movimiento sindical argentino,* 2:230; Pereira, *Formação do PCB,* pp. 28–30; Santillán, *La F.O.R.A.,* pp. 79, 210, 213, 221–222, 237, 269–272; Dulles, *Anarchists and Communists in Brazil,* pp. 60–65, 107, 121–123, 338; Marianetti, *Las luchas sociales en Mendoza,* p. 94; Babini, *Enero de 1919,* pp. 23–25; Pintos, *Historia del movimiento obrero del Uruguay,* p. 130; Dean, *Industrialization of São Paulo,* p. 165.

38 On the Chilean organization, see James O. Morris, *Elites, Intellectuals and Consensus: A Study of the Social Question and the Industrial Relations System in Chile* (Ithaca, N.Y., 1966), chap. 7; on Brazil, see Dean, *Industrialization of São Paulo,* pp. 162–166; Fausto, *Trabalho urbano e conflito social,* pp. 223–244; and the action of the Santos owner in Sheldon L. Maram, "Anarchists, Immigrants, and the Brazilian Labor Movement, 1890–1920" (Ph.D. diss., History, University of California, Santa Barbara, 1972), p. 35.

39 On these organizations in Argentina, see Tomás Amadeo, *Los sindicatos en el extranjero y en la República Argentina* (Buenos Aires, 1922); in Uruguay, Pintos, *Historia del movimiento obrero del Uruguay,* p. 174; in Chile, Ramírez Necochea, *Origen y formación del Partido Comunista de Chile,* pp. 110–111.

40 Abadie-Aicardi, *Economía y sociedad de Bolivia,* p. 108, on Bolivia; Brazilian data from Dean, *Industrialization of São Paulo,* pp. 151–152; on Cuba, see Raymond Buell *et al., Problems of the New Cuba: Report of the Commission on Cuban Affairs of the Foreign Policy Association* (Baltimore, Md., 1935), p. 78; on Chile, see Lagos Valenzuela, *Bosquejo histórico,* p. 35; and Barría Serón, *Los movimientos sociales de Chile,* pp. 38–42, 81; on Peru, see Martínez de la Torre, *Apuntes para una interpretación marxista,* 1:63–65. Workers and their families lived on these low salaries by supplementing their incomes with home-grown foods and homemade items. This unpaid labor, in reality, forms a part of the workers' salary. It accounts for the ability of capitalists to pay starvation wages. It also partially explains wage differentials between societies where workers can or do produce their own food and those in which they do not.

41 Leôncio Martins Rodrigues, *Conflito industrial e sindicalismo no Brasil* (São Paulo, 1966), pp. 143–144. On general legislation, see Oficina Internacional de Trabajo, *Legislación social de América Latina,* 2 vols. (Geneva, 1928); and the U.S. Department of Labor's *Monthly Labor Review* (Washington, D.C.), which contains a special section on foreign legislation by area.

42 Juan E. Pivel Devoto, *Uruguay Independiente* (Buenos Aires, 1949), pp.

227–239; Russell H. Fitzgibbon, *Uruguay: Portrait of a Democracy* (London, 1956), pp. 128–134.

[43] A typical statement is Arturo Alessandri, *Recuerdos de gobierno* (Santiago, 1951), p. 389; details on his social policies in Pike, *Chile and the United States*, pp. 170–181; Morris, *Elites, Intellectuals and Consensus*; or Ricardo Donoso, *Alessandri, agitator y demolador*, 2 vols., 2d ed. (Mexico City–Buenos Aires, 1952), vol. 1.

[44] *El Obrero Ferroviario*, March 1, 1921, and August 1, 1922, cited in Heidi Goldberg, "La Unión Ferroviaria: From Radicalism to Reform: The Birth of a Labor Elite" (MS, Yale University, 1975), pp. 18, 22.

[45] Social legislation in Alejandro M. Unsain, *Ordenamiento de las leyes obreras argentinas* (Buenos Aires, 1943). On labor in general, see Marotta, *El movimiento sindical argentino*, vol. 2, chaps. 13–21; for railroad workers and the Radicals, see Paul B. Goodwin, *Los ferrocarriles británicos y la U.C.R., 1916–1930* (Buenos Aires, 1974), esp. pp. 75–82. Two interesting liberal interpretations of Radicalism and its class relationships are Walter Little, "Radical Populism and the Conservative Elite, 1912–1930," in *Argentina in the Twentieth Century*, David Rock, ed. (Pittsburgh, 1975), pp. 66–87; and David Rock, *Politics in Argentina, 1890–1930: The Rise and Fall of Radicalism* (Cambridge, Eng., 1975).

[46] López, *Historia del movimiento social*, pp. 328–340; Rodolfo Puiggrós, *El Yrigoyenismo* (Buenos Aires, 1965), p. 210; Marotta, *El movimiento sindical argentino*, vol. 2, chap. 9.

[47] Morris, *Elites, Intellectuals and Consensus*, chaps. 5–6; Pike, *Chile and the United States*, p. 174; Jobet, *Ensayo crítico*, pp. 164–166.

[48] See Robert J. Alexander, *Labor Relations in Argentina, Brazil and Chile* (New York, 1962).

[49] On these two struggles, see José Peter, *Historia y luchas de los obreros de la carne* (Buenos Aires, 1947); Rufino Gómez, *La gran huelga petrolera de Comodoro Rivadavia (1931–1932)* (Buenos Aires, 1973).

[50] On this period, see Luis Aguilar, *Cuba 1933: Prologue to Revolution* (Ithaca, N.Y., 1972); Fabio Grobart, "The Cuban Working Class Movement From 1925 to 1933," *Science & Society* 29, no. 1 (Spring 1975): 73–103; Mirta Rosell, ed., *Luchas obreras contra Machado* (Havana, 1973); José R. Tabares del Real, *La revolución del 30, sus dos últimos años* (Havana, 1971); and Evelio Tellería, *Los congresos obreros en Cuba* (Havana, 1973), pp. 105–198. Portions of this section appeared as part of "The Workers' Struggle: 1850–1961," *Cuba Review* 4, no. 1 (July 1974): 3–10, 31.

[51] Buell, *Problems of the New Cuba*, p. 190; Grupo Cubano, *Estudio sobre Cuba*, p. 548; Tellería, *Los congresos en Cuba*, pp. 49–80.

[52] Carleton Beals, *The Crime of Cuba* (Philadelphia, 1933), p. 247–248, cites 147 labor leaders killed in these years.

[53] Rosell, ed., *Luchas obreras contra Machado*, p. 18.

54 Robert F. Smith, *The United States and Cuba: Business and Diplomacy, 1917–1960* (New York, 1960), pp. 24–29.
55 Quotes from Grobart, "The Cuban Working Class Movement," p. 96.
56 Rosell, ed., *Luchas obreras contra Machado,* p. 22; Buell, *Problems of the New Cuba,* p. 190.
57 Buell, *Problems of the New Cuba,* pp. 74–75; also see "Breve historia de la lucha en el central 'Mabay' desde su fundación hasta el año 1933," in Rosell, ed., *Luchas obreras contra Machado,* pp. 379–385, for one sugar worker's personal testimony.
58 Mario Riera Hernández, *Historial obrero cubano, 1574–1965* (Miami, 1965), pp. 97–98; Tellería, *Los congresos obreros en Cuba,* pp. 199–266.
59 Grupo Cubano, *Estudio sobre Cuba,* p. 727; Buell, *Problems of the New Cuba,* p. 182; Charles A. Page, "The Development of Organized Labor in Cuba" (Ph.D. diss., Latin American Studies, University of California at Los Angeles, 1952), pp. 87–88.

3

MEXICO: CO-OPTATION AND REPRESSION, 1910–1970

At the turn of the century, the Mexican labor movement displayed characteristics found throughout Latin America. After 1910, however, local events moved it in new directions. The Revolution of 1910 and the ensuing chaotic years served to accelerate the explosive and expansive period, which quickly passed into the co-optive–repressive stage. The sequence that occurred in Mexico before 1930 prefigured patterns that developed elsewhere after that date. The Mexican case is thus in one sense unique; at the same time, it conforms to the general historical evolution of Latin American labor. Thus Mexico offers an example of a transition between the expansive and explosive and co-optive–repressive periods. It also is the first case chronologically in which local variables make it necessary to discuss labor in a national rather than a continental context.

A few general observations are needed to identify larger trends and to set national events within a global context. The Revolution forced structural changes that transformed the composition of the ruling and working classes and therefore also changed their relationship. An urban-based bourgeoisie emerged dedicated to classic capitalist development. That group both overlapped and tended to supplant the traditional agrarian elites. It did not, however, change the basic form of the bourgeois state inherited from the era of Porfirio Díaz (1876–1911).

The shuffling within the ruling class and the disruption caused by the Revolution gave working-class organizations an opportunity to expand. Labor formed one of the few potential power blocs within Mexican society. The precarious balance of forces during the violent revolutionary period meant that until the late 1930s labor support could provide vital backing for those seeking power.

By the same token, potential working-class hostility presented a distinct threat to all regimes. Accordingly, almost from the inception of the Revolution, its leaders made conscious efforts to subordinate labor and to prevent the development of an independent working-class movement. When the tactic of co-opting labor failed, they forcefully repressed it. Thus, at the time when other Latin American ruling classes had just initiated co-optive–repressive measures (see Chapter 2), these procedures had become the norm in Mexico.

The gradual expansion of industry and mechanized agriculture after 1920 demanded more disciplined and skilled workers. This, in turn, dictated new state strategies toward labor, culminating in the building of an official labor movement. Then as now, that movement carefully channeled workers' demands and kept labor peace. In return, the rank and file, most of them in the dynamic economic sectors, received limited material gains, and a corrupt labor bureaucracy received handsome pay-offs for its role as government agent. Workers outside the state system had little or no access to economic or social gains. Those who disagreed with set policies or who threatened to upset the enforced internal stability were labeled enemies of the Revolution. Because the state used nationalism to justify the sacrifices that it demanded of workers, it branded all dissidents "Communists" and saw "international conspiracies" orchestrated from Moscow or, more recently, Havana behind every social protest.

Mexico's dependent position within the world capitalist system played a major role in determining state labor policy. As we have seen, both foreign capital and foreign ideologies entered Mexico before 1910. After that, due to the Revolution, the Depression, and World War II, the country entered a period of lessened economic dependence, although foreign capital, technology, and ideas still largely determined the pace of national capitalist growth. In the postwar period, U.S. capital moved into Mexico at an accelerating rate; by 1970, direct U.S. investment totaled $2.2 billion, or 79 percent of all foreign capital in Mexico. Today, trade still relies heavily on the U.S. market, and tourism is a major earner of necessary foreign exchange. U.S. capital goods and primary products for manufacturing constitute over 80 percent of all Mexican imports, and bonds and loans from U.S. and international bankers finance internal expansion. U.S. policy decisions thus continue to have a vital effect on the Mexican economy.

After 1944, the state's independent development efforts slowed, and government activities became increasingly integrated with the policies of U.S.-based transnational corporations. In turn, the Mexican bourgeoisie associated itself with foreign capital rather than assuming an independent position. Like its counterparts elsewhere, this class performs a double function: It must ensure enough surplus to satisfy foreign economic interests and to secure continued investment and financing, and it must see that sufficient surplus remains for its own enrichment. That explains the apparent contradiction of wealth and poverty within Mexican society. Between 1955 and 1965, for example, foreign investment totaled $886 million. Net total income on all foreign investment reached $1.7 billion, of which less than 20 percent remained in the country as reinvestment, meaning that almost $500 million left Mexico. Nationally, 5 percent of all families get 36 percent of all income, and 10 percent get over half of all income. At the other end of the scale, the bottom 60 percent of all families receive only 20 percent of all income. Annual per capita income in rural areas is $120, and infant mortality stands at a high 60.7 per 1,000 births. Almost 75 percent of the population has less than four years of education. Housing and other social services remain grossly inadequate; 24 million people have no running water in their homes.[1]

VIOLENT REVOLUTION AND LABOR, 1910–1918

Objective conditions during the repressive thirty-five-year Díaz regime mirrored those found in other countries. Textile workers, for example, normally toiled fourteen hours a day, with only two forty-five-minute breaks, and rural custom dictated a sunup-to-sundown routine. Almost no legal protection existed, and the law heavily favored capitalists and rural landowners. Accidents abounded—in one mining complex alone, over 500 workers died during a five-year period. Housing remained substandard, wages consistently lagged behind inflation, and working-class efforts to unite and to protest met repression.

Despite the obstacles placed in their way, workers began to organize in the late nineteenth century. After 1900, a host of labor organizations and worker-oriented parties appeared. Numerous strikes erupted, the most famous being the miners' strike at Cananea, the textile upheaval at Orizaba, and the 1908 railroad strike. All ended in violence. The government continued to consider any social disturbance a matter for local or federal police, but the increasing agitation did not go unnoticed by Díaz and other prominent Mexicans. The president personally commissioned a report on the labor situation in order to plan for the trouble he was sure would follow.[2]

In 1910, the internal political situation changed. An anti-Díaz opposition headed by the Liberal Francisco Madero forced Díaz from office by 1911. Instead of an orderly transition, however, this event initiated a power struggle that degenerated into a decade of civil war. In reality, growing discontent in all sectors of society toppled Díaz. The dictator's friends monopolized government posts, excluding younger ruling-class members from power. Many Mexicans resented the fact that foreigners drained the country's riches through their huge land and mining concessions (foreigners owned approximately one-seventh of Mexico's land by 1910). Members of the emerging bourgeoisie in provincial centers such as the northern industrial city of Monterrey chafed under rigid government centralization; they asked for more local autonomy, for a voice in national affairs, and for additional resources to be diverted their way. A series of economic recessions after 1900, plus inflation, eroded the position of middle-sector groups. They, too, welcomed Madero's promise of constitutional government, thinking it would bring them relief. Finally, a deep-seated rage boiled among workers and peasants; and when the Revolution began, they voiced demands for social justice.

Four central strands dominated the Revolution: a nationalist upsurge, the struggle for social justice, the desire for effective representation, and a strong anticlericalism. However, each power group interpreted these strands differently. To the bourgeoisie, nationalism meant that they, not foreigners, should exploit the nation's wealth; proletarians thought of it in terms of an end to the favored status that foreigners enjoyed in salaries and jobs, a curbing of the abuses suffered by workers for foreign-owned companies, and the development of the nation's riches for all on an equal (or more equal) basis. The ruling class interpreted social justice as the establishment of a liberal bourgeois state; workers saw it as including adequate job and living conditions, equality before the law, and sometimes, the building of a socialist society; peasants hoped that it meant land and the chance to cultivate that land peacefully. Anticlericalism, rooted in the nineteenth-century Liberal battles against the church, permeated the Revolution, and the religious issue plagued Mexico until the 1930s. These differing interpretations led to conflict over who held decision-making powers and dominated the fight for state control in the Revolution's early years.

An ever changing balance of forces emerged during these years. Madero succeeded Díaz as president but was assassinated in 1913. Meanwhile, Venustiano Carranza, Alvaro Obregón, and Francisco ("Pancho") Villa rebelled in the north. They called themselves Constitutionalists because they condemned Madero's murder and said they followed his adherence to the 1857 Constitution. Within a year, Carranza occupied the capital; but he retreated to Veracruz to survive threats posed by Emiliano Zapata's peasant forces to the south and by Villa, now operating alone. Carranza's armies gradually proved to be the strongest, and they eventually retook the capital. By 1918, fighting subsided, and Carranza became president, only to fall when he attempted to impose a hand-picked successor. The election of Obregón in 1920 opened a new era, ending the Revolution's most violent period.

The role of the working class and organized labor during this period is subject to debate. Some scholars claim that workers figured significantly in events immediately after 1910; others suggest that they remained largely indifferent. Although workers in several areas did back Madero, a majority probably stayed on the sidelines. All scholars agree that peasants contributed importantly, particularly in the south, where they bore the brunt of the fighting. Nevertheless, specific working-class groups made meaningful contributions. At the same time, often unrelated to the Revolution, activists used this period to organize.[3]

Numerous labor organizations sprang into existence during the Revolution's first years. By 1911, bakers, cabinetmakers, carpenters, shoemakers, stonecutters, tailors, typographers, and others had formed or re-formed associations. In addition, textile workers, miners, and railroaders strengthened already functioning groups. A majority of the workers' organizations operated in Mexico City, but working-class activity grew in most provincial centers, too. Miners' unions spread across the northern states, and the printing trades federation included affiliates in five states and the capital. Railroad workers, among the first to organize, expanded their network and attempted to form a national confederation. Organizations in Mexico City and Veracruz also tried to unite workers nationally but failed because of the overall frailty of working-class organization and a lack of communication caused by wartime conditions.

Ideological differences divided the labor movement in Mexico just as they did elsewhere in Latin America. Anarchists, anarcho-syndicalists, reformists, and Socialists vied to establish their points of view. Similarly, small groups representing differing tendencies sometimes existed within the same trade or in a particular city or state. Mutualist organizations also competed for workers' allegiance, and the Catholic reform movement presented workers with yet another alternative. Nevertheless, the vast majority of workers remained unorganized.[4] Many of Mexico's 853,350 industrial workers had only recently entered the labor force, and because of their lack of experience, they still accepted rural paternalism. Even among organized workers, a revolutionary outlook hardly existed. In 1916, for example, after the company partially granted demands for higher pay and improved job conditions, a representative of Mexico City streetcar workers thanked the general manager in these words: "I am honored in two different ways: in the first place in addressing my humble words to a chief so honorable as you; in the second place because I come in the name of my companions to present you our eternal gratitude, because of the increase in wages you have conceded us."[5]

In truth, developments after 1910 failed to inspire workers' involvement in the Revolution. As a Liberal, Madero turned away from radical groups. He sought to reform the existing system, not change it. He clearly stated that strikes should not interrupt the economy, and he cracked down on militants. In recognition of the emerging labor problem, he did create an official labor office but saw it as a deradicalizing influence and limited its functions to mediating conflicts, promoting labor-management harmony, and providing employment. Thus, "by 1913, the hostility of management for unions and the failure to achieve meaningful industrial reform had hurt the morale of labor and eroded its faith in the administration."[6]

Among labor organizations that developed after 1910, the Casa del Obrero Mundial (House of the World Worker) emerged as a leading body. Founded by anarchosyndicalists in 1912, it soon included representatives of varying persuasions drawn from Mexico City's leading unions and from other centers of working-class activity. On May 1, 1913, it sponsored a demonstration that attracted about 20,000 workers. Orators called for an eight-hour day and a weekly day of rest and attacked the government for its antiworker policies. In response, the authorities canceled Casa public meetings, arrested some of its leaders, and deported a number of its foreign members. In the middle of 1914, after the Casa's continued campaign for workers' rights, the government closed it, again detaining several leaders. However, the fortunes of war intervened to revive it. In July 1914, Constitutionalist forces headed by Carranza and Obregón took Mexico City. Obregón, a shrewd politician, recognized the value of labor support. He reopened the Casa and donated a building for its headquarters.[7]

Despite his distrust of all radicals and workers, Carranza opportunistically moved toward a rapprochement with labor at the urging of Obregón and in response to his declining fortunes on the battlefield. He issued a decree promising that social victories would follow military ones and vowed to pass "legislation to better the condition of peasants, workers, miners, and the working class in general."[8] He then decreed far-reaching agrarian reform. Carranza hoped that these moves would marshal working-class support and blunt the appeal of Zapata's radical agrarian, anti-imperialist program, which had attracted many labor activists.

The Carranza-Obregón government followed up its promises with action. When workers of the foreign-owned Mexico City power company struck, the government turned over the company to workers and named Luis N. Morones general manager. Morones, a rising young union leader, would later play a major role in assuring government control over labor. At the same time, Carranza gave the Casa 15,000 pesos for needy workers. The strategy paid dividends. After a series of unfruitful discussions, the Casa and the Constitutionalists signed a formal pact in February 1915. The Casa agreed to support the government by forming workers' battalions, in return, it received freedom to organize and assurances that decrees concerning workers would be implemented after the war.[9]

The pact had several consequences. By allying itself with the government, the Casa abandoned its apolitical position for a strategy not unlike that of workers' politics practiced by the Argentine FORA IX (see p. 61). That stance alienated radical members, who either refused to fight or joined Zapata. Casa members later formed one important organizing nucleus within the working class; consequently, this deradicalization helped to shape the movement in a reformist direction. The pact also placed the Casa at the service of a political movement rather than in a vanguard position. It thus accepted the limits of bourgeois politics and rejected the concept of a revolutionary working-class movement. As one commentator has aptly said: anarchists understood the Revolution's bourgeois nature but failed to formulate an adequate strategy to combat it; the rest of organized labor failed to grasp the point clearly, thinking to move the Revolution from within.[10]

The Casa formed seven battalions that more than once served on the shooting front. All the time, Casa followers actively organized. By 1915, it claimed thirty-six affiliated branches and over 80,000 members, the majority of them in Mexico City. Not all workers flocked to the Casa's banners. In textile zones, workers forcefully resisted its advances. The reasons are unclear, but perhaps those who had participated in the 1907 strikes saw the contradiction of aiding Carranza, a former Díaz supporter and large landholder, to establish a bourgeois constitutional order against the Zapatistas' program of social justice. Many also just preferred to remain on the job rather than get involved in the war.

Carranza's distrust of the Casa quickly showed itself. As soon as practical, he disarmed the Casa forces and discharged them. Relations between the Casa and Carranza steadily deteriorated, and he increasingly used force against workers and militants. After 1916, he crushed general strikes in Veracruz and Tampico, ended a railroad stoppage by drafting strikers into the army, and parried two general strike threats in Mexico City. On that occasion, he declared martial law and ordered all participants tried by military justice. The failure of the general strikes and government pressures gradually eroded the Casa's position and it declined. Other labor organizations throughout the country survived the government offensive but in weakened condition. In all probability, only Obregón's intervention prevented the movement's total destruction.[11]

Although brief, the Casa's role was important. Future labor leaders gained experience under its banner, and it served as a movement clearinghouse. Its policy of collaboration with the government, however, set a crucial precedent, orienting labor away from an independent policy and leading the movement down a path that sectors of Mexican labor have followed ever since.

But the Constitutionalists could not ignore labor or an increasingly vocal working class. As a result, these years produced Mexico's first labor legislation, almost all of it passed by local governors. Sometimes, popular pressure forced its passage; in other instances, it represented an attempt to rally mass support. By 1916, seven Mexican states had promulgated some labor laws and the state of Veracruz formulated a comprehensive program that included minimum wages, improvements in working hours and conditions, overtime pay, and accident compensation.[12]

The 1917 Constitution marked a high point in labor legislation. No workers' representatives attended the Constitutional Convention, but some labor organizations sent suggestions to sympathetic delegates. A small pro-labor bloc first defeated Carranza's conservative proposals and then convinced the assembly of the need for a separate labor article. The fact that Catholics had formulated a labor program helped convince many conservatives that not all social legislation represented a radical step, and the spirit of compromise shown at the gathering also aided the reformers' cause.

In final form, the Constitution's labor provisions in Article 123 covered a range of topics. They guaranteed an eight-hour day, stipulated that minors under twelve could not work, set conditions for children under fourteen and women, outlawed discounts and fines, prohibited the use of scrip, and banned the much-hated company stores. They also mandated overtime pay, set safety and hygienic standards, obliged companies in rural areas to build schools, and imposed heavy penalties for illegal firings.

More important, the Constitution set guidelines for labor organization and relationships between capital, labor, and the government. It guaranteed both employers and all workers the right to organize. It did not require unionization, but if a majority of workers in a given workplace organized, they then could represent all workers there. The document outlined a complicated machinery for settling disputes through Conciliation and Arbitration Boards composed of one worker, one employer, and one government appointee. These boards ruled on the legality of strikes and worked toward negotiated settlements; their decisions could not be appealed. Strikers had to give ten days' notice if employed in a public-service industry and six days' notice otherwise. During legal strikes, employers had to pay workers, a clause designed to encourage a quick end to legal disputes.

The Constitution contained several drawbacks for labor. Despite the fact that it guaranteed basic rights, their effectiveness depended upon the government. It held a deciding vote on the boards, it ruled on the legality of any action, and it granted or withheld legal status from unions. Thus labor's ability to operate depended largely upon official good will. Furthermore, Article 123 and its correlates confined working-class action to material improvements. Labor could mobilize only to adjust the workers' relative economic position, not to change fundamental power relationships. Any action outside these bounds became unconstitutional and thus illegal, which subjected labor to state repression. Then, too, the Constitution only set guidelines for action. The federal government had to regulate each part of Article 123, a task that took until 1931. Until then, individual states enforced and passed labor legislation. As a result, wide variations existed from area to area, although in most states conservatives saw to it that the law favored their interests. Other clauses remained inoperative. Profit sharing, for example, did not become a reality until the 1960s, and then only on a limited scale.[13]

The Constitution thus nourished the seeds of co-optation and repression first planted by Madero and his successors. A neutral state could use existing legal procedures to equalize opposing interest groups; but states are not neutral. Their laws—or the interpretation of them—reflect existing class relationships. The Revolution's leadership since 1910 has represented the ruling class. As the beneficiary of capitalism, it has sought to maintain and strengthen it. Thus, Mexican governments have confined conflict within the capitalist arena, although labor has occasionally received some favored treatment.

LABOR ENCHAINED: THE ERA OF CROM, 1918–1934

As stability gradually returned after 1916, a number of labor organizations called for a central body. Over fifty delegates attended a Veracruz congress at which they signed a solidarity pact and drafted a program for a national confederation. The proposed organization pledged itself to direct action based on class struggle in order to achieve the socialization of the means of production, called for the formation of unions to defend and win workers' rights, and advocated an apolitical stance. However, it advised only limited use of general strikes. Ideological splits between radicals and reformers soon doomed the attempt at unity. Another congress, sponsored by the Casa and some anarchist societies, met late in 1917. Representatives of five unions and two federations from Mexico City, twenty-three organizations from twelve states, and the recently formed Partido Socialista Obrero (PSO), including its founder, Morones, attended the meeting. Despite sharp clashes between anarchists, reformists oriented toward electoral politics, and revolutionary syndicalists, the congress approved an eight-point program of basic workers' rights. However, it failed to form a viable labor organization.[14]

These attempts did not go unnoticed by Carranza, who feared that radical elements would succeed in uniting and controlling the growing labor movement. Accordingly, he laid plans to check the threat by getting the provincial governor of Coahuila and several friendly labor groups to call a third labor congress at Saltillo in 1918. The fact that anarchists of all persuasions boycotted the gathering reduced factionalism; and moderates, led by Morones, won a majority. The assembled delegates then agreed to form the Confederación Regional Obrera Mexicana (CROM). Its statutes committed members to a nonelectoral position and left them free to administer their internal affairs subject only to a mutual solidarity pact. They also opened the way for collaboration with the government by stating that CROM would participate in assuring compliance with the fundamental laws of the land and would seek to resolve workers' problems on its own only if the government did not show itself attentive to those issues.

Other CROM declarations strengthened its nonrevolutionary position. It failed to call for the socialization of the means of production; instead it merely demanded sharing the wealth and land distribution, thus accepting private property. In 1923, it took a nationalist stand, placing the welfare of the working class second to that of the nation. Two years later, CROM agreed to mute any radical demands in order not to frighten away foreign capital. This statement by a leading CROM affiliate is typical of the organization's attitude: "We are not talking about destroying capitalism, but of joining capital and labor in harmony."[15] In view of CROM's stands, no wonder the Mexican president in 1925 guaranteed the Ford Motor Company that it would have no problems with labor if it invested in the country.

CROM's statutes called for a confederative democracy. In reality, a small group known as the Grupo Acción, which numbered about twenty members, dictated policy and strategy. Under

Morones's leadership, the clique controlled CROM's Central Committee, which, in turn, spoke for the main body. The Partido Laborista Mexicano (PLM), founded in 1919 by Morones, formed CROM's political arm. Morones's earlier experience with the PSO, which ran candidates unsuccessfully in 1917, led him to a "multiple action" strategy for labor that envisioned simultaneous union, social, and political action. The PLM fulfilled the political function; its program called for the eventual socialization of the means of production but stipulated that electoral politics could achieve workers' goals. The leadership encouraged but did not require CROM members to join the party.[16]

The PLM and Grupo Acción derived their influence from the close relationship they forged with the Revolution's two most important leaders, Plutarco Elías Calles and Obregón. In August 1919, for example, PLM leaders signed a secret pact with Obregón. They agreed to swing CROM's support to Obregón's presidential candidacy. In return, Obregón agreed to consult CROM on reforms affecting workers, to appoint a friendly minister of labor, and to accept advice in naming a minister of agriculture. He further pledged to implement Article 123 of the Constitution and to support CROM's organizational and propaganda activities. Armed with this accord, CROM and PLM leaders (who were mostly the same persons) set about entrenching themselves in the labor movement and the government, a feat they accomplished during the presidencies of Obregón (1920–1924) and Calles (1924–1928). Both named CROMistas to government posts and assured their election to national and local offices. CROM often helped in the electoral process by supplying organizers to rally voters and strong-arm squads to intimidate the opposition. The PLM at its apogee in 1927 boasted 40 out of 272 representatives in the Chamber of Deputies, and almost one-fourth of the Senate. Party members also occupied several state governorships, municipal posts, offices in state legislatures, and for a time, the governorship of the Federal District. Most important, Calles tapped Morones for the post of minister of labor, giving the PLM, CROM, and especially the Grupo Acción a power base inside the government.

Morones soon became the second most powerful person in Mexico; some believed his power equal to the president's.[17]

Morones and his cronies lost no time exploiting their advantages. They used government influence and union positions to build a carefully controlled CROM. On the side, they cynically shook down companies over contracts for their own gain and skimmed off a healthy share of union dues. All the time, they posed as champions of labor and of the Mexican worker. CROM members did reap certain economic benefits in terms of higher-than-average salaries through collective contracts, job protection, and limited social services. But Morones kept labor demands carefully controlled. For example, when bank clerks asked for CROM support in a strike, he denied the request, claiming that they asked for too much control over the bank policy. Leadership seldom if ever consulted the rank and file on major or minor policy decisions. In fact, it opposed attempts to educate workers in revolutionary ideas, saying that workers could not yet safely assimilate such concepts. That dictum, of course, prevented the development of future leaders from within the ranks and kept militancy at the desired low level.[18]

Government protection aided CROM's growth. Employers learned that trouble with the confederation meant trouble with the government. They therefore usually acquiesced quickly to CROM's contract demands or agreed to unionize their workers. During the initial years of Obregón's presidency, unionization proceeded slowly because the president allowed the individual states to handle labor matters, and for the most part they did not encourage organization. Obregón sympathized with labor demands as long as they remained peaceful, but he could side with workers only at the risk of alienating both foreign capital and powerful local capitalists. In Obregón's final years and during Calles's term, however, labor's ranks grew. According to its own estimate, CROM membership reached 50,000 in 1920, 1.5 million in 1925, and 2 million by 1929. CROM concentrated its efforts among urban industrial workers but also accepted nonindustrial members, including intellectuals, domestics, and even prostitutes. It also organized workers in the countryside.

Sporadic opposition arose inside CROM. The imposition of local officials from the top sometimes provoked unrest among the rank and file and also alienated those wishing to climb the hierarchical ladder. Leadership's nonmilitant stands, their obvious personal wealth, and their total subordination to the government led members to question the value of remaining in the confederation. By the early 1920s, almost all radicals had either left CROM or been purged for challenging existing policies. Yet even mildly progressive members questioned CROM acts such as naming Calles honorary president and giving him the title "socialist worker" or the crowning of a beauty queen, "Miss First of May," to celebrate that workers' holiday. Still, until the end of Calles's term in 1928, CROM's strength seemed undiminished.[19]

CROM staunchily opposed all other labor organizations and used government machinery or force against them. CROM printers refused to set manifestoes for rival groups, confederation members booed non-CROM actors off the stage, general strikes suddenly erupted in places where unaffiliated unions proposed to hold meetings or conventions, and the government denied permission for demonstrations by groups not enrolled in the official confederation. When oil workers paralyzed the Tampico fields during 1926, Minister of Labor Morones rescinded the striking union's legal status, citing the "lack of union discipline." His action paved the way for CROM strikebreakers, supported by troops, to replace the strikers.[20]

CROM's efforts to destroy or take over rival unions did not always succeed. Where local government did not favor CROM, independent unions and labor organizations managed to resist. Railroad workers formed one of the strongest independent groups. Although CROM won over some small unions, the industry in general remained outside its grasp. During a 1926–1927 strike, the confederation hastily formed its own union and supplied strikebreakers. As in other cases, CROM insisted that foreign influences (i.e., Communists) caused the disruption and used nationalistic appeals in its campaign to crush the strike. The effort prevented the non-CROM rail union from winning its demands, but the defeated union continued its independent existence. In 1927, CROM plans again failed, this time among the miners. It supplied scabs to break a strike called by the militant miners' federation in the state of Jalisco. When violence erupted, the state governor, a former railroad worker who disliked CROM, denied federal troops access to the province. Without the support of the local government, CROM could not undermine the movement. Similar events occurred in Tamaulipas, where Governor Emilio Portes Gil blocked CROM attempts to organize.[21]

A number of other working-class organizations remained outside of CROM's orbit. One of these, the Confederación General de Trabajo (CGT), founded around 1920, endorsed a revolutionary syndicalist position. It took a strictly apolitical stance, attacking both the government and CROM as reformist enemies of the proletariat. It appealed to all workers and endorsed strikes, boycotts, and sabotage as valid tactical weapons, even advocating armed confrontation in response to government repression. In 1923, it advised workers to occupy factories if threatened with mass firings, although it later modified its position by proposing workers' control when an establishment closed. That same year, the CGT endorsed Adolfo de la Huerta's brief uprising against the government; and many of its members, along with other groups of workers who had suffered government persecution, joined the rebel army. The exact membership of the CGT is impossible to determine, but it attracted support among textile workers in and around Mexico City, transport workers, and a scattering of other unions.[22]

Catholics also refused to enter CROM, although CROM made overtures in their direction. Despite CROM and government opposition, the Catholic movement claimed 392 workers' organizations with 22,137 members by 1926; but after that date, membership slowly declined. As elsewhere, Catholics advocated a gradualist approach, although Catholics did negotiate salary increases for workers in several cases. A Catholic attempt to organize peasants also made little headway.

Several other non-CROM federations existed. The Mexican Communist Party, for example, after briefly supporting the CGT, founded a federation that claimed eighteen unions; when it collapsed, a new Communist federation was formed in 1929.[23]

Railroad and electrical workers formed the two largest groups unaffiliated with any other labor confederation. Railroaders had organized during the Díaz period and in 1920 founded a confederation that adopted a reformist program. Slowly, however, the workers realized the inadequacy of nonmilitant tactics in a hostile political climate, particularly after confrontations with Obregón in 1921 and with CROM in 1926 and 1927. Communists played a key role in spreading this idea, and gradually, sentiment for a united industry-wide organization spread. Organizers constantly reminded workers that unity bred strength and argued that isolated strikes only led to defeat. They emphasized the fact that the industry's strategic importance gave workers power and that their high level of skill made them hard to replace. When the companies fired 11,000 people during 1931, workers responded by founding the Sindicato de Trabajadores Ferrocarrileros de la República Mexicana (STFRM), which united 35,000 railroaders. The organization's charter reflected past struggles by specifically condemning government- and company-sponsored unions.

Electrical workers organized a nonmilitant confederation containing about 4,000 persons. Its statutes outlined a reformist program dedicated to social and economic improvement; and almost totally ignored the national working class and larger social issues. Almost from its inception, the confederation negotiated contracts through a workers' and employers' commission. [24]

Independent unions that resisted the temptation to affiliate with CROM in order to maintain their freedom of action led a precarious life; many disappeared when they failed to seek CROM's protection. Ideological struggles often racked these organizations. For example, within a ten-year period, the Mexico City streetcar workers' union supported the Casa; joined, left, and then rejoined CROM; twice declared itself independent; affiliated with the CGT; and finally split into three separate unions. [25]

Paralleling developments elsewhere on the continent, the Mexican movement spread to the countryside. The strongest regional rural organizations functioned in Veracruz. There, a league of agrarian communities (Liga de Comunidades Agrarias) was formed in 1923 and spread rapidly. In 1926, it merged with similar groups in other areas to form the Liga Nacional Campesina (National Peasants' League), which by 1929 claimed 300,000 members representing every state, a claim that was surely exaggerated. It opposed any government attempt to impose an agrarian program on peasants. It maintained close ties with the Communist Party and could muster significant support for local issues in several states.[26]

CROM maintained its position as the most powerful labor body during the 1920s by consistently allying itself with the individual in power: first Obregón, then Calles. The situation became complicated when Calles's term drew to a close. Obregón wished to run for a second time. Morones also harbored a desire to become president, and for a brief time Calles apparently toyed with the idea of running again. He realized, however, that opposition from the military and agrarian forces, which backed Obregón, was too strong and therefore accepted Obregón's candidacy as inevitable. CROM, or rather Morones and his circle, viewed this event with apprehension. Obregón had earlier rallied rural forces against CROM. Furthermore, he had issued strong statements citing the need to oust corrupt labor leaders, and everyone knew to whom this referred. After some hesitation, Morones offered Obregón support, but the revolutionary chief rejected the bid. Obregón's victory in the election left Morones in a difficult position, even though CROM and the PLM had belatedly endorsed his candidacy.

Shortly after the election, a right-wing Catholic assassinated the president-elect. Although no one actually proved his involvement, Morones came under considerable suspicion. He had used similar tactics in the past, and he stood to lose power if Obregón took office. Under pressure, Calles finally asked all PLM members to resign their government posts, which most soon did.[27]

That signal of official disfavor resulted in mass defections from both CROM and the PLM. The process accelerated when interim President Emilio Portes Gil (1928–1929), an avowed enemy of Morones, withdrew all government support. For a brief time, the new president even flirted with the CGT and the Communist confederation, both of which modified their positions by indicating that they would accept a working relationship with the government. Morones, never one to accept defeat gracefully, refused to compromise, and CROM remained alienated from government circles.

In reality, Portes Gil fronted for Calles, now the Revolution's undisputed leader. Their drive against CROM and their temporary support for other labor groups constituted a preliminary step to forming a national political party that would include all groups. They wished to undermine labor's strength in order to prevent the possible formation of a working-class political party and to prepare for labor's incorporation into the new party on terms they could dictate. They applied similar tactics to the agrarian movement. After 1929, the government increasingly pressured militant rural unions, at times openly persecuting the national agrarian leagues when they attempted any independent action. Portes Gil also stepped up the pace of government distribution of land and issued strong statements on agrarian reform. By 1934, most rural organizations had been brought under government control. Through these tactics, the new party, the Partido Nacional Revolucionario (PNR), managed to incorporate both urban and rural sectors. The party helped finance its activities by appropriating forced contributions from government employees that had formerly been turned over to CROM.[28]

The other presidents named and controlled by Calles to fill out Obregón's term (which ended in 1934) maintained a hostile attitude toward CROM. By the end of 1930, printing and textile workers and five other federations withdrew. In 1929, CROM dissidents founded a separate organization; and Vicente Lombardo Toledano, a rising star on the labor horizon, openly called for the dissolution of the rapidly disintegrating Labor Party. Three years later, a "purified" CROM was formed, but confederation die-hards continued to maintain the old organization. In 1932, it still claimed 1 million members, but it could no longer muster significant labor support. The era of CROM and Morones had passed.[29]

CROM's demise left a divided labor movement. Weaker unions disappeared when deprived of government protection. Others sought regional affiliation or joined one of CROM's rivals. And the Depression caused many workers to withdraw from unions. The CGT benefited most from the changed situation; by 1931, it claimed ninety-six affiliates, with a total of some 80,000 members. Nevertheless, labor remained badly fragmented. In the southwest textile zone, for example, workers split into a CROM organization of 10,000 to 12,000 members; one belonging to the CGT, which counted 8,000 to 10,000 workers; and a local federation representing 7,000 to 8,000 members. Small autonomous unions also operated in the area.[30]

Governments passed only minimal labor legislation after 1917, so few workers received the full benefits of Article 123. Obregón issued no labor laws, and discussions about profit sharing and social insurance led nowhere. After 1924, this situation changed as the ruling class, along with its representative, the revolutionary government, consolidated its position. Until 1929, individual states promulgated most labor laws. Advanced labor codes existed in Puebla, Veracruz, Yucatán, and Zacatecas; but most legislation stacked the legal deck in favor of employers, reflecting local power structures. Several minor laws also governed workers in the Federal District. Two projects to issue a national labor code, in 1924 and 1928, failed.

The judicial branch of government hindered the passage of legislation. From 1917 to 1923, the Supreme Court refused to recognize the Conciliation and Arbitration Boards as binding decision makers in labor disputes. In 1924, however, it reversed that opinion; and in 1925, a government decree implemented some provisions of Article 123. In 1929, a national convention of workers and employers met to discuss interpretations of the article. Soon after, a constitutional amendment gave the government authority to rule on all labor matters. In 1931, the National Federal Labor Law formally inaugurated the co-optive–repressive period in the legal sphere. Communists, independents, and some of the remaining CROM unions protested the law, saying that it centralized control in government hands and severely restricted labor's rights.[31]

The law indeed increased legal controls over labor. It took a more conservative position than many state laws and in some features resembled the corporatist labor code passed in Mussolini's

Italy. In broad outline, it followed the mainstream of ruling-class thinking that labor should not develop independently but that the state should oversee labor-capital relations. Within this framework, two lines of thought existed, both of which fit under the new law. One, favored by people like Obregón, believed that government should arbitrate between the working and capitalist classes. Until labor coalesced into an organized force, however, the state might favor its cause. The second school, propounded by Calles especially after 1928, envisioned a basically neutral state. If the capitalists proved stronger than labor, this did not concern the state in its role as legal administrator. These positions really shared the common goal of assuring that labor did not hinder capitalist development. In the long run, both held that capital and labor would eventually fuse into a harmonious polity. By extension, therefore, acts against the government transgressed against all Mexican society. Both strands survived after 1930, but most governments subscribed to the position championed by Calles.

The law itself upheld most rights specified in the Constitution. It stipulated one union per workplace and outlined the conditions under which both workers' and employers' groups could legally form. Only legal unions could strike or sign collective contracts. Employers had to accept these if a union so desired, and they could not discharge workers during a legal stoppage. Workers could also call solidarity strikes. The code prohibited compulsory unionization and a closed shop. A majority of workers needed to approve any collective actions. An agreement between two-thirds of the employers and covering two-thirds of the workers in a single industry in a particular region automatically extended to all employers and workers in that industry and region. The code instituted minimum wages for urban and rural labor, fixed every six months by local boards made up of one worker, one employer, and one government representative. Conciliation and Arbitration Boards had a similar composition, and their decisions could not be appealed.

The law gave the government widespread powers. By ruling a strike illegal, the government could sanction the use of force against an action or a union. During illegal strikes, collective contracts lost validity, allowing owners to fire workers. The government also could use force to reopen a factory or public service illegally paralyzed. Binding arbitration enabled the authorities virtually to dictate settlements. The code encouraged unionization, but only within careful limits. Workers received job protection by belonging to a union, but if expelled from the union, they could be legally dismissed. Employers collected union dues and passed them directly to union officials, assuring unions of economic stability but also preventing rank-and-file protest through the withholding of dues. Article 245 of the code prohibited unions from participating in politics or religious matters, further limiting activities to purely economic issues. Article 260 clearly demonstrated the code's spirit by saying that strikes should "seek an equilibrium of power to harmonize the rights of labor with those of capital."[32]

As far as the size of labor organizations is concerned, any evaluation based on statistical material is risky because most organizations overstated their membership. Similarly, wage or price studies are limited to particular industries or specific geographic areas. Nevertheless, sufficient data exist to venture some tentative conclusions. Although CROM claimed 50,000 members in 1920, another source estimated that there were only 54,000 organized workers in all of Mexico. Of these, 22,000 belonged to railroad unions, and from 8,000 to 10,000 belonged to independent unions. This leaves less than 25,000 persons in CROM. The same source reckoned that in 1927, when CROM boasted 1.8 million members, it in fact had only 13,000 dues payers. The obvious inflation in CROM's evaluation derived in part from its desire to appear to be a strong force but also from the fact that it counted all workers in a particular industry or factory if part of that work force belonged to an affiliated union. Still, even if the organization had only 13,000 dues payers, its membership could have amounted to five or six times that number. Figures for other organizations are also vague. The CGT's claim to 80,000 adherents, if calculated on the same basis as CROM's, appears reasonable. More indicative of labor's strength is the fact that in 1930 some 14.9 million Mexicans toiled in the industrial, transport, and communications sectors. Of these, 1.8 million, or 5.5 percent, belonged to an organization. In comparative terms, then, the Mexican movement's numerical

TABLE 6.   WAGES OF RAILROAD AND TEXTILE WORKERS, SELECTED YEARS
(Pesos)

	Wages							
	1909	1912	1919	1924	1926	1929	1930	1932
Railroads	1.85	1.90	—	—	4.21	4.38	—	—
Textiles	—	—	1.70	2.18	—	—	3.08	3.58

SOURCE: Marjorie Clark, *Organized Labor in Mexico* (Chapel Hill, N.C., 1934), pp. 180, 192.

TABLE 7.   TEXTILE STRIKES AS PERCENTAGE OF NATIONAL STRIKES, 1920–1925

	Percentage		Percentage
1920	41	1923	58
1921	52	1924	24
1922	71	1925	23

SOURCE: Clark, *Organized Labor in Mexico*, p. 119.

strength in the 1920s surpassed that found in other Latin American nations.[33]

Wage data show that, with some exceptions, workers earned low wages and achieved few economic gains in the Revolution's first twenty-five years. Studies of the Guanajuato mining region indicate that skilled workers earned less in 1920 than they had in 1908 and that semiskilled labor earned approximately the same. The National Department of Labor calculated that in 40 percent of the municipalities workers made 25 to 50 centavos a day during the 1920s; whereas in 1910, they had earned 42.5 centavos daily. Yet Table 6 shows that railroad and textile workers' wages improved. Why this disparity? Both groups maintained active and generally strong unions, calling frequent strikes, as shown in Table 7. For the most

TABLE 8. STRIKE DATA, 1920–1934
(By Presidential Terms)

	Obregón 1920–1924	Calles 1924–1928	Calles 1928–1934
Number of legal strikes[a]	206.5	56.5	19.3
Strikers per strike[a]	404.5	137.8	122.5
Number won by workers	242	43	136
Number won by employers	137	21	130

[a] Figures are yearly averages.
SOURCE: Guadalupe Rivera Marín, *El mercado de trabajo: Relaciones obrero-patronales* (Mexico City, 1955), table 55, p. 143.

part, they also remained outside CROM. It thus appears that these workers managed real economic gains through militant action. Both sectors also possessed a long tradition of action, dating back before 1910, indicating that they translated collective experience into concrete gains.[34]

The workday for the average Mexican shortened a little. In 1928, Morones claimed that 39 percent of all workers had won an eight-hour day, but later observers suggest that this figure is too high. Reports from the countryside indicate that peons still labored from sunup to sundown, as they did during the Díaz period.[35]

The strike information given in Table 8 provides a base from which to extrapolate. The steady drop in legal strikes after 1924 corresponds to the labor-government interaction. During Obregón's administration, CROM consolidated its position. At first, this required CROM's calling of strikes to show employers its power and that it had government support. During Calles's term, however, often just the appearance of pickets carrying CROM's red-and-black banner ensured a settlement, causing the drop in the number of total strikes called. At the same time, government pressure on non-CROM unions resulted in few strikes by these unions. After 1928, worker disorganization and unfriendly governments further reduced workers' activity. The average number of strikers per strike reveals similar trends. During Obregón's term, labor organized larger establishments; during Calles's presidency, it operated primarily against smaller ones. The lesser number of persons per strike after 1928 indicates the movement's reduced scope. The ratio of strike victories for labor and capital also demonstrates labor's changing position. Before 1929, labor won twice as many conflicts as it lost. The proportion then dropped to half. The balance did not tip in favor of employers for three reasons. First, independent unions sometimes mustered substantial support on the local level that allowed them to strike and win. Second, the state labor bureaucracy did not dissolve immediately in 1928 and sometimes succeeded in aiding strike movements. Third, Calles and the PNR wished to control labor, not destroy it. Allowing workers some triumphs statistically demonstrated state "neutrality" and reminded workers of the government's power.

By 1934, the dominant trends in relations between the state and labor had already formed. The legal system contained mechanisms for controlling labor, and the government had developed a co-optive–repressive strategy outside the law. Important segments of labor cooperated with the state, securing in return limited benefits for union members and lucrative posts for collaborationist leaders. Although notable pockets of strength existed, opposition remained fragmented. Despite official claims, most workers remained outside the labor network, living under conditions that had changed little since 1910.

LABOR AND CÁRDENAS, 1934–1940

Labor had reason to applaud the inauguration of Lázaro Cárdenas in 1934. As governor of Michoacán, he had proved progressive in labor matters. Furthermore, PNR declarations and its Six-Year Plan indicated a favorable disposition toward labor. The party's program called for the implementation of both Article 27 on agrarian reform and Article 123, stating that "confronting the class struggle inherent in the system of production in which we live, the Party and the Government have the duty of contributing to the strengthening of the syndicalist organizations of the working classes."[36] And during his campaign, Cárdenas pledged to fulfill that obligation.

These statements, however, must be placed within their historical context. The Depression had battered Mexico's economy, and as conditions worsened, social unrest raised the specter of 1910. Therefore, Cárdenas faced a difficult problem. The bourgeoisie demanded measures to revitalize the economy and protect their profits; the working class agitated to improve its deteriorating economic situation. Cárdenas resolved the apparent dilemma by using redistributive policies to prevent immediate social dislocation. Simultaneously, he strengthened the economy through long-term structural reforms that gave the state increased controls over all sectors of society, including labor.[37]

As a natural reflection of Cárdenas's policies, contradictions abounded during his presidency. At times, he appeared to favor workers over capitalists; at other times, capitalists over labor. Sometimes he played nationalist by challenging foreign capital; on other occasions, he protected foreign investment. Each move, however, led toward a single goal: preservation and strengthening of Mexico's industrial and agricultural capitalism. Within six years, he accomplished this goal, first blunting the challenge posed by urban labor and the rural proletariat and then incorporating each into the ruling party, thus bringing them under government control. This process opened the way for renewed economic expansion in the late 1930s and assured consolidation of the now relatively unified industrial and agrarian bourgeoisie in power after 1940.

In 1934, the labor movement remained divided. The CGT and CROM continued to function, but the newly founded Confederación General de Obreros y Campesinos de Mexico (CGOCM) became the strongest organization. Under the guiding hand of Lombardo Toledano, it adopted a revolutionary syndicalist line, seeking to organize all the working class into a single confederation independent of the government or electoral politics. At first, it declined to support Cárdenas, but soon official encouragement and the need for labor unity led it to modify this position.[38]

Economic conditions and perhaps the expectation of a more tolerant regime led to sharp increases in actions by workers during

1934. Strikes multiplied and reached record numbers in the first months of 1935. For a time, the bourgeoisie feared a social revolt, and its representatives called for strong state measures. No single organization led this massive outburst, but labor leaders of all persuasions took the opportunity to organize and agreed on the need for working-class unity in view of the expected capitalist counteroffensive. At the First Mexican Industrial Congress in 1934, for example, labor voted as a bloc despite internal disagreements, indicating a desire for cooperation and a realization of the importance of unity at this crucial juncture.[39]

Cárdenas represented the younger reformers within the ruling party who disagreed with the conservatives, led by Calles. The latter wished to continue the policy of repression, urging the government to take measures to protect profits by holding the line against workers' demands. Cárdenas saw the inadequacy of these methods. Instead, he proposed to expand the state's role in developing the economy and to strengthen it by increasing purchasing power and building in guarantees against the repetition of widespread dislocation. This, in turn, involved encouraging a labor movement under state control and oriented toward purely economic goals.

Just after Cárdenas took office in 1935, matters came to a head when three major strikes occurred involving foreign-owned companies. Petroleum workers struck against noncompliance with national labor laws, and tramway and power company workers in Mexico City demanded higher salaries and better job conditions. When the Conciliation and Arbitration Board ruled in favor of the tramway workers, conservatives took a stand against a government that they branded "socialistic" and that they feared would drive out foreign capital and put a serious crimp in all profits. Calles issued a major declaration saying that in view of the government's support for workers, strikes endangering the nation's economic health showed labor's ingratitude and could be called treasonous. In his version of the national interest, workers' problems took second place.

Labor leaders understood the real nature of this challenge and, led by the CGOCM, formed the National Committee for Proletarian Defense. It included all important labor groups except the CGT and CROM. The CROM organization sided with Calles, hoping for a return to favor if he won the power struggle. The committee branded Calles a "traitor to the Revolution" and an "enemy of the working class," announcing that its own interpretation of the national interest differed from his. In addition, they staged a massive demonstration and invited Cárdenas to speak. In response, the president backed labor's right to secure its just due through legal channels and affirmed his intent to carry the Revolution forward by implementing its labor and agrarian programs. He also called for the creation of a central labor confederation. His stand forced party members to choose sides. Cárdenas emerged strongest, and both Calles and Morones departed for exile in the United States.[40]

A bitter labor conflict in Monterrey soon presented Cárdenas with an opportunity to demonstrate good will toward labor and to formulate a labor policy. He settled the dispute in the workers' favor but then carefully drew the limits within which labor could operate. He first warned owners: "I recommend to the employers that they comply with the law in good faith, cease intervening in the workers' organizations, and give to them the economic well being to which they have a right . . . because oppression, industrial tyranny, unsatisfied needs, and unnecessary agitation are the explosive forces which at any given time can bring the violent disturbances you so fear." [41] Having demonstrated an understanding of the potential benefits in terms of social peace deriving from granting labor's most pressing demands, he outlined a fourteen-point program for labor and capital. Although the government should act as arbiter between the two, it would, at this time, naturally side with labor as the weaker force in order to ensure a social balance. Strikes only harmed both sides and, more important, Mexico. Therefore, disputes should be settled peacefully. Capitalists who objected to labor's legitimate demands could turn their establishments over to the state or to the workers in return for just compensation. However, labor demands must consider the economic capacity of each company. Cárdenas again urged workers to form a central confederation and promised that the government would consult it on labor matters. And in answer to conservatives, he specifically denied that any Communist threat existed, pointing out that Communists represented only a small faction within organized labor.

These declarations set the tone for Cárdenas's labor policy, which, despite the conservatives' protests, merely represented a continuation of previous tendencies. He adhered strictly to the proposition that the party ruled supreme, made all decisions, and tolerated no independent pressure groups. His position, like Obregón's, held that the government should intervene to smooth conflicts rather than allow a natural interplay of forces. He thus courted labor by acceding to its immediate demands while controlling it through state agencies. But within these limits, Cárdenas favored labor more than any other president.

The CGOCM again took the initiative in following Cárdenas's suggestions, and it helped form a new central organization, the Confederación de Trabajadores de Mexico (CTM). Its Declaration of Principles called for a classless society but stated that national liberation came first: "The final aim . . . is the abolition of the capitalist system. Nevertheless, since Mexico is subject to imperialist domination, before arriving at that final aim it is necessary to achieve the political and economic freedom of the country."[42] At the same time, in contradiction with the above passage, the declaration carefully noted that the confederation did not seek to abolish private property. The CTM's program precluded collaboration with the government, came out against the intervention of third parties in labor disputes, and stated that it was not Communist.

By 1936, however, the CTM's Central Committee had embarked on a course of collaboration with the government that was ratified by the CTM's first congress a year later. Confederation leaders argued that labor must co-operate with progressive forces against the conservatives and creeping fascism in order to promote national development, which would eventually allow it to secure its long-range goals.

The CTM reaped immediate benefits. Official agencies supplied financial aid, and men favorable to its cause occupied political offices at national, state, and local levels. The government helped finance a CTM university designed to raise the consciousness of workers and to train future leaders. It also poured money into technical education programs to upgrade workers' skills; the programs both served the needs of the emerging light and heavy industrial sector and permitted larger numbers of CTM members to hold higher-paying jobs. Under the leadership of Lombardo Toledano, a close confidant of Cárdenas, the CTM kept growing. Communist-controlled unions withdrew briefly in 1937 but quickly rejoined the confederation in the name of popular front unity.[43]

Rival labor groups often, but not always, faced official disfavor. For example, government bureaucrats and official agencies tended to hand down unfavorable rulings when non-CTM members were involved. But the government also limited the CTM's scope. As it would do in the agrarian sector, it prohibited the confederation from organizing public employees, decreeing that they must form a separate grouping. This, of course, allowed the government more control over its own workers and at the same time curbed the CTM's strength.

In 1938, Cárdenas built his own popular front by founding the Partido de la Revolución Mexicana (PRM), which replaced the PNR. The party divided along corporatist lines into four sectors: labor, peasants, military, and a generalized popular sector that included elite groups as well as government employees and other members of the middle sectors. Unlike the PNR, it incorporated and gave institutionalized expression to all important segments of Mexican society. Cárdenas hoped to reap several advantages: to channel input from the country's main power blocs and reduce military influence, to legitimize the decision-making power of the revolutionary leadership, and to facilitate control over the groups by keeping them divided and dependent on the government, reducing the possibility that they could unite against the established leadership. Within a year, the PRM claimed some 4 million members (2.5 million peasants, 1.25 million workers, and 500,000 in the popular sector).[44]

Labor enjoyed a special relationship with the state and the chief

TABLE 9.   STRIKE DATA, 1935–1940

	Number
Strikes[a]	478.3
Strikers[a]	61,422
Strikes Won by Workers	1,596
Strikes Won by Employers	434

[a] Figures are yearly averages.
SOURCE: Rivera Marín, *El mercado de trabajo*, table 55, p. 143.

executive. As a result, it gained more freedom to organize and usually won favorable decisions from government agencies. Table 9 shows that strike activity increased and that the proportion of strikes won by workers surged to a record high (see Table 8 for a comparison). The movement also expanded. Unions increased from roughly 2,000 in 1934 to about 5,000 in 1939–1940; membership reached 600,000 by the end of Cárdenas's term, although the CTM claimed in 1939 that it represented 3,594 groups and 945,913 workers. Whereas in 1930, only 5.5 percent of the economically active population belonged to a union, ten years later the figure stood at 14.5 percent. Owners' associations grew, too; Cárdenas required that they, like any other interest group, organize as a part of the corporatist state.[45]

Strikes followed a predictable pattern. Labor, encouraged by a friendly government and by CTM leaders, initiated an action and then asked for arbitration. Either the government responded through the legal machinery or else the president's office would handle the matter. In many cases, workers gained some of their demands. Labor also won collective contracts. For example, bakery, sugar, and textile workers in the capital all struck. In each case, the final settlement included a collective contract that, with some local variations, became the industry standard.[46]

Cárdenas, however, made sure of government initiative in labor matters. Workers could begin an action, but positive results depended upon favorable rulings from official agencies or the president. Cárdenas favored the CTM but protected other labor groups as a check on the confederation's power. The textile industry presented a typical case. In that sector, violence repeatedly flared between CTM and CROM members. Cárdenas personally arranged temporary truces between warring factions and sent troops to enforce them. In 1938, government mediation brought relative peace; a settlement stipulated industry-wide wage levels, equal pay for equal work, promotion by seniority, and a closed shop, which protected both CTM and CROM unionists. The government thus restored labor peace, awarded workers concrete gains, and kept a balance between rival union forces.[47]

Conflicts in the railroad and oil industries illustrate Cárdenas's willingness to implement advanced solutions to labor questions within the confines of established policies. In the middle of 1936, when a board outlawed their strike, railroad unions accepted the decision and ordered members back to work. However, they continued to agitate for pay raises and more than once disrupted service. Cárdenas finally ended this situation by invoking the Expropriation Law of 1936. He placed the railways under state management, turning the system over to the workers for a five-year period starting May 1, 1938. Critics pictured this action as "creeping socialism," but in reality it only made railroad workers state employees. The experiment proved short-lived: Avila Camacho, Mexico's next president, ended it. Nor did it prove successful from labor's viewpoint. Economic problems stemming from a high debt ratio, low freight charges set to benefit foreign exporters of raw materials, and a lack of administrative experience prevented significant improvements in operations. Some said that Cárdenas intended the experiment to fail as proof that workers' control did not work.[48]

The petroleum conflict developed into an even more tense situation. The Expropriation Law implemented the Constitution, ruling that subsoil rights belong to the state as sovereign power. This left in doubt the legal status of properties that foreign oil companies had "purchased" before the Revolution. Prolonged negotiations during the 1920s failed to resolve the problem. Up until 1936, the companies had prevented workers' attempts to organize; but this situation changed when several groups of workers, aided by outside organizers and veterans of previous union battles, formed a union that promptly joined the CTM.

The new union initiated a militant campaign to secure a collective contract and substantial economic and job improvements. The companies resisted, and the union threatened a general strike. During the 1920s, Mexico had ranked as the world's third-largest oil producer, and oil revenues had provided an economic backing for Obregón's regime. After that, production fell steadily, partly as a result of conflict between the government and the companies. Cárdenas hoped to expand the industry as part of Mexican industrialization and saw this confrontation as a way to settle the issue. He induced both sides to negotiate and persuaded the workers to postpone the strike. But the protagonists remained intransigent, and the workers struck in May 1936. The Conciliation and Arbitration Board promptly declared the action illegal. The workers then invoked a clause in the labor law which stipulated that a government-nominated commission could determine whether workers' demands fell within the reasonable capacity of an industry to pay. Upon examining these findings, the board would then rule on the conflict, subject to appeal.

The companies, seeking to avoid the entire process, protested and again objected when the commission supported the workers and condemned company practices. The companies refused to accept the ruling and appealed to the Supreme Court, which upheld the verdict. The contest sharpened when the companies refused to obey the board ruling despite the Supreme Court decision. The CTM's official organ now proclaimed that the struggle had become "a protest of the Mexican masses, led by organized workers, against their foreign overlords." In reality, labor demands at this stage took second place to the confrontation between Cárdenas, as head of state, and foreign capitalists.[49]

Backed almost unanimously by public opinion, Cárdenas applied the Expropriation Law in March 1938. Labor hailed the move as a victory and staged a mass rally in support of the decision. However, the oil workers' hopes soon turned to frustration. The new state company refused to meet their demands under the government's reorganization plan, and in 1940 the Conciliation and Arbitration Board ruled against them. The CTM supported Cárdenas throughout, first against the foreign companies and then against the oil workers after nationalization, a stance that led the oil unions to withdraw from the confederation. In his final years, Cárdenas took stronger stands against labor. For example, he forcefully broke a miners' strike by using federal troops, once again receiving CTM praise for steps to counter persons acting "against Mexico's interest."

Cárdenas reaped concrete gains from these public stands. He appeared as the champion of Mexican nationalism against foreign companies and their exploitation of Mexican workers. He solidified his alliance with organized labor, particularly the CTM. And through state intervention, he preserved the government's role as supreme arbiter over labor. The examples of the railroad and oil industries should not, however, be interpreted as signs of a desire to nationalize industry. In March 1936, Cárdenas assured businessmen and bankers that few industries would be expropriated. Similarly, after the oil expropriation, he rushed to assure foreign investors that he would not invoke the same solution in other cases, and he delivered on both pledges.[50]

Cárdenas's agrarian policies mirrored his urban labor policies. Consonant with his campaign pronouncements, he accelerated the pace of agrarian reform and distributed almost twice as much land as all previous presidents combined. That still left some 35 percent of the rural population landless, but it dampened rural unrest. On the other hand, in true Cárdenas style, large estates dedicated to commercial agriculture also expanded during these years.

Cárdenas encouraged rural unionization. The party, not the CTM, handled this task through the Confederación Nacional Campesina (CNC). By 1938, the CNC boasted thirty-eight peasant leagues, which later joined the party. The CTM, and Lombardo Toledano in particular, wished to undertake rural organizing, but Cárdenas persuaded it to abandon this effort and to recommend that all agrarian affiliates resign and join the CNC.

The two groups maintained consultative ties, but their separation ensured easier government control over both, another example of Cárdenas's dual policy.

In rural conflicts, Cárdenas followed the patterns he used in urban struggles. In the La Laguna district, he supported peasants against large landlords and called in CTM organizers to bolster their efforts. The intervention proved effective, and many peasants acquired land. Yet most large estates (70 percent of them foreign-owned) remained intact. Similarly, during the conflict at Los Mochis in Sinaloa, workers received land, but the property of the U.S.-based United Sugar Company went untouched.[51]

Available data allow for some generalizations about labor's economic situation. Salaries in the thirteen largest industrial establishments increased 97 percent between 1934 and 1940; those of urban workers in general rose 32.2 percent; the average minimum rural salary advanced only 19.3 percent. In Mexico City, prices of foodstuffs rose 56 percent, and prices of clothing climbed 68.5 percent. Prices probably increased less outside the capital. These figures suggest that industrial workers in the leading sectors improved their economic position but that urban labor in general and rural workers did not. In turn, those in larger urban workplaces gained more than the average worker. Significant differences existed within the working class. Most workers earned the legal minimum or less. On the other hand, those workers in the nine leading industrial establishments who made the lowest salaries received almost twice as much as the minimum, and those in the highest pay brackets earned four times that figure.[52]

These data clearly indicate the outline of official labor policy. Workers in sectors vital to Mexico's economic development, who also usually belonged to the CTM, received rising economic benefits. By granting these, the government hoped to buy industrial peace and raise productivity. This tactic also demonstrated to workers the advantage of CTM membership and showed confederation leaders the rewards of a friendly relationship with the government and Cárdenas.

Cárdenas has been viewed as a radical, an interpretation strengthened by the fact that he followed and preceded conservatives in office. But the years from 1934 to 1940 fit naturally into the flow of historical events. Cárdenas actually continued trends begun in the 1920s. He kept labor subordinate to the ruling party while undercutting it by splitting urban industrial workers from rural and government workers. He sometimes favored labor, but only to cool class antagonisms. He made it clear that the state held the real power and that only with government approval could labor win economic benefits or operate freely. Labor, in turn, continued to conform to the rules of the game set by the party. Organizations within the structure could win some economic and legal benefits. At all times, however, Cárdenas emphasized that the national interest included the rights of capitalists and the right of private property. After Cárdenas, Mexican governments formally linked to imperialist powers and representing an increasingly unified bourgeoisie tipped the scale further in favor of capital over labor.

LABOR AND THE STATE SINCE 1940

Presidents since 1940 have concentrated on accelerating capitalist industrial and agricultural development. The ruling party (the PNR became the Partido de la Revolución Institucional, or PRI, in 1946) acts as a clearinghouse for all officially recognized interests, and a small clique makes all decisions. Within this inner circle, the president has the most influence, serving as the official link among groups and supreme arbiter over national affairs. PRI labor policy has continued past practices of co-optation and repression.

The question of Cárdenas's successor loomed large. For a time, Lombardo Toledano emerged as a possible candidate, but the army vetoed that suggestion, believing him too radical. Finally, the conservative Manuel Avila Camacho received the party's backing. The CTM announced support for him in 1938 and duly received thirty-two seats in the Congress. The change of presidents coincided with the outbreak of World War II. During that crisis, the interests of labor and government momentarily meshed. Both agreed on supporting the war effort to defeat fascism and on building national industry to avoid shortages and create a stronger national economy. The government also saw an opportunity to increase the power of the capitalist class at labor's expense. Both thus called for unity under nationalistic slogans.[53]

This campaign soon resulted in a national unity pact between capital and labor signed by the CTM, CROM, and CGT, which together represented the vast majority of organized workers. The signers agreed to submit all disputes directly to the Ministry of Labor. Labor leaders further pledged full co-operation in the "battle of production" to secure Mexico's economic independence and to suspend interunion fights. Workers' representatives said they would call strikes or institute work actions only in extreme situations and that they would accept presidential arbitration in all cases. Only a few independent unions, such as the electricians' union, did not sign the pact, and it proved sufficient to keep labor peace. From 1941 through 1943, the number of strikes and strikers declined precipitously from the levels previously logged under Cárdenas.[54]

Labor unrest at the end of the war was foreshadowed in the form of increased stoppages during 1944. However, the pattern of capital-labor co-operation continued. Labor now joined in an un-written alliance with the Cámara Nacional de la Industria de Transformación, an industrialists' association that included the most progressive members of the rapidly expanding industrial bourgeoisie. In contrast with other employers' groups, which re-fused to maintain relations with labor, the Cámara thought that co-operation between labor and capital could ensure a smoothly functioning economy. Both sides agreed to work for Mexico's full economic independence through the development of the national economy and for higher national material and cultural standards. To this end, industry would modernize by using technology and capital from advanced nations, a somewhat contradictory statement in view of the agreement's commitment to economic independence. In reality, foreign investment only increased Mexico's dependence on advanced economics; modern technology led to capital-intensive operations that created fewer jobs than the older labor-intensive systems. The pact also provided for the peaceful solution of labor conflicts through collective bargaining.[55]

Why did the leading labor organizations sign this agreement? The CTM leadership grew increasingly reformist after the war. Leftists and other militants either gradually retired from the organization or were removed. The largest purge took place in 1948 as a direct result of the Cold War, when the government, under U.S. pressure, acted to remove all Communists or Marxists from the confederation. Reformists hoped that the pact would secure labor peace and industrial growth. Labor peace would assure the government's good will, which in turn gave them benefits in the form of political offices and lucrative union posts. Industrial growth would result in economic benefits for their followers, who represented an elite group of workers in the advanced sectors. Nor did these expectations prove wrong. The joint commission created to arbitrate conflicts functioned smoothly. In 1949, for example, only 2 of more than 200 cases brought before the commission required further litigation before settlement. At the same time, workers in most key industries received higher wages than the rest of the labor force, and the corrupt leaders reaped handsome personal rewards.[56]

Two additional factors account for labor's decreased militancy in the 1940s. First, government legislation gradually implemented provisions originally laid out by the Constitution and the Federal Labor Law of 1931 and, at the same time, increased penalties for those not conforming to official dictates. In 1943, for example, in the face of rapidly rising living costs and workers' discontent, laws supplemented the income of those earning less than the legal minimum and guaranteed a periodic revision in minimum wages. In 1944, the government created the long-promised social security system, which slowly expanded to cover 1.1 million persons by 1952. However, most of the beneficiaries belonged to the unionized sector, and less than 100,000 lived in rural areas. On the other hand, the labor law's 1942 revision further limited labor autonomy, and subsequent modifications continued to erode labor's rights. For example, new provisions made it easier to fire workers and restricted the rights of public employees to strike. The government also passed the Law of Social Dissolution, which set penalties for any attempt to "dissolve" Mexican society. The law failed to specify what acts fell into this category, thus allowing the authorities to interpret it freely. Originally passed against the fascist threat, the law remained on the books for use against all protestors.[57]

Second, outside the CTM, labor remained divided. The division prevented the formation of a progressive working-class front to combat the confederation's reformist policies. Lombardo Toledano, after failing to move the CTM out of the PRI, founded a separate labor organization and then a political party. In 1946–1947, a second schism occurred when the more progressive unions, including rail workers, miners, petroleum workers, and electricians, withdrew to form the Central Unica de Trabajadores (CUT). But the new organization did not endorse class struggle; it merely stated that it wished to function without government support or interference. It, in turn, soon split. First rail workers and then other unions resigned under heavy official pressures. Government employees, one of the largest groups, also failed to unite. Because they formed part of the party's popular sector, authorities denied them the right to unionize or to form a new sector within the party in 1946 and again in 1950. The revolutionary leadership thus remained consistent in its policy of dividing workers and preventing the formation of independent labor blocs.[58]

Divisions within labor's ranks continued after 1950, sometimes encouraged by the party because they facilitated government control. In the mid-1950s, the labor sector divided. The more conservative elements formed the Bloque Unido Obrero (BUO), a loose grouping of confederations and unions headed by the CTM until it was dissolved in 1966. A number of smaller organizations formed an anti-BUO bloc. Both remained closely linked to the PRI, differing principally over economic issues. The anti-BUO bloc campaigned against "corrupt labor leadership," but in practice limited its actions to rhetoric. CTM dissidents also founded two new confederations, but they remained in the PRI. Nevertheless, the CTM continued to be the leading labor body, enrolling from 70 to 90 percent of all unionized workers.[59]

In 1960, the government formed the Central Nacional de

Trabajadores, which claimed 400,000 members and declared itself a nationalist organization independent of employers but subject (as always) to the state. When that group faltered, the party tried again in 1965, orchestrating the formation of an Asamblea Nacional Revolucionario del Proletariado, which incorporated the same old corrupt bureaucracy and representatives of the state. By 1970, yet another group sprang into existence, the Comisión Nacional Tripartita, which incorporated representatives of labor, capital, and government for the purpose of discussing mutual economic issues. Each of these developments coincided with a new presidential succession and represented the attempt by the incoming officeholder to build a national organization to smooth labor relations. Labor dissent inside the CTM grew markedly after 1958, and the creation of new organizations reflected the hope of reorganizing labor into a confederation that might gain greater appeal among workers. Their failure resulted from the fact that the same persons occupied leadership posts and that workers distrusted both those bureaucrats and all state initiatives.[60]

In the agrarian sector, the CNC now dominates all organized activity. Its prime function is not to unionize peasants but to mobilize rural support for the PRI. Like its urban counterpart, the CTM, the CNC maintains a more or less united agrarian front for the party and settles local disputes peaceably whenever possible. In 1963, twelve peasant organizations tried to form an independent group, but it foundered within two years. More recently, however, agrarian unrest has grown in several states.[61]

In order to maintain the fiction that it operates autonomously, the CTM sometimes opposes government policies. In 1954 and 1958, for example, it initially refused to accept government wage standards and demanded higher raises than those proposed. In both cases, most labor organizations operated within the rules, using legal means to express their grievances. In 1954, the CTM even threatened a general strike before backing down after government assurances that it would consider the group's demands. Similarly, in 1974, when the annual inflation rate exceeded 20 percent, labor threatened to strike to protest wage increases of less than that amount. As usual, the CTM eventually called off the action and agreed to a compromise figure. Throughout these crises, the state maintained the initiative and dictated solutions. In all cases, however, the rank and file acted more militantly than the leadership. During 1958, dissidents captured control of several unions by appealing to the membership over the heads of the bureaucracy. That brought quick action, and the government ousted the dissidents once the storm of protest subsided or else used force to crush those workers who did not accept state decisions.

At the heart of the system lies corruption backed by force. Progovernment leaders use union funds and live lavishly at the expense of the rank and file. A select few receive high political posts in Congress, state governments, or the government bureaucracy. The CTM garners the majority of these sinecures; the party distributes the rest among friendly non-CTM labor groups. The government and the labor bureaucracy use numerous legal and illegal mechanisms of control. On the lowest level, union leaders rely on interpersonal relationships. Industrial jobs pay comparatively well and are scarce within a labor-surplus economy in which unemployment and underemployment are estimated at 30 to 40 percent. Officials apportion these jobs to recommended persons, ones highly unlikely to oppose their rule. Furthermore, recalcitrant unionists can be expelled from an organization and as a consequence lose their jobs. The bureaucracy can censor all materials sent to workers, thereby preventing the circulation of dissenting views. They also recruit future leaders, thus assuring that only co-operative persons rise within the hierarchy. Union leaders seldom attempt to build consciousness among the rank and file. Most contracts are renewed every two years. Little union political activity takes place during the intervals between contract negotiations. The leaders speak for the unions, and agreements in many cases are not subject to ratification by the rank and file. Thus the average union member pays dues and follows orders.

If antigovernment forces gain control of a local, the national officers can usually depose them by refusing to recognize their election on some technical ground. A case in point occurred in the oil industry in 1958. Dissidents won two Mexico City locals and gained recognition by staging demonstrations that showed widespread support by workers. But the revolt lasted only a short time. Within two years, legal maneuverings backed by government pressure drove the "rebel" leaders from office. Teachers also succeeded in forming independent unions for a time, but in 1960, they succumbed after a series of unfavorable legal rulings.

The government can intervene in union affairs in numerous ways. It can use official agencies. Conciliation and Arbitration Boards take one of three rulings on strikes under their jurisdiction: that an action is illegal, that it is "nonexistent" (i.e., has no legal basis to exist), or that it is legal. The first alternative allows employers to fire workers at will; if workers continue to strike, they then risk direct military or police intervention. If a strike is ruled nonexistent, which usually occurs when the board deems the strike harmful to the balance between labor and capital, then workers must normalize operations in forty-eight hours. In either case, no lost pay is recouped. Only if a strike is legalized does the employer pay for days lost. Board decisions concerning strikes often take considerable time; a strike may last weeks before a decision is reached. Given these risks, it is obviously safer to settle matters peaceably or else secure assurances of the government's good will before beginning an action.

Other steps, such as the refusal to recognize an organization, can keep unions in line. This move prevents unions from striking legally or bargaining collectively. In 1949, for example, the government denied recognition to Lombardo Toledano's newly formed confederation on the ground that it illegally included rural groups. In reality, the government disliked the group's leftist politics. The government can also choose extralegal tactics. For example, it aided friendly leaders when dissidents threatened to take over the mineworkers' confederation by blocking their attendance at the national convention. Progovernment leaders then easily secured a majority and saved their positions. Force, probably used more often than is commonly acknowledged, is yet another weapon in the government's arsenal. Under the Law of Social Dissolution, authorities can jail and try "subversives" for acting against state interests. All nonconformists run the risk of personal injury at the hands of union thugs.[62]

The case of the railroad unions provides a study in dissent. Mexican rail workers traditionally maintained an independent position. During the 1920s, they successfully fought CROM attempts to absorb their unions. In the late 1940s, they broke with the CTM and led the way in forming the CUT. Their internal strength resulted in part from the workers' unique position. Their organization ranked as the largest single labor entity, with over 70,000 members, and encompassed practically all workers in the industry. In addition, it controlled a vital sector of the economy. After the union's show of independence in 1948, however, the government proceeded to arrest its leaders and purge most progressives. Those acts paved the way for the election of Jesús Díaz de León, nicknamed "El Charro," to head the union. He soon turned the union officials into docile government supporters through the heavy-handed use of force and outright bribery. His example became the prototype for corrupt leaders, and that style of control is still known as *charrismo*.

By 1958, however, many of those purged from office had strengthened their rank-and-file support. Dissidents took the lead that year in demanding salary increases by forming an ad hoc commission on wages led by Demetrio Vallejo, a pro-Communist. The commission showed that real wages had dropped 40 percent since 1948 and insisted on substantial rectification. After a short strike against one line, the government partially capitulated. It unilaterally granted increases that surpassed those originally offered but still below the commission's demand. Commission members then asked for recognition as the union's leadership on the basis of their role in the struggle. The government deposed old-line officials and called elections, but barred Vallejo from running for office. Unrest and wildcat strikes continued until the government approved free elections, which Vallejo won by an overwhelming majority.

Supported by the rank and file, Vallejo now attempted to secure a uniform industry-wide settlement. After futile negotiations, a call for a general strike went out in conformity with Mexican law. Before the strike, which the government firmly opposed, the BUO called mass rallies to back the government. As usual, workers attending these demonstrations received the day off with pay and free transportation. The BUO then claimed that this "spontaneous" demonstration showed that workers sided with the party against the railroad union.

The strike, however, began at the appointed time. At that point, the government moved forcefully, declaring the strike illegal. Federal troops occupied national and local union buildings, soldiers forced strikers back to work at gunpoint, and authorities arrested some 3,000 workers, including all the newly elected officials. Simultaneously, it initiated a massive campaign to discredit the strike leaders. The press assured the public that "international Communism" lay behind the strike, and secret police turned up "subversive" materials at union headquarters. As crowning proof, the government expelled two Soviet diplomats with whom Vallejo had supposedly met regularly.

Repression was not confined to the railroaders; the government also arrested leaders from the petroleum, teachers, and communications workers' unions because they had shown signs of backing the rail workers. Almost overnight, an anti-Vallejo faction appeared in the railroad union and received official blessings. Vallejo, along with other strike leaders, came to trial under the Law of Social Dissolution in 1963, after being imprisoned for five years. He received a sixteen-year sentence for conspiracy and sabotage; his companions received lesser terms. An international campaign eventually secured his release in 1968.[63]

The scenario during other working-class protests has not been substantially different. Teachers' agitation, the 1964–1965 doctors' strike, and the internationally famous student strike of 1968 all met harsh responses. The 1968 massacre of students and workers in Mexico City is merely one incident in a long chain of state violence against dissent.[64]

The level of organization and the general economic situation of the working class reflect government attitudes. As Table 10 shows, the number of unionized workers and organizations has grown. However, the relative level of unionization has declined, after remaining steady from 1950 to 1955. This trend is, in part, the result of a slowing down in the number of new jobs in highly

TABLE 10.   NUMBER OF UNIONIZED WORKERS AND UNIONS, 1940–1969

	Number of Unionized Workers	Percentage of All Workers	Number of Unions
1940	605,433	8.6	—
1950	817,381	9.1	—
1955	979,991	8.7	—
1960	1,298,025	7.5	9,675
1965	1,697,258	7.4	12,733
1969	1,793,553	7.3	14,159

SOURCES: Calculated from Pablo González Casanova, *La democracia en México* (Mexico City, 1969), p. 304, and Estados Unidos Mexicanos, Secretaria de Industria y Comercio, Dirección General de Estadística, *Anuario estadístico compendiado de los Estados Unidos Mexicanos,* 1970 (Mexico City, 1971), p. 145. See also the general discussion of problems concerning statistics in Michael D. Everett, "The Role of the Mexican Trade Unions, 1950–1963" (Ph.D. diss., economics, Washington University, 1967), p. 81; Roberto de la Cerda Silva, *El movimiento obrero en México* (Mexico City, 1961), p. 147; and Horace B. Davis, "Numerical Strength of Mexican Unions," *Southwest Social Science Quarterly* 35, no. 1 (June 1954): 48–55.

unionized sectors (industry) and a rapid growth of those less unionized (services). At present, approximately 14 million persons in the labor force do not belong to a union. Organized labor thus forms a small portion of the working class. At the same time, the number of unions has risen faster than union membership. In other words, individual unions are becoming smaller on the average, a fact that facilitates government control. Smaller organizations, unless backed by the labor movement as a whole, are easier to bring into line with official policy.

The strength of individual unions and confederations cannot be accurately determined because the only available figures on membership are exaggerated. In 1958, for example, government sources listed 1.2 million union members; the PRI labor sector claimed that the BUO included almost 1.9 million workers, of which 1.5 million belonged to the CTM; and the anti-BUO bloc

TABLE 11.   STRIKE DATA, 1935–1969
(By Presidential Terms)

	Average Number of Strikes	Average Number of Strikers
Cárdenas (1935–1940)	478	61,422
Avila Camacho (1941–1946)	387	55,314
Alemán (1947–1952)	108	19,250
Ruíz Cortines (1953–1958)	248	25,057
López Mateos (1959–1964)	403	44,465
Díaz Ordaz (1965–1970)	124	2,886

SOURCES: González Casanova, *La democracia en México*, pp. 183–184; International Labour Office, *Yearbook of Labour Statistics* (Geneva, 1972), p. 747.

boasted that it had about 250,000 followers. Not all these claims can be correct. Overall, the CTM probably includes somewhere between 70 and 90 percent of those unionized. Non-CTM organizations claimed 25.7 percent of organized workers in 1950 and 30.5 percent in 1960, indicating a slight trend away from CTM membership during that period.[65]

Existing data on strike activity suggest other trends. Since 1940, the government has strongly encouraged peaceful settlement of disputes along established guidelines. In general, that policy has proved successful. The progovernment bureaucracy has co-operated fully, and arbitration boards have usually declared stoppages by militant unions or those seeking benefits above the guidelines to be either illegal or nonexistent. In 1957, for example, of 13,364 conflicts submitted to the boards, only 193 developed into strikes; in 1970, these bodies ruled on 26,377 disputes, but only 206 strikes occurred.[66]

Table 11 shows that strike activity decreased after 1940, reaching a low point between 1947 and 1958. Moreover, between 1941 and 1950, labor managed outright victories in only 301 strikes, whereas employers triumphed in 359.[67] This marked the first time that labor lost a majority of the actions that resulted in clear-cut

TABLE 12.   URBAN AND RURAL MINIMUM SALARIES, 1935–1962

	Percent
Increase in minimum urban salary	1,032.1
Increase in minimum rural salary	906.4
Increase in cost of living, Mexico City	986.2

SOURCE: Secretaria de la Presidencia, *Cinquenta años de revolución en cifras* (Mexico City, 1963), p. 112.

decisions. Activity rose briefly during the presidency of Adolfo López Mateos, as workers protested against spiraling inflation. Since then, however, the government has clamped down as measured by new lows reached in the period from 1965 to 1970. Since the total number of persons unionized has gone up along with the number of unions, it is clear that proportionately fewer and fewer workers are able or willing to voice *legal* protest.

Wages vary substantially from industry to industry, from area to area, and between rural and urban workers. Minimum-wage levels provide guidelines, but large numbers of workers earn less than the minimum levels. Furthermore, official data often fail to reflect actual cost-of-living rises. Still, available statistical series suggest several generalizations on living standards.

Table 12 indicates that urban salaries increased somewhat more than the overall cost of living but that rural salaries at best kept pace (assuming that the cost of living in rural areas rose less than it did in Mexico City). Other figures cast further light on the matter of salaries. In 1956, the average urban minimum salary stood at 7.86 pesos a day. A breakdown of income levels for that year shows that 78.2 percent of the population made less than 750 pesos annually, which amounts to about 2.5 pesos a day. Another 18.3 percent earned between 751 and 2,000 pesos. Even if the latter group represents urban labor, the average wage would amount to under 7 pesos a day if all persons in the group earned 2,000 pesos annually, a supposition that is obviously untrue. It therefore seems safe to assume that many workers earn less than the minimum and do not receive mandated increments under minimum-wage legislation. The figures in Table 12 thus represent an optimistic interpretation of the real situation.[68]

Other data show mixed results. One study concluded that average salaries increased 216 percent between 1930 and 1950 and that the cost of living rose 256 percent, leaving real salary levels 9 percent lower in 1950. Another study found that from 1940 to 1960 real industrial wages fell 6 percent and the minimum agrarian salary declined 45 percent in real terms. Scattered figures for 1962 to 1970, on the other hand, show a 50 percent income rise in the manufacturing sector while the cost of living increased slightly more than 30 percent. Workers in highly organized sectors, such as transportation (64 percent unionized), electricity (100 percent unionized), extractive industries (68 percent unionized), or in the chemical sector, where foreign capital predominates, receive better salaries than others. However, these workers represent only one-seventh of the total nonagricultural labor force and thus form a sort of labor elite.[69]

Income distribution figures support the conclusion that most families live on precariously low incomes. A study of urban conditions in 1961–1962 concluded that 94.6 percent of all families (not individual workers) earned under 3,000 pesos yearly. In other words, most families barely took in more than the supposed minimum wage for an individual worker. Mexico thus is a typical underdeveloped area. A small group of higher paid workers exists in the dynamic sectors, and these sectors generate much of the capital accumulated by the national and foreign bourgeoisie. Workers who belong to a union earn more and live better than those who do not, but their numbers are tightly controlled, and they represent a shrinking percentage of the work force. New industry is capital- rather than labor-intensive because it must compete within the world capitalist markets. Unions may therefore have reached a limit of relative expansion. Existing organizations cannot expand their membership as fast as the population growth (now over 3 percent a year and one of the highest in the world) without a radical shift in investment patterns or government social policies. Because this is unlikely, the social and economic gap between union and nonunion workers will surely continue to grow.[70]

Conclusion

Many factors weigh against any significant change in the near future. The policy of co-optation–repression shows few signs of seriously breaking down, and workers face many obstacles. Legal controls severely hamper opposition movements. Unions outside official groups have not attracted a large permanent following. The composition of the labor force also hinders the growth of militancy. Workers from the countryside have little or no union experience and are easily absorbed into the official system. The CTM even recruits in rural areas to ensure that workers join its ranks. Movement from a rural to an urban setting may mean an immediate improvement in economic terms and therefore temporary satisfaction. The fact that the service sector (only 4.2 percent organized) is the fastest-growing segment of the work force also restricts possibilities. Workers in this area have proved traditionally hard to organize, in part because many hold only temporary or part-time jobs. At the same time, the government continues to meet at least some of the workers' most pressing demands. The social security system has expanded, and in 1962 a primitive profit-sharing arrangement went into effect. Workers in key industries receive salary increases that at least approximate increases in the cost of living. And the authorities effectively use official propaganda to make workers think that the Revolution has their welfare in mind.[71]

On the other hand, the potential for increased working-class militancy in Mexico exists. Inflation, a product of the world economic situation and beyond the government's control, is currently running at about 20 percent a year. That casts doubts on the ability of the ruling class to allow even organized labor wage increases that match the rise in the cost of living and also continue the process of capital accumulation. In 1976, for example, the government granted wage increases of 23 percent, or 7 percent less than the official inflation rate. The disparity of income levels within the working class grows and how long workers outside the system will accept accelerating differences is problematical. Underemployment and unemployment now afflict half the work force of 16 million, and the economy generates many fewer jobs than the 800,000 needed to provide work for those entering the labor market each year. Furthermore, Mexico's foreign debt now stands at $24 billion (versus $3.5 billion in 1970), and repayment will place severe constraints on future government budgets and, therefore, economic policies.[72]

Social unrest has recently become one of the most important issues within Mexico. In rural areas, invasions of large estates have increased in frequency, particularly in the northwest. Four million landless migrants now seek the means to earn a living and their numbers grow every year. Urban labor too is restless and illegal strikes are becoming more frequent. Left opposition groups operate in many unions, including those once considered safely under government control. Workers also continue to organize outside the official labor movement.

The government, however, shows no signs of changing its policies. Luis Echeverría (1970–1976) came to office with a liberal program designed to relieve growing social and economic pressures, but an increasingly vocal right-wing faction within the party blocked most of his efforts. Mexico's current president, José López Portillo (inaugurated December 1, 1976), represents this group, and he has clearly stated his intention to strengthen the traditional alliance of government with business and foreign capital. He has already announced an austerity program. Thus the patterns formed during the decades after 1910 appear likely to continue, but repression rather than co-optation will become the principal response to working-class and peasant demands.[73]

NOTES

[1] For a general history, see James D. Cockcroft, "Mexico," in *Latin America: The Struggle with Dependency and Beyond*, Ronald H. Chilcote and Joel C. Edelstein, eds. (Cambridge, Mass., 1974), pp. 233–303, income and investment statistics from pp. 259, 277, 302–303; total net foreign-income figures derived from the Banco de México in 1967 include profits remitted abroad and profits reinvested, interest, royalties, and other payments. See also Juan Felipe Leal, "The Mexican State, 1915–73: An Historical Interpretation," *Latin American Perspectives* 2, no. 2 (Summer 1975): 48–63, and David Barkin, "Mexico's Albatross: The U.S. Economy," ibid., pp. 64–80; documentation on official pronouncements and media handling of dissent in Evelyn P. Stevens, *Protest and Response in Mexico* (Cambridge, Mass., 1974).

[2] In addition to the sources cited in Chapter 2 on the period up to 1910, see Ramón Eduardo Ruiz, *Labor and the Ambivalent Revolutionaries: Mexico, 1911–23* (Baltimore, Md., 1976), chaps. 1–2; Barry Carr, *El movimiento obrero y la política en México, 1910–1929*, 2 vols. (Mexico City, 1976), vol. 1, chap. 2.

[3] Compare James D. Cockcroft, *Intellectual Precursors of the Mexican Revolution 1900–1913* (Austin, Tex., 1969); Rodney D. Anderson, "Mexican Workers and the Politics of Revolution," *Hispanic American Historical Review* 54, no. 1 (February 1974): 94–113; and Ruiz, *Labor and the Ambivalent Revolutionaries*.

[4] Luis Araiza, *Historia del movimiento obrero mexicano*, 4 vols. (Mexico City, n.d.), 3:9–10; Roberto de la Cerda Silva, *El movimiento obrero en México* (Mexico City, 1961), pp. 105–107; Marjorie Clark, *Organized Labor in Mexico* (Chapel Hill, N.C., 1934), pp. 21–22. On Catholics, see Genaro María González, *Catolicismo y revolución* (Mexico City, 1961), pp. 310–312; José Castillos y Piña, *Cuestiones sociales* (Mexico City, 1934), pp. 221–238; Alfonso López Aparicio, *El movimiento obrero en México* (Mexico City, 1952), pp. 137–140.

[5] Cited in Clark, *Organized Labor in Mexico*, p. 37.

[6] Ruiz, *Labor and the Ambivalent Revolutionaries*, p. 38.

[7] Best single source on the Casa, although a favorable interpretation, is Rosendo Salazar, *La Casa del Obrero Mundial* (Mexico City, 1962), and *Líderes y sindicatos* (Mexico City, 1953). John Mason Hart's as yet unpublished work, which I have not seen, should shed new light on the Casa and its dealings with the government.

[8] Clark, *Organized Labor in Mexico*, p. 27.

[9] Cerda Silva, *El movimiento obrero en México*, p. 115; Leafar Agetro, *Las luchas proletarias en Veracruz* (Mexico City, 1942), pp. 159–161,

has a complete text of the pact; Robert P. Millon, *Zapata: The Ideology of a Peasant Revolutionary* (New York, 1969), pp. 80–82.

10 Jean Meyer, "Los obreros en la revolución mexicana: los 'Batallones rojos,' " *Historia Mexicana* 21, no. 1 (July–September 1971): 1–37; Severo Iglesias, *Sindicalismo y socialismo en México* (Mexico City, 1970), p. 49; Ruiz, *Labor and the Ambivalent Revolutionaries*, pp. 52–53.

11 Araiza, *Historia del movimiento obrero mexicano*, 3:6; Salazar, *La Casa del Obrero Mundial*, pp. 27–28; Clark, *Organized Labor in Mexico*, p. 40.

12 López Aparicio, *El movimiento obrero mexicano*, pp. 137–140; Agetro, *Las luchas proletarias en Veracruz*, pp. 167–171; Ruiz, *Labor and the Ambivalent Revolutionaries*, pp. 63–64.

13 On the Constitution and implementation, see Clark, *Organized Labor in Mexico*, p. 48; Oscar C. Alvarez, *La cuestión social en México* (Mexico City, 1950), p. 108; Guadalupe Rivera Marín, *El mercado de trabajo, relaciones obrero-patronales* (Mexico City, 1955); Ruiz, *Labor and the Ambivalent Revolutionaries*, pp. 66–69; on profit sharing, see Susan Kaufman Purcell, *The Mexican Profit Sharing Decision: Politics in an Authoritarian Regime* (Berkeley, Calif., 1976).

14 Iglesias, *Sindicalismo y socialismo en México*, pp. 39–40; Araiza, *Historia del movimiento obrero mexicano*, 3:189–191.

15 Quote from Iglesias, *Sindicalismo y socialismo en México*, pp. 66–67; on U.S. business and the Ford Motor Company, see Robert Freeman Smith, *The United States and Revolutionary Nationalism in Mexico, 1916–1932* (Chicago, 1972), pp. 230–231.

16 On the Saltillo Congress and CROM, see Camile Nick Buford, "A Biography of Luis N. Morones, Mexican Labor and Political Leader" (Ph.D. diss., History, Louisiana State University, 1971), pp. 17, 19–21, 32–33; Ricardo Treviño, *El espionaje comunista y la evolución doctrinaria del movimiento obrero en México* (Mexico City, 1952), pp. 105–109; Iglesias, *Sindicalismo y socialismo en México*, pp. 43, 66; Araiza, *Historia del movimiento obrero mexicano*, vol. 4; Clark, *Organized Labor in Mexico*, p. 61; Carr, *El movimiento obrero y la política en México*, vol. 1, chap. 3.

17 The Pact's main provisions are given in Buford, "Biography of Luis N. Morones," pp. 34–35, 86; López Aparicio, *El movimiento obrero en México*, p. 182.

18 Buford, "Biography of Luis N. Morones," p. 93; Maximino Zaragoza-Carbajal, "Vicente Lombardo Toledano: His Role in the Socio-Political Evolution of Mexico Since the 1930's" (Ph.D. diss., Political Science, University of St. Louis, 1971), p. 104.

19 On CROM in general, see Clark, *Organized Labor in Mexico*, pp. 108–118, and 65–67 on membership figures; also Buford, "Biography of Luis

N. Morones," p. 99; Iglesias, *Sindicalismo y socialismo en Mexico*, p. 67; Rosendo Salazar, *Los primeros de Mayo en México* (Mexico City, 1965), p. 102.

20 See Agetro, *Las luchas proletarias en Veracruz*, p. 188–189, for details on petroleum workers.

21 Buford, "Biography of Luis N. Morones," pp. 45, 94–95. On railroad workers, see Marcelo N. Rodea, *Historia del movimiento obrero ferrocarrilero en México (1890–1943)* (Mexico City, 1944), pp. 247–249; Mario Gill, *Los ferrocarrileros* (Mexico City, 1971), pp. 46–48, 69–71.

22 Detailed information on the CGT is in Araiza, *Historia del movimiento obrero mexicano*, vol. 4; Iglesias, *Sindicalismo y socialismo en México*, pp. 63–65.

23 Joaquín Márquez Montiel, S.J., *La doctrina social de la iglesia y la legislación obrera mexicana* (Mexico City, 1939), p. 55; López Aparicio, *El movimiento obrero en México*, pp. 188–189; Clark, *Organized Labor in Mexico*, pp. 88–89. On the Communist Party, see Karl M. Schmitt, *Communism in Mexico. A Study in Political Frustration* (Austin, Tex., 1965), an unsympathetic account; see also Harry Bernstein, "Marxismo en Mexico, 1917–1925," *Historia Mexicana* 7, no. 4 (April–June, 1958): 497–516.

24 On railroads, see Rodea, *Historia del movimiento obrero ferrocarrilero en México*, esp. chaps. 2–3; Gill, *Los ferrocarrileros*, pp. 44–52. On electrical workers, Clark, *Organized Labor in Mexico*, p. 164, and Mark E. Thompson, "The Development of Unionism Among Mexican Electrical Workers" (Ph.D. diss., Cornell School of Industrial and Labor Relations, 1966), chaps. 3 and 4, trace the union to 1932.

25 Clark, *Organized Labor in Mexico*, p. 85.

26 Ibid., pp. 154–160; Agetro, *Las luchas proletarias en Veracruz,* pp. 102–117; L. Vincent Padgett, *The Mexican Political System* (Boston, 1966), pp. 110–111.

27 Robert E. Scott, *Mexican Government in Transition* (Urbana, Ill., 1966), pp. 110–111; Clark, *Organized Labor in Mexico*, pp. 122–123; López Aparicio, *El movimiento obrero en México*, pp 190–191; Buford, "Biography of Luis N. Morones," pp. 148–156; on Calles and labor, and on Calles, Obregón, and CROM, see Carr, *El movimiento obrero y la política en México*, vol. 2, chaps. 1, 2, 4.

28 Clark, *Organized Labor in Mexico*, pp. 154–160.

29 Ibid., pp. 134–139; López Aparicio, *El movimiento obrero en México*, pp. 210–213; Robert P. Millon, *Mexican Marxist: Vicente Lombardo Toledano* (Chapel Hill, N.C., 1966), p. 267.

30 López Aparicio, *El movimiento obrero en México*, p. 212; Clark, *Organized Labor in Mexico*, p. 193.

31 Clark, *Organized Labor in Mexico*, p. 110; Padgett, *Mexican Political*

System, p. 166; Arthur Neef, *Labor in Mexico* (Bureau of Labor Statistics, Report No. 251) (Washington, D.C., 1963), pp. 50–54, has a detailed discussion of the law; Cerda Silva, *El movimiento obrero en México*, pp. 136–137.

32 Iglesias, *Sindicalismo y socialismo en México*, p. 103.

33 Clark, *Organized Labor in Mexico*, pp. 65–67; Cerda Silva, *El movimiento obrero en México*, p. 140; Rivera Marín, *El mercado de trabajo*, p. 84.

34 Charles C. Cumberland, *Mexico: The Struggle for Modernity* (New York, 1968), p. 251; Labor Department information cited in William English Walling, *The Mexican Question* (New York, 1927), p. 45.

35 See Clark, *Organized Labor in Mexico*, p. 119.

36 Joe Ashby, *Organized Labor and the Mexican Revolution Under Lázaro Cárdenas* (Chapel Hill, N.C., 1967), p. 22.

37 Ibid., pp. 22, 182, 192; Arnaldo Córdoba, *La política de masas del cardenismo* (Mexico City, 1974); and Arturo Anguiano, *El estado y la política obrera del cardenismo* (Mexico City, 1975). Many sources have noted the broad similarity between the policies of Cárdenas and Franklin D. Roosevelt. Unemployment jumped from 90,000 to 340,000 between 1929 and 1932; see Córdoba, *La política de masas del cardenismo*, p. 17.

38 Iglesias, *Sindicalismo y socialismo en México*, pp. 71–73; Zaragoza-Carabajal, "Vicente Lombardo Toledano," pp. 105–106; Córdoba, *La política de masas del cardenismo*, p. 69.

39 Strike data in James W. Wilkie, *The Mexican Revolution: Federal Expenditure and Social Change Since 1910* (Berkeley, Calif., and Los Angeles, 1970), p. 184; Ashby, *Organized Labor and the Mexican Revolution*, p. 23.

40 Millon, *Mexican Marxist*, p. 118; López Aparicio, *El movimiento obrero en México*, p. 214; Ashby, *Organized Labor and the Mexican Revolution*, pp. 14–28.

41 Ashby, *Organized Labor and the Mexican Revolution*, pp. 32–35; Antonio Alonso, *El movimiento ferrocarrilero en México, 1958/1959* (Mexico City, 1972), pp. 39–40.

42 On the CTM's early years, see Confederación de Trabajadores de México, *Confederación de Trabajadores de México, 1936/1941* (Mexico City, 1942), esp. pp. 12–80.

43 Buford, "Biography of Luis N. Morones," p. 194; Zaragoza-Carabajal, "Vicente Lombardo Toledano," pp. 129–131; see also the *Mexican Labor News*, published monthly in Mexico City by the workers' university; *Mexican Labor News* (May 1937): 1.

44 Millon, *Mexican Marxist*, p. 128; Scott, *Mexican Government in Transition*, pp. 130–131.

45 Cerda Silva, *El movimiento obrero en México*, p. 147; CTM claims

made at its annual congress, in Confederación de Trabajadores de México, *Confederación de Trabajadores de México*, p. 491; Secretaria de la Presidencia, *50 años de revolución en cifras* (Mexico City, 1963), p. 161.

[46] On these struggles and those of textile workers, see Ashby *Organized Labor and the Mexican Revolution*, pp. 98–121.

[47] Buford, "Biography of Luis N. Morones," pp. 213–224, 216–217; the *Mexican Labor News* carried detailed accounts of interunion fights in almost every issue during these years.

[48] Gill, *Los ferrocarrileros*, pp. 79–123; Anguiano, *El estado y la política obrera del cardenismo*, p. 91.

[49] Quote from *Mexican Labor News* (June 1937): 1; Ashby, *Organized Labor and the Mexican Revolution*, pp. 182–269, covers labor and the oil controversy; a pro-Company view is William E. McMahon, *Two Strikes and Out* (Garden City, N.Y., 1939).

[50] Cockcroft, "Mexico," pp. 267–268, 274.

[51] On La Laguna specifically, see Ashby, *Organized Labor and the Mexican Revolution*, pp. 144–179; on the CNC, Moisés González Navarro, *La Confederación Nacional Campesina: Un grupo de presión en la reforma agraria mexicana* (Mexico City, 1968), pp. 87–184; on Cárdenas's agrarian policies in general, Eyler Simpson, *The Ejido: Mexico's Way Out* (Chapel Hill, N.C., 1937); and Nathan L. Whetten, *Rural Mexico* (Chicago, 1948).

[52] Secretaria de la Presidencia, *50 años de revolución en cifras*, p. 112; López Aparicio, *El movimiento obrero en México*, p. 217; Pedro Merla, *El costo de la vida obrera en México* (Mexico City, 1942), p. 7.

[53] Details in Edwin Lieuwen, *Mexican Militarism: The Political Rise and Fall of the Revolutionary Army, 1910–1941* (Albuquerque, N.M., 1968), pp. 127–131.

[54] On the shift to a policy of industrialization and its roots under Cárdenas, see Sanford A. Mosk, *Industrial Revolution in Mexico* (Berkeley, Calif., and Los Angeles, 1950); text of the pact in López Aparicio, *El movimiento obrero en México*, p. 230; Vicente Lombardo Toledano, *The CTAL and the War* (Mexico City, 1945), contains his defense of the agreement; strikes in Wilkie, *Mexican Revolution*, p. 184.

[55] López Aparicio, *El movimiento obrero en México*, p. 232.

[56] Iglesias, *Sindicalismo y socialismo en México*, p. 131; Michael D. Everett, "The Role of the Mexican Trade Unions, 1950–1963" (Ph.D. diss., Economics, Washington University, St. Louis, 1967), pp. 8, 28.

[57] Padgett, *Mexican Political System*, pp. 167–169; Wilkie, *Mexican Revolution*, p. 94; Everett, "Role of the Mexican Trade Unions," p. 51.

[58] Everett, "Role of the Mexican Trade Unions," p. 80.

[59] On these splits and temporary groupings, see Scott, *Mexican Government*

in Transition, pp. 162–168; Iglesias, *Sindicalismo y socialismo en México,* pp. 134–135; Everett, "Role of the Mexican Trade Unions," pp. 34–35, 52–53, 80–100, 174; Neef, *Labor in Mexico,* pp. 87–92.

60 On recent trends, see Raúl Trejo Delarbe, "The Mexican Labor Movement, 1917–1975," *Latin American Perspectives* 3, no. 1 (Winter 1976): 133–153.

61 See González Navarro, *La Confederación Nacional Campesina,* chaps. 10–12.

62 On the above conflicts and government repression, see Everett, "Role of the Mexican Trade Unions," pp. 8–10, 21–35, 55–57, 70–74, 117–132; Iglesias, *Sindicalismo y socialismo en México,* pp. 136–139; Pablo González Casanova, *La democracia en México* (Mexico City, 1969), p. 26.

63 On rail workers, see Gill, *Los ferrocarrileros,* and especially Alonso, *El movimiento ferrocarrilero en México.* Electrical workers have also gained some autonomy from the state; see Thompson, "Development of Unionism Among Mexican Electrical Workers"; and [Sindicato de Trabajadores Electricistas de la República Mexicana], *Insurgencia obrera y nacionalismo revolucionario* (Mexico City, 1973), a selection of editorials and articles from *Solidaridad,* the official magazine of the electrical workers' union.

64 On students, Ramón Ramírez, *El movimiento estudiantil de México: Julio–diciembre de 1968* (Mexico City, 1969), 2 vols.; and United States Committee for Justice to Latin American Political Prisoners, *The Students Speak* (New York, 1968); and on railroads, doctors, and the students' movement as well as repression and the media, see Stevens, *Protest and Response in Mexico.*

65 Everett, "Role of the Mexican Trade Unions," p. 94; Alonso, *El movimiento ferrocarrilero en México,* p. 101.

66 Howard F. Cline, *Mexico, Revolution to Evolution: 1940–1960* (New York, 1963), p. 226; Estados Unidos Mexicanos, *Anuario,* pp. 146–151.

67 Rivera Marín, *El mercado de trabajo,* pp. 232–235. Won-lost totals do not match strike totals in Table 11 because some conflicts reached no decision.

68 Ifigenía de Navarrete, *La distribución del ingreso y el desarrollo económico de México* (Mexico City, 1960); see also Antonio Ugalde, *Power and Conflict in a Mexican Community* (Albuquerque, N.M., 1970), p. 21.

69 Rivera Marín, *El mercado de trabajo,* p. 141; Everett, "Role of the Mexican Trade Unions," p. 64; González Casanova, *La democracia en México,* p. 303; Estados Unidos Mexicanos, *Anuario,* pp. 158–176; International Labour Office, *Yearbook of Labour Statistics,* pp. 570, 592; Cockcroft, "Mexico," p. 275.

70 Robert I. Rhodes, "Mexico—A Model for Development?" *Science and*

Society 24, no. 1 (Spring 1970): 63; Stephen R. Niblo, "Progress and the Standard of Living in Contemporary Mexico," *Latin American Perspectives* 2, no. 2 (Summer 1975): 109–124, examines the deteriorating standard of living.

[71] Ugalde, *Power and Conflict in a Mexican Community*, a study of labor in Ensenada, clearly indicates the economic thrust of unions and their essentially conservative nature in regard to confronting the system. He also says that local leaders, at least in his sample, are far less corrupt than national officials.

[72] See, for example, *The New York Times*, Dec. 1, 1976, p. A17.

[73] Ibid., Dec. 26, 1976, p. 17.

4

LABOR AND POPULISM: ARGENTINA AND BRAZIL

The Depression inaugurated the co-optive–repressive period for most of Latin America, although the period's specific characteristics differed depending upon both the international dimension and local circumstances. In Mexico, for example, the 1910 Revolution hastened the process; in other areas, the 1930s determined the contours of co-optation and repression. In several countries, populism emerged as the dominant mechanism through which those in power dealt with the working class and labor.

The term *populist* describes a variety of Latin American regimes since the 1930s. Most agree that populism is "a political movement opposed to the status quo and supported by the mass of the urban working class and sometimes the peasantry as well as nonworking class elements." Recent research has pinpointed the key elements of populism by concluding that politicians from the ruling class or petty bourgeoisie lead populist movements and that, despite rhetoric to the contrary, they serve the class aims of these politicians. Populism is nationalistic in content and thus may involve real or potential conflict at an international level. It ultimately serves to *weaken* working-class organization by restricting its autonomous development, and in that sense does not attack existing structures. In reality, conflict arising around populist movements represents intraclass struggles on a national or extranational level rather than interclass warfare, as is often supposed.[1]

Populism in Latin America is often identified with individual politicians. It has no systematic ideology; rather, it usually adopts a loose set of concepts to fit a particular case or occasion and displays itself through a political style. This chapter looks at populism during the period of Juan D. Perón in Argentina (1943–1955), and during the regimes of Getúlio Vargas (1930–1945, 1950–1954) and João Goulart (1961–1964) in Brazil.

These cases, of course, represent only three examples. In Chile, the Popular Front period and its aftermath (1938–1948) can be viewed as populist. Similarly, the Cárdenas years share many characteristics found in populist periods elsewhere, but Cárdenas is best understood within the Mexican context. Perón and Vargas stand out most distinctly within the historical development of their nations. Significantly, all the examples cited here occurred in the 1930s, but populist regimes and parties have continued to exist throughout Latin America.[2]

To understand populism's origins, it is necessary to examine events generated by the Depression, which facilitated its rise. The economic crash brought a sharp contraction of world trade. Between 1930 and 1933, the volume of world exports fell 25 percent, and its total value plummeted over 50 percent. The Latin American nations, along with other exporters of primary products, suffered greatly. Mass liquidation of foreign investment worsened the situation. Latin America's import capacity shrank severely. In the period from 1930 to 1934, it declined 37 percent from the previous five-year period; between 1935 and 1939, it declined 27 percent. Every nation except Argentina defaulted on its foreign debt service, further curtailing available external financing.[3]

Table 13 shows the Depression's impact in Argentina and Brazil. Argentina's agricultural and pastoral exports enjoyed a relatively stable demand, and furthermore, production (area sown or animals marketed) could be varied on an annual basis. Argentina suffered less than other nations, and its economy recovered by the late 1930s. Markets for Brazil's main export, coffee, shrank rapidly, but coffee trees grew berries every year. As a result, economic activity plummeted and recovered only gradually.

After 1930, two central problems concerned national governments: how to prevent economic collapse and how to avoid massive social unrest. In Argentina and Brazil, as elsewhere in Latin America, military regimes seized power. Gradually, however, defensive strategies for survival gave way to programs designed to meet the crisis actively on a long-term basis. The Depression

TABLE 13. VARIATIONS IN AVERAGE ANNUAL IMPORT CAPACITY,
1930–1939
(Percentage Variation from 1925–1929)

	Argentina	Brazil
1930–1934	−27	−35
1935–1939	−11	−32

SOURCE: Celso Furtado, *Economic Development of Latin America* (Cambridge, Eng., 1970), table 5.3, p. 41.

underscored the vulnerability of export economies to the vagaries of world capitalism, and industrialization appeared to be a way to remedy that circumstance. Those in power hoped that industrial expansion would generate internal economic growth and ease the impact of the crisis. They also saw it as a means to lessen dependency upon the developed nations. Both countries embarked on industrialization programs, entering the so-called import-substitution stage, during which local industry produced manufactures previously imported. The resulting growth in manufacturing, in turn, led to rapid urbanization aided by a depression in the agricultural sector which drove people into cities in search of better opportunities or just the means of survival. This mass of urban newcomers played an important role in populist politics and the development of organized labor.

The problem of financing industrial development soon arose. Nowhere in Latin America did an industrial bourgeoisie exist either capable of or willing to undertake this mammoth task alone, and external financing could not be obtained. Expanded state participation, however, provided an alternative. Accordingly, in the 1930s, state economic intervention increased, and governments actively sought ways to raise needed investment capital and build the required infrastructure. One method was the imposition of regressive wage policies that forced the working class and peasantry to contribute yet greater amounts to internal capital accumulation.

Industrialization financed primarily by the local working class required new labor strategies. Industry needed skilled and disciplined workers, but it also needed a reserve pool of labor to maintain low wages. Strict control over the working class could assure both. Populist politicians thought they could best accomplish this goal by tightly controlling surviving unions or by creating them where none existed. Labor organizations performed several functions in that formulation. They tied workers directly to state agencies that administered labor laws, thus facilitating the implementation of government policy. Through wage policies and distribution of social services to union members, they also served as vehicles for controlling the rate of capital accumulation and raising or lowering purchasing power. Furthermore, government co-optation and repression (as in Mexico) theoretically prevented any serious challenge by organized labor or the working class.

Nationalism became the dominant ideology used to justify these measures, and industrialization quickly became a national panacea. The Depression threatened the viability of national society, and it originated abroad. As a result, almost all sectors of the population thought that the economy should be strengthened against the possibility of such occurrences in the future, and they readily accepted nationalist ideologies. Official propaganda spun the myth that all citizens would ultimately benefit equally from industrial growth but warned that it entailed grave sacrifices. Workers occupied an assigned place in the scheme as the ultimate producers (but not yet consumers) of wealth; they supposedly ensured their children's future by tightening their own belts, a process repeated every generation. Capitalists, however, reaped immediate rewards. They acquired needed capital to invest and accumulated profits as compensation for the risks of entrepreneurship. Official propaganda proclaimed that any ideology which even obliquely threatened industrialization smacked of treason. Before 1930, Communism and anarchism represented godless attempts to undermine family, property, and morals; after 1930, bourgeois ideologies contended that Communism and anarchism also menaced free enterprise, the capitalist system, and therefore the state's ability to provide wealth for all.

The ways in which each ruling class could accomplish its goals varied according to two additional factors: the structure and strength of the working-class movement and the degree of cohesion within the bourgeoisie.[4] The Depression affected Argentina least of any Latin American nation. Labor there had attained a high level of organization before 1930. The elite remained unified, in the sense that the agricultural-pastoral sector dominated an industrial sector composed mainly of foreigners. At the time, agrarian exporters felt that limited national industrial development to fill the gap left by a reduced capacity to import did not harm their interests. They thus backed regimes that espoused controlled industrialization. Because no strong or unified central labor organization existed after 1930, the government could effectively repress labor. However, the militancy of a working class possessing a long tradition of struggle could remain dormant only for a limited time. Labor unrest and working-class mobilization increased during the late 1930s, but workers' demands fell on deaf ears. Perón built his populist coalition in the 1940s by tapping workers' discontent before it exploded. He extended social and economic benefits to the working class, but at the same time, he carefully controlled organized labor and discouraged autonomous working-class expression. Perón's policies favored national industry and workers over traditional agrarian interests, but he never challenged the capitalist basis of Argentine society.

In Brazil, the elite split between the old oligarchy centered in São Paulo and those opposed to it, including urbanized middle groups. Labor remained poorly organized because of effective repression throughout the 1920s. Vargas therefore faced no strong working-class opposition upon seizing power. After taking steps to bolster the economy, he proceeded to create a state-controlled labor movement that facilitated industrialization and provided him with mass support when needed. At the same time, he assured social peace and labor co-operation in a period of local capital accumulation. Vargas's hands-off policy in the countryside temporarily calmed agrarian interests, and like Perón, he attempted no radical changes of the prevailing socioeconomic system.

In the 1930s and 1940s, local capital enjoyed a *relative* autonomy in relation to world capitalism and imperialism. The

Depression loosened ties of dependency. The war brought mixed results for Latin America. Producers of strategic materials and primary products needed for the war effort profited from foreign sales, but industrialization slowed as the 1940s advanced. At the urging of the United States, some governments transferred funds into war-related production, but capital and intermediate goods could not be imported. However, between 1929 and 1947, industrialization made significant strides. That sector grew from 22.85 to 32.40 percent of gross domestic product in Argentina and from 11.7 to 23.1 percent of GDP in Brazil. Existing pockets of local capital expanded and new ones formed.[5]

After the war and European recovery, the era of relative freedom ended. Led by the United States, foreign capital actively re-established hegemony over underdeveloped areas. The process involved two steps: increased investment (now more and more in manufacturing) and the creation or maintenance of conditions that allowed maximization of profits and minimization of risks. It required governments that followed acceptable policies with regard to the investment of foreign capital, such as adequate infrastructure, free profit remittances, monopoly positions, and low import duties. It also demanded both a quiescent and stable working class and peasantry that could provide adequately trained and disciplined personnel and at least a minimum of local purchasing power.[6]

Spearheaded by the United States, international capitalism and its local allies no longer tolerated governments or movements that threatened "safe investment climates." They considered populist regimes particularly undesirable because such regimes advocated nationalism and mobilized workers, forces that might oppose foreign domination. Imperialist powers therefore worked against populist regimes or at least tried to nullify their nationalist policies and purge them of their working-class component. Failing this, they sought to water down nationalist economic policies and to see that only procapitalist working-class organizations survived (see Chapter 6). The fact that by 1955 governments favorable to imperialist wishes replaced two of the populist regimes discussed here attests to the success of these efforts. Similarly, foreign pressures also helped snuff out Goulart in 1964.

LABOR AND POPULISM IN ARGENTINA:
THE RISE AND FALL OF PERÓN, 1930–1955

Depression and Realignment, 1930–1943

The conservative military coup of 1930 represented the interests of the landed oligarchy that had been threatened by the drastic fall in exports to Great Britain and Europe. Succeeding governments continued to reflect those interests, and elections simply rubber-stamped official candidates. Most opposition parties at first opposed conservative rule but later either openly or tacitly endorsed the fraudulent electoral process, confining themselves to ineffectual verbal protests or isolated political acts.[7]

The landed bourgeoisie faced a series of economic problems. The drop in exports severely curtailed foreign exchange earnings and therefore the nation's capacity to import. Continued imports meant huge budget deficits and, sooner or later, default on external obligations, which exporters wished to avoid in order not to antagonize overseas buyers. Conversely, any prolonged reduction in imports would result in domestic shortages, inflationary pressures, and social unrest. Limited national industrialization of the import-substitution variety seemed a way out of the dilemma. To meet the immediate economic crisis, governments after 1930 implemented measures for *contained* national industrialization, including commercial and monetary controls, massive public works projects to build infrastructure, and state production boards, all of which signaled increased state participation within a carefully regulated economy. By 1935, the downward cycle bottomed out. Simultaneously, the agrarian oligarchy assured its own continued prosperity through the Roca-Runciman Pact of 1933 (renewed in 1936). These agreements guaranteed Argentine beef entry into British markets at set prices. In return, British capital gained greater control over the export process and concessions primarily within the transport sector.

The industrial sector of the economy grew rapidly, and by 1943 industry ranked as the leading contributor to national income, overtaking agriculture. The number of industrial establishments increased from 37,362 in 1935 to 52,445 in 1941, many of them small firms financed by national capital. As a result, imports within the total supply of goods fell from 52.9 percent in 1929 to 34.9 percent in 1938 and continued downward in the following years. However, during the 1930s, local industrialists had no national political role. In 1935, foreigners made up 60 percent of all entrepreneurs, and many more were of immigrant origin. As foreigners, they could not vote, and they remained unattached to any political bodies. Furthermore, their recent appearance as a national interest group had not given them time to articulate their views in an organized manner.[8]

As industrial production climbed, the number of industrial workers increased, from 435,816 in 1935 to 684,497 in 1941; the service sector expanded similarly. Those thrown out of work by the Depression and persons entering the labor market from the urban population represented a portion of this increase, but so did rural workers who migrated to the cities. Between 1936 and 1943, an average of 72,000 persons arrived annually in greater Buenos Aires from the interior. That mass, along with newly employed people, would play a key role in Perón's rise to power after 1943.[9]

The Depression coincided with a period of declining labor activism. Two important confederations existed in 1930, but neither could respond to the economic crisis. The anarchosyndicalist FORA had lost its earlier potency. The newly founded CGT (Confederación General de Trabajo), combining Socialists and syndicalists, had been formed only a few days after the coup. At that time, CGT officials adhered to an apolitical position and wished to consolidate the organization; therefore, they formulated no set position toward the military junta and petitioned it to allow the exercise of democratic rights.

Initially, the military repressed only those working-class groups that opposed its anticonstitutional rule, namely, the Communists and anarchists. Soon, however, particularly after an attempted Radical countercoup in 1932, it moved against all opposition. It now jailed and deported labor leaders and dissolved many unions as "illicit associations." Government goons and rightwing "patriotic" organizations such as the Unión Cívica combined to smash workers' demonstrations and break strikes.

In the face of this offensive, labor remained disorganized. The governing interim National Labor Committee of the CGT still had not formally constituted the body. At the 1932 meeting, the committee called for more social legislation and for civil liberties, but it presented no plan for setting up the confederation. Behind this indecision lay fundamental disagreements. Syndicalists, who controlled the committee, believe in autonomous worker action. Socialists, who probably had the largest following among unionized workers, wished labor to express its demands through their party. They thus worked against the creation of a strong, independent CGT. Communists remained outside the CGT and attempted to organize separately. In 1935, however, they changed strategy and adopted a modified popular front platform by joining the confederation. Their presence only complicated internal rivalries.[10]

By 1935, the committee still had not called a constituent assembly. In that year, a group of unions predominantly sympathetic to the Socialist position declared the committee defunct and organized a convention that formally inaugurated the CGT in 1936. Hard-line syndicalists refused to accept this pre-emptive action and formed a splinter confederation. The CGT, however, still remained divided. In 1942, it split after a hotly contested election. A CGT No. 1 included those following a "laborist" position, which urged the formation of a workers' party outside the confederation. A CGT No. 2 grouped persons who wanted the confederation to represent the labor arm of either the Socialist or Communist Party. Within this faction Socialists predominated, but a strong Communist minority existed. Thus, at the time of the 1943 military coup, rival factions fought within the CGT while syndicalists and independent unions also vied for workers' support.[11]

Despite these divisions, working-class activity expanded after 1935. The Communists proved the most dynamic group in the revival. While others quibbled over what to do, Communists organized, particularly among those who had never belonged to a labor group. They helped form a series of new unions and federations, among which the construction workers' federation ranked strongest. Five years after its founding in 1936, the federation incorporated almost 50,000 workers, or half of those regularly employed in the industry. Metalworkers and textile workers also unionized, aided by Communist Party members. By 1940, the Communist bloc represented an important minority within the ranks of organized labor, one able to challenge the dominant position of the conservative transport workers' unions led by La Fraternidad and the Unión Ferroviaria.[12]

Organized labor grew to include nearly one-third of all industrial workers. By 1936, there were 296 unions claiming 369,969 members; five years later, official figures listed 356 organizations with 441,412 members. The CGT boasted 217 affiliated entities and 320,681 adherents, or about 70 percent of all those organized and 60 percent of all unions. The syndicalist confederation represented fewer than 25,000 workers in 31 unions; 83 independent organizations numbered 82,638 persons. Labor also achieved qualitative advances. Industry-wide organizations slowly replaced craft unions, and workers formed national unions and federations. In addition, local and provincial groupings extended their contacts to become an integral part of national networks among construction, textile, and power workers.[13]

Despite many heroic struggles, workers won few gains in these years. Table 14 indicates that strike activity declined during the early 1930s from an already reduced level of the late 1920s. After 1935, however, strikes and the number of strikers rose as labor revived from the Depression and government repression. The data also suggest that after 1935 only the largest unions or federations initiated strikes against a government committed to labor peace maintained by force. The information in Table 15 indicates that those striking received lower-than-average wages. Thus, the suggestion arises that the locus of labor activity lay among those newly unionized, such as construction workers, who not only represented a substantial group but also remained badly paid because of their lack of organization before 1935. A comparison between levels of industrial employment and the number of strikers in Table 14 reveals another dimension of the situation.

TABLE 14.   STRIKES, STRIKERS, AND INDUSTRIAL EMPLOYMENT,
1926–1941
(By Index Numbers)

Year	Strikes	Strikers	Year	Industrial Employment
1926–1930	100	100	1929	100
1930–1935	62.5	86.4	1935	119.6
1936–1939	71.3	146.6	1941	140.6

SOURCE: Miguel Murmis and Juan Carlos Portantiero, *Estudios sobre los orígenes del peronismo*/1 (Buenos Aires, 1971), p. 87.

TABLE 15.   REAL WAGES, ALL WORKERS COMPARED TO STRIKERS,
1929–1939
(By Index Numbers)

	Real Wages			Real Wages	
	All Workers	Strikers		All Workers	Strikers
1929	100	100	1935	101	71.4
1931	98	100.3	1937	96	77.9
1933	96	89.9	1939	97	67.8

SOURCE: Murmis and Portantiero, *Orígenes del peronismo*, p. 87.

Before 1935, relatively fewer workers in the labor force dared take action; but after that date, the relative numbers surpassed those of the pre-1930 period. Table 15 throws yet more light on labor activity during the 1930s. Wages lagged behind inflation, which partly accounts for the fact that wage demands motivated 85 to 90 percent of all strikes. And as Table 16 shows, most strikes failed. Simultaneously, the number of workers covered by collective bargaining agreements declined after 1936, indicating that substantial numbers among the working class either remained un-

TABLE 16.   PERCENTAGE OF STRIKES WON AND LOST OR UNRESOLVED,
1934–1939

| | Strikes | | | Strikes | |
	Won	Lost or Unresolved		Won	Lost or Unresolved
1934	2.4	97.6	1937	8.2	91.8
1935	55.8	44.2	1938	11.3	88.7
1936	14.7	85.3	1939	18.4	81.6

SOURCE: Murmis and Portantiero, *Orígenes del peronismo*, p. 89.

organized or could not muster sufficient strength to win their demands from employers.[14]

Nor did the meager social legislation passed during this period alter most workers' lives. For example, laws sanctioned the already accepted five-and-a-half-day week and gave people slightly more protection from indiscriminate firings, but enforcement remained sporadic and court decisions consistently went against labor. Other evidence suggests that most of the working class experienced little improvement in the quality of its life. The workday, which averaged about nine hours in 1900, lengthened in the 1930s as employers took advantage of unemployment and the fact that most workers remained unorganized and lacked access to legal protection. In greater Buenos Aires at least, rapid urbanization served only to further depress living conditions. One survey calculated that 60 percent of all working-class families lived in one room and that another 30 percent dwelt in two rooms.[15]

By the early 1940s, increased production fostered a growing group of national capitalists. Official policies aided their emergence through fiscal measures as well as by enforcing low wage levels, hindering working-class organizations, and preventing serious disruptions of the work process. By 1943, however, the period of national capital accumulation financed largely by the working class began to reach its limits, and signs of labor discontent were gathering on the horizon in the form of unmet demands dating from 1930.

The Military Coup and Perón's Rise to Power, 1943–1946

A military junta came to power through a bloodless coup in 1943. It imposed a state of siege, outlawed all political parties, and postponed elections scheduled for 1944. Although influenced by pro-Axis sentiment, the military operated primarily nationalistically, projecting a leadership role for Argentina within Latin America and in world affairs. This meant countering U.S. and British influence inside Argentina and that of Brazil in South America. The junta sought to prevent a return to oligarchical (and pro-British) rule by canceling the elections. It planned continued national industrial growth with an emphasis on heavy industry designed to loosen the nation's ties to advanced industrial powers.

On the labor front, the junta dissolved the CGT No. 2 as "Communist inspired" and then intervened in the Unión Ferroviaria and La Fraternidad, the two most powerful members of the CGT No. 1, forcing both to withdraw from the organization. These events led most labor leaders, who at first had adopted a neutral attitude toward the coup, to oppose the junta. But their stance soon began to change as the junta's labor policies moved in a more favorable direction.

Gradually, Colonel Juan D. Perón emerged as the leading figure within the new government. In October 1943, he became head of the National Labor Department (shortly thereafter upgraded to a ministry), which now had jurisdiction over the whole country. Perón had met with labor leaders even before his appointment, and he continued to do so, forging permanent links with many of them. Once he took over the Labor Department, Perón's influence spread among both leadership and rank and file. In late 1943, he supported a meat packers' strike and helped the union win its first collective bargaining contract. In December, he suspended the unpopular Law of Professional Associations, which gave the government extensive power of intervention in union affairs. At the same time, he cultivated allies among the military and by 1944 occupied two additional government positions, minister of war and vice-president.[16]

During the next two years, Perón actively courted and won labor support. He promulgated social and labor legislation and supported labor demands and friendly working-class organizations. Decrees extended and improved the social security system, which by 1946 covered nearly 1.5 million persons. Other measures raised retirement benefits, protected workers against arbitrary dismissal, broadened accident insurance, and lengthened paid vacations. The government also froze urban rents and extended the system of labor courts. Further, it instituted a year-end extra month's salary for all workers. The Statute of the Peón, Argentina's first comprehensive rural legislation, guaranteed fixed minimum wages for all permanent farm workers and granted them paid holidays, free medical services, and job protection. Within two years, the government led by Perón implemented much of the legislation that labor had demanded during the preceding decade and toughened the enforcement of both existing and new laws.[17]

Perón also moved decisively into labor politics. He encouraged the formation of unions among previously unorganized groups such as Tucumán sugar workers or those in the Mendoza wine industry. He personally intervened in labor disputes, helping workers gain recognition for their unions and collective contracts. At the time, however, the government attempted no real income distribution (see Table 17, p. 169); it confined itself to the legal and organizational spheres. Perón's maneuvers placed many labor leaders in a quandary. If they refused his help, they risked the loss of gains for their organizations and a workers' revolt. By accepting aid from the Labor Ministry, they became beholden to Perón or saw their leadership position weakened because many workers credited Perón for any gains. Perón's stand against Communists and Socialists sharpened their dilemma. He branded both as "foreign imports"; by extension, all who disagreed with his policies ran the risk of being called "unpatriotic." Therefore, many labor leaders co-operated with the government, and Perón's personal following among workers grew rapidly.

As Perón expanded his white- and blue-collar base, opposition arose among business, Socialist and Communist labor, and finally the military. Agrarian and business interests linked to the foreign-oriented export-import sector objected to the government's policies because they saw these as strengthening labor and costing them profits. In the middle of 1945, a manifesto signed by leading business organizations condemned the new social legislation. Encouraged by the Labor Ministry, unions quickly responded by issuing a counterdeclaration and calling a massive demonstration. At the rally, CGT banners proclaimed, "In defense of the benefits received from the Minister of Labor," which clearly showed that the CGT leaders acknowledged the source of their recent gains. When business openly defied the government by not paying the year-end bonus in December, Perón forced them to comply with the law.[18]

Significant opposition existed within the ranks of labor. In September 1945, the Socialist-leaning La Fraternidad, shoemakers, and textile unions withdrew from the CGT, which had become increasingly identified with support for Perón. Socialists and Communists urged workers to join antigovernment demonstrations to protest military rule and more specifically the failure to call elections and to take a pro-Allied stand in the war. In response, Perón tightened his control over labor. By using pressure and cashing in on favors owed to him by labor leaders, he placed a loyal sympathizer as secretary-general of the CGT. At the same time, he issued a new Law of Professional Associations. It stipulated that only one union could exist in each branch of industry and that it would represent all workers in that industry. It gave the ministry power to legalize unions, and only those so recognized could bargain collectively. In contrast with most Latin American labor legislation, it did not allow the government to intervene directly in unions, but the CGT could discipline them. It also specified circumstances in which labor could act as a political pressure group. The law thus greatly increased government control over labor and paved the way for Perón's political use of the movement.[19]

By far the most serious threat to Perón arose from within the military. Many officers felt uneasy about his growing personal power and obvious political ambitions. In October 1945, this faction forced Perón to resign all posts and withdraw from public life. A week-long crisis ensued, and an emergency labor committee quickly formed. Some argued for an immediate and indefinite general strike until Perón returned; others believed that his dismissal meant no fundamental change in policy and that confrontation would only jeopardize labor's gains. After a close vote, the emergency committee issued a strike call for October 17, although workers in many parts of the country had already initiated work stoppages in support of Perón. On that day, thousands of workers converged on downtown Buenos Aires chanting Peronist slogans. Perón's enemies capitulated, and he appeared before the wildly cheering mass of workers as proof of his return. This victory consolidated Perón's position. In turn, the successful mobilization gave workers a new sense of their own power.[20]

Shortly afterward, the government called elections for early 1946. Two blocs emerged as the leading contenders: Perón and his allies on one side and the traditional political forces on the other. Perón's backers coalesced around the Partido Laborista, which was headed by many of those who had mobilized workers in October. Modeled on the recently victorious British Labour Party, its appearance marked the triumph of those who thought labor should form a separate political power group. The party quickly proclaimed Perón its candidate and formulated a reformist, mildly nationalistic platform. Dissident factions drawn from the traditional parties also supported Perón, as did some nationalist groups. An opposition coalition that included Radicals, Conservatives, Socialists, and Communists soon formed.[21]

Few thought that Perón could compete against the combined forces of the traditional parties, but events proved otherwise. The fraudulent electoral practices of the 1930s had discredited the Oligarchy and the Radicals. Perón appeared to offer a new alternative to old politics. Many voted not so much for Perón as against established parties. Perón's image as a nationalist also appealed to Argentines, in contrast with the pro-British Oligarchy. This image gained more credence when the U.S. State Department, which feared any form of nationalism, attempted to influence the election by releasing a Blue Book connecting Perón with Fascist sympathizers. Issued under the aegis of Spruille Braden, then undersecretary of state for Latin America and former ambassador to

Argentina, the publication became a major campaign issue. Perón's supporters used the slogan "Braden or Perón" to indicate that voters must choose between imperialism and Argentina. A vast majority of workers supported Perón. Labor leaders worked hard to secure voters for the Labor Party candidate. Many who belonged to Socialist- and even Communist-oriented unions opted for Perón because they believed that he favored continued gains for workers. The refusal of business to pay the year-end bonus in 1945 and Perón's successful intervention dramatically underscored this point. Dissident Radicals also brought substantial numbers of voters into the Peronist camp. And Perón skillfully manipulated state resources to his advantage, using his official position to gain maximum media exposure.[22]

The final returns showed 1,527,230 votes for Perón and 1,207,155 for the opposition. Peronist candidates won control of the Senate and the Chamber of Deputies, every provincial governorship, and substantial blocs in most provincial assemblies. Even the Oligarchy, at least until the final results were known, admitted that the elections had taken place without coercion.

Peronist Populism in Power: The Early Years, 1946–1950

After 1943, Perón carefully built a coalition out of diverse interest groups and class fractions. At first, he managed to satisfy all elements in the coalition through his domestic and foreign policies. He personally mediated between the various blocs. At the same time, he used government agencies and an increasingly captive legislature to control or crush the opposition.

The coalition housed a broad spectrum. Many in the armed forces agreed that Argentina should emphasize national industrial development and that the country must become an independent power in continental and world politics. Small and medium industrial and commercial sectors favored domestic industrial expansion because they benefited directly from it. A growing bureaucracy also supported Perón and his idea of increased state participation. Significant elements within the Catholic church backed the regime, particularly after the government granted the church substantial influence in state education. Nationalists from varied political and class backgrounds approved of Perón's policies, as did some traditional politicians who saw Peronism as a vehicle for personal advancement. But workers constituted the largest numerical bloc within the coalition. They, too, approved plans for industrialization because, at least during Perón's early years, they reaped gains from it. Perón's personality, a shared interest in domestic economic development, and material pay-offs held the coalition together. An expanding economic base allowed Perón to satisfy short-run demands and prevent internal tensions or outright divisions. When economic troubles hit Argentina, however, the coalition broke apart, and its dissolution eventually resulted in Perón's ouster.[23]

In outline, Peronist economic policy aimed at stimulating national commerce and industry (mostly light industry) through a transfer of resources from the agricultural to the industrial sector. International demand for pastoral and agricultural products remained high, and the state controlled the export-marketing process. The government thus retained a major portion of the surplus earned by exports and funneled it into the industrial sector or spent it in other areas. At the same time, Perón used the huge wartime balances of previously blocked currencies to subsidize exports and to nationalize foreign-owned companies in the service sector (railroads, light and power companies, telephones, and so forth). State industrial credit banks created in 1944 and the central bank nationalized in 1946 distributed credit, import licenses, and foreign exchange to industrialists and the commercial sector.

Industry grew in response to these favorable policies and as a result of a conscious effort to enlarge the home market through income redistribution. The number of establishments increased from 59,675 in 1943 to 81,599 in 1950, and the total of industrial workers swelled from 820,470 to 1,115,597 in the same period. Real wages for skilled and unskilled workers climbed steadily after 1946, as did the workers' share of national income (Table 17). In addition, fringe benefits increased because of expanded social services. Within the working class, real incomes of unskilled workers and those in newer, more dynamic industries grew fastest. These workers, in turn, tended to be among those only recently

TABLE 17. WAGES AND SALARIES IN INDUSTRY, 1943–1950

		Real Wages	
		Skilled Workers	Unskilled Workers
	Percent of	(Index Numbers)	(Index Numbers)
Year	National Income		
1943	44.1	100.0	100.0
1944	44.8	105.1	107.1
1945	45.9	86.5	98.5
1946	45.2	90.8	105.2
1947	46.6	103.9	108.8
1948	50.2	123.6	137.0
1949	56.1	118.4	134.3
1950	56.7	113.2	126.8

SOURCE: Bertram Silverman, "Labor Ideology and Economic Development in the Peronist Epoch," *Studies in Comparative International Development* 4, no. 11 (1968–1969): 243, 245.

employed in the industrial sector and unionized during Perón's rise to power. Not coincidentally, they also numbered among the regime's strongest supporters, acting as a counterbalance to the older unions, which either drifted into opposition after 1946 or maintained serious reservations about the hierarchical structures that curbed independent action. Personal consumption increased among all segments of the population, rising 7.5 percent annually. Moreover, after 1945, the economy generated almost full employment, with the public sector incorporating many of those who did not find jobs elsewhere.[24]

Although workers increased their share of national income, the industrial and agrarian sectors garnered larger absolute total returns. Labor's share rose relative to that of the rest of society, but economic expansion allowed all other sectors to earn more income. Industrialists gained more than agriculturalists, but the agriculturalists' share trailed only relative to those of others. Agrarian opposition to Perón stemmed from the fact that government controls limited profits during a period of prosperity, not because landowners lost money on their investment.

Social legislation and labor organizing complemented the state's distributive policies. The social security system continued to grow, and the government started numerous low-cost housing projects and built public works in working-class districts. It also incorporated new groups into the legal system. In 1947, part-time agricultural workers, later joined by tenant farmers and sharecroppers, received the legal protection given to other workers. The ranks of organized labor swelled. In 1946, about 500,000 persons belonged to a union; by 1951, the figure stood at over 2.5 million.

In 1946, labor appeared in a good position to influence national politics. However, that did not occur. Perón allowed working-class leaders and organizations little or no autonomy. By 1950, the alliance between labor and Perón had become a one-way proposition, with Perón in full command. Soon after his inauguration, he curbed the power of Labor Party members who wanted an independent movement. He dissolved the party and then created the Peronist Party, leaving no doubt about the new organization's function and orientation. Although the Labor Party continued to exist on paper until 1948, it no longer spoke for significant numbers of workers. Some party members continued to struggle within the Peronist Party, but they found themselves shunted aside by opportunist politicians who increasingly monopolized party posts.

After 1946, Perón pursued a dual labor policy. On one hand, he sought to eradicate or neutralize all opposition; on the other, he actively built his own loyal following. The government, for example, financed Peronist slates in union elections, hastily formed and awarded recognition to Peronist unions in order to deprive unfriendly organizations of their legal status, and suspended the charters of unions that did not obey official dictates. Labor leaders who followed orders received positions within the Labor Ministry, union posts, or some other reward.

These tactics proved largely effective. By 1950, anti-Peronist forces remained in control of only a few organizations, mostly in the transport sector. In 1951, Perón delivered a crippling blow to one bastion of opposition. When rail workers struck in defiance of official policies, he drafted the strikers into the army, forcing them back to work under the threat of summary military justice.

Throughout these years, those opposing the regime frequently operated clandestinely inside their unions and not infrequently ended up in jail or, worse, victims of violence. Some chose to go underground or exiled themselves in Uruguay. Even unions supporting the government risked its wrath if they acted independently. Tucumán sugar workers, one of the most independent Peronist groups, struck without official sanction in 1949. The government quickly repressed their action and then imposed a new leadership on their federation. At the same time, it granted the demands made by the strikers. Such attitudes clearly indicated that Perón alone disposed and that he tolerated no autonomous labor activity.

The CGT gradually emerged as the central vehicle for official labor policy. At first, older unions that tended to sympathize less with Perón formed a majority within the confederation. Newer organizations, most of them solidly committed to the government, eventually gained control over the CGT through their ability to outvote the more established unions. Once in command, they unhesitatingly implemented orders from the top. If a union showed signs of not conforming to government wishes, the CGT corrected the situation. Usually, it charged the union with internal irregularities and placed loyal leaders in the union's top posts. In the case of the meat packers, the CGT intervened even though the union did not legally belong to the confederation. In 1950, the CGT capped its drift into the Peronist camp by openly declaring adherence to Peronist doctrine and to the movement's leader.[25]

A steady stream of propaganda glorified Perón as the benefactor of the working class. Workers also occupied a central place in *justicialismo*, Peronism's official ideology. It emphasized the dignity of work and the role of workers in forging a strong nation. Typical rhetoric included such pronouncements as "There is only one class of men for the Peronist cause: the Workers" and "The two main branches of Peronism are Social Justice and Social Welfare." The Declaration of Rights of Workers, which was written into the 1951 Constitution, summarized official policy in ten planks: the right to work, the right to a just wage, the right to job training, the right to adequate working conditions, the right to preserve physical and moral health, the right to well-being, the right to social security, the right to family protection, the right to economic improvement, and the right to defend professional interests, specifically including the formation of trade unions.[26]

Peronist doctrine developed a vision of society and the historical process. It condemned both capitalism and "dogmatic socialism" as inadequate. Capitalism bred inequalities of wealth and privilege; socialism denied basic human freedoms. *Justicialismo*, of course, did neither. In the Peronist scheme, the state existed for the purpose of balancing capital and labor, siding temporarily with whichever was weakest. It held that all classes could exist peacefully together, admitting that class antagonisms existed but denying the necessity for class struggle. The state as a neutral force could oversee peaceful social change. By extension, Peronism condoned private property and proposed no alternatives to the traditional mechanisms of the free market, private enterprise, or collective bargaining, differing from classical capitalism in these areas only in postulating a substantial state role and enlarged state sector.

The Collapse of Peronist Populism, 1950–1955

By 1950, the economy no longer generated sufficient surplus to distribute among the various elements within the coalition. Perón reacted by adjusting his policies so as to alienate as few supporters as possible, but he succeeded only in weakening his following among all sectors. When the government moved to strengthen control over potential opposition, its support further eroded. The coalition gradually disintegrated, and a conservative coup ousted Perón with surprising ease in September 1955. Not even labor tried to save him.

A faltering economy lay at the heart of the crisis. Prosperity rested on the export of agricultural products to finance imports of needed raw materials and capital goods. By 1950, Argentina's international trade position had seriously deteriorated. As long as prosperity lasted, the government could both raise wages and satisfy demands for increased profits, muting class antagonisms. But the country faced obstacles not entirely of its own making. U.S. dominance of the world economy worked to Argentina's disadvantage. Subsidized U.S. agricultural exports competed with Argentine products in European markets and, in conjunction with joint purchasing agreements among the Allies, kept world prices low. More importantly, the United States excluded Argentine imports and embargoed shipments of many vital capital goods to that country. The policy flowed from U.S. hostility toward Argentine noncompliance with U.S. hemispheric goals during the war and from opposition to Perón's economic nationalism. This excerpt from a telegram sent by the State Department to the chargé d'affaires in Buenos Aires summarizes U.S. policy: "Export of capital goods should be kept at present minimum—it is essential not to permit the expansion of Argentine heavy industry. . . ."[27] As a result, Argentina could not secure the imports to rebuild and expand its industrial plants.

After the world recovery from wartime conditions, continued U.S. subsidies of agricultural products kept international commodity prices low, but those of industrial raw materials and capital goods tended to rise. Thus Argentina had to earn larger amounts of foreign exchange precisely at a time when it received less for its exports. Furthermore, the volume of products available for export declined. Natural disasters, including a severe drought in 1950, had cut sharply into agricultural production. In addition, landowners deliberately curtailed output and investment or withheld grains and livestock from the government-controlled market.

Perón's domestic policies hastened the economic crisis. He spent balances accrued during the war largely in unproductive ways, among them nationalizations of utilities and railroads. He also used the surplus derived from exports for propaganda at home and abroad and for political pay-offs to union bureaucrats and other groups. Huge sums went into conspicuous consumption, most of it for Perón's personal glorification. He thus drained funds that could have been utilized for domestic investment. According to one source, 74 percent of the total increase in fixed capital during Perón's rule went into nonproductive activities.[28]

By 1950, the government budget began to show deficits, and Perón had to devise new ways to hold the coalition together. He shifted priorities from the industrial to the agricultural sector in order to stimulate domestic production and therefore the volume of exports. He strengthened controls over potential sources of opposition, including labor, the university system, and the Peronist Party, moving toward a corporative structure in order to further the centralization of power. He apportioned necessary reductions in government services and spending among all groups. Finally, he sought outside aid in the form of foreign loans and then foreign investment to revive the flagging economy. This policy switch, a product of the contradiction arising from nationalist development efforts within the world capitalist system, opened the door for foreign corporations. By the 1960s, transnationals monopolized key economic sectors, forcing out or subordinating national capitals.

These responses, although logical in economic and social terms, proved Perón's undoing. The agrarian sector remained unalterably against him. Industrialists and labor resented the cutbacks. The flirtation with foreign capital, notably a $60 million loan from the United States and a contract with Standard Oil of New Jersey to develop Argentine natural resources, alienated nationalists. These moves also whetted the appetite of foreign capital, which continued to oppose him while actively encouraging those sectors of Argentine society that it thought would favor their interests. Increasing social controls marked by the curtailment of civil liberties and more direct government interference in all phases of life also eroded Perón's base. Slowly, the coalition fell apart. After several abortive plots, a military uprising ousted Perón. Argentina's new rulers represented the conservative, proimperialist landowners and industrialists now convinced that only massive foreign investment could renew industrial growth. Their economic plan called for a reduction in labor's share of national income and conditions for easy capital accumulation by foreign and local capitalists. The new government thus solidly opposed Perón's policies and quickly initiated measures against workers.

Labor did not mobilize massively during the coup. An examination of relationships between government and labor after 1950 explains why. As Table 18 shows, both skilled and unskilled industrial workers suffered declines in real wages after 1949 as Perón shifted resources away from industry and into agriculture. Rural

TABLE 18.   REAL WAGES IN INDUSTRY, 1948–1955
(By Index Numbers, 1943 = 100)

	Real Wages	
Year	Skilled Worker	Unskilled Worker
1948	123.6	137.0
1949	118.4	134.3
1950	113.2	126.8
1951	94.4	110.9
1952	87.5	102.1
1953	87.9	102.5
1954	95.2	115.7
1955	86.5	105.8

SOURCE: Silverman, "Labor Ideology and Economic Development in the Peronist Epoch," pp. 245, 247.

workers, whose salaries rose even more than those of urban workers before 1950, also saw their real wages reduced. The decline in real income lowered the collective standard of living, which adversely affected domestic industry and commerce. Between 1946 and 1948, for example, the index of retail sales in greater Buenos Aires rose 26.2 percent. However, the next year it fell 18 percent, and by 1954 it sunk to less than one-third of its 1948 peak. Partly because of the continued expansion of the social security system and the slow fall in social services and fringe benefits, most workers still lived materially better in 1955 than they had a decade earlier. But the sudden drop in disposable income contrasted sharply with gains made after 1945 and caused many workers to question their unconditional support for Perón, especially in view of the increasingly authoritarian measures enacted by the government.[29]

Perón tried to bolster his position by bringing new groups into the coalition. Eva Duarte de Perón, his wife, made the most important contribution in this sphere. A much-maligned figure still not thoroughly understood in terms of her role as a strong woman in a male-dominated society, she particularly championed the cause of working-class women. In 1951, she encouraged legislation that awarded women the right to vote. They exercised that right for the first time in the 1952 elections, which returned her husband to office. Eva Perón also acted as one of the strongest links between the president and the labor movement. She personally met with labor leaders and thousands of workers to explain the motives underlying Peronist policies and to discuss strategy and tactics. Her strong sense of social justice did much to strengthen the impression that Peronism truly favored the working class. Eva's untimely death from cancer in 1952 deprived Perón of a valuable ally and contributed to the gradual erosion of workers' support.[30]

After 1950, signs of labor opposition to the government increased. The Comité Obrero Argentino de Sindicatos Independientes (Argentine Workers' Committee of Independent Unions, or COASI) coordinated many activities against Perón and Peronism. Formed in 1945 by Socialists and independents, the committee functioned openly until Perón closed it in 1949, after which it moved its operations to Montevideo. Backed by the AFL-CIO, which had broken relations with the CGT in 1944, calling it a "fascist" organization, COASI clandestinely organized what it called the "democratic" labor forces. It also generated voluminous propaganda against Perón on the international scene and later supported the anti-Peronist forces in 1955. Communists and assorted other independents also opposed the regime, maintaining considerable strength in many unions. In 1950, for example, port and maritime workers struck for six weeks before retreating in the face of official pressures. Perón also crushed the strikes mounted by railroad workers in 1950–1951, finally intervening in La Fraternidad and placing subservient labor leaders at its head. Such measures, however, failed to silence critics. For example, an open manifesto signed by fifty-six labor leaders in the early 1950s protested the government's centralizing tendencies and called for union autonomy.[31]

Discontent and defiance appeared even within the ranks of Peronist labor organizations. After 1949, workers at times moved against the orders of union leaders and repudiated contracts signed by officially designated representatives. In Buenos Aires, graphic arts workers struck several times despite constant police repression and the opposition of their own leaders. Such incidents symbolized the widening split between union bureaucrats pledged to Perón and the rank and file. Widespread labor protests also greeted the government decree that mandated biannual instead of annual contract negotiations. The longer time span virtually ensured that wage adjustments could not catch up with inflation.

However, the extent of workers' discontent should not be overestimated. Strikes frequently sought limited economic goals or were aimed against a particular employer. They did not always represent a real protest against Perón. The sugar workers in Tucumán, for example, voted overwhelmingly for Peronist candidates only one month after the authorities had forcibly beaten back their strike. Most observers judged that the results of the union elections accurately reflected the sentiment of the rank and file. Fortified by a constant barrage of official propaganda, Perón retained his image as defender of the workers, and he could cite the concrete gains made since 1943 to justify the claim. Moreover, no meaningful alternative existed for most workers. The traditional political parties remained discredited, and the Communist Party, outlawed since the early 1940s, could operate only clandestinely. Opposition to Perón from within Peronist ranks existed, but not as a cohesive force within the labor movement.

The surprisingly easy overthrow of the regime by dissident military officers has been interpreted as a sign that Peronism's mass base no longer existed. Perón did lose support among industrialists, merchants, middle groups, and nationalists, but the evidence concerning workers is less clear. In the middle of 1955, after an abortive coup, labor leaders met with the president and asked for arms to defend the regime. Perón refused the request. Even during his final hours, he did not ask the 3-million-member CGT to mobilize. Perón thus stayed within the populist mold, preferring almost sure defeat rather than trying to gain a victory aided by armed workers, for such an event might have signaled the advent of real power for the working class.

LABOR AND POPULISM IN BRAZIL: THE ERA OF
GETÚLIO VARGAS, 1930–1955, AND RADICAL POPULISM
UNDER JOÃO GOULART, 1961–1964

The First Vargas Period, 1930–1945

Like its Argentine counterpart, Brazilian populism is closely associated with one man. The figure of Getúlio Vargas overshadows Brazilian history from 1930 to 1955, during which time populist patterns emerged that closely resembled those in Argentina. Like Perón, Vargas built a state-controlled labor movement to accommodate domestic industrialization and as potential support against his enemies. He, too, eventually created a political party largely based on labor. Finally, he suffered a fate similar to Perón's: the armed forces, which represented conservative and proimperialist interests, overthrew him.

The economic crisis of 1930 marked the fall of the oligarchic regime headed by agrarian elites centered in São Paulo. Their corrupt rule ignored urban areas and the emergent middle groups that had grown increasingly discontented during the 1920s. Fraudulent elections in 1930 and inept handling of the crisis led the Aliança Liberal (which lost the elections) to seize power in a civilian-military movement, establishing a provisional government headed by Vargas. The Aliança represented a reformist coalition composed of sections of the bourgeoisie opposed to the São Paulo oligarchy, elements from the military, and urban middle groups. As the Aliança's candidate, Vargas had enunciated his position on the social question. He urged a comprehensive labor code in accord with agreements signed at Versailles after World War I but made it clear that reforms would come from above and that labor should not hope for autonomy.

Labor did not support the Aliança. Constant repression in the 1920s and then the Depression severely reduced working-class activity and existing organizations. Only the Communist Party recruited workers, through a labor confederation and their electoral arm, the Workers' and Peasants' Bloc. They did not endorse Vargas because he represented just another bourgeois political movement. Furthermore, Vargas appealed to workers as individuals but not to labor as a whole. A few labor leaders joined the Aliança, but most remained neutral. Similarly, with one or two exceptions, labor played almost no role in the 1930 revolution.[32]

Once in power, Vargas pursued a dual labor policy. He curbed or crushed all potential working-class opposition. His appointed representatives in São Paulo moved swiftly against strikes by using troops, closing unions, prohibiting rallies, and deporting leaders. In early 1931, the government withdrew official recognition from all labor organizations, forcing them to reapply for legal status. The move allowed the government to recognize only those unions it considered safe. Vargas, however, wished to do more than just suppress labor. The São Paulo elite represented his main enemy, and the strongest labor organizations also operated in that city and state. At the very least, Vargas needed labor's neutrality in case of open conflict. Simultaneously with the crackdown in São Paulo, the government raised wages and decreed basic labor legislation. Through these moves, Vargas hoped to assure social peace during the depths of the economic crisis. They also represented the first steps toward building a labor movement that would co-operate fully with the state and therefore capital and thus mediate class conflict.

As Vargas developed plans for industrialization, he applied to the rest of the country tactics similar to those implemented in São Paulo. Between 1930 and 1936, he created Brazil's first Ministry of Labor and retirement and pension institutes covering a majority of urban workers. Other measures regulated work conditions, curtailed nightwork, mandated paid vacations, and created disability insurance. The pension and retirement systems were later expanded to provide emergency health and hospitalization insurance and to issue mortgages and make housing loans. Finally, Vargas formed a minimum-wage commission.

The 1934 Constitution embodied most legislation passed after 1930. It guaranteed the right to join unions, although it did not make membership compulsory. Unions could not support political parties or candidates nor issue political propaganda, but they could draw up labor contracts and maintain a variety of services such as schools, clinics, and co-operatives. The ministry retained extensive control over unions. It could recognize or withhold recognition, it had access to all records, and its officials could attend meetings. Most important, the government agency could intervene in any union and replace elected officers with its own agents. These measures aimed at creating a labor movement that would respond to industry's needs. The legislation lowered social costs, eased investment problems, and brightened the profit picture. At the same time, strong state control could impose wage scales on workers and keep any protest within acceptable limits.[33]

Vargas encouraged unionization, emphasizing the theme of class collaboration and clearly enunciating the government's role as mediator between labor and capital. However, many employers failed to appreciate the long-range benefits of Vargas's policies and opposed all measures designed to help labor organize. Their opposition served to enhance Vargas's image as friend of the worker. By 1935, over 500 unions existed, a majority in Rio or São Paulo, with a scattering over the rest of the country. Originally, only union members received mandated benefits, a provision that encouraged the formation of unions, but after 1934 these benefits applied to all workers. At the same time, the number of unionized workers grew considerably.[34]

The Constituent Assembly elected Vargas president in 1934 for a four-year term. Soon after, political forces began maneuvering with an eye to the elections scheduled for 1938. The Communist Party increased its activities among workers and on the national political scene. It led protests, for example, against Vargas's labor laws, correctly labeling them a device to squash independent worker action. Although Communist unions operated outside the legal system, after 1935 the party attempted to form a single labor bloc. In that year, a labor unity congress met. Communists held a minority position at the gathering, but many participants sympathized with their goals and Communist caucuses operated within most important unions. The congress accomplished no concrete results, but it showed renewed labor activity and represented a step toward autonomous working-class action.[35]

The Communists' major effort, however, went into organizing the Aliança Nacional Libertadora (ANL), a kind of popular front. Its basic program called for the nationalization of foreign enterprises, the cancellation of foreign debts held by capitalist powers, guaranteed individual liberties, limited land reform, and the right to popular democratic government. The ANL never became a vehicle for mass mobilization, although its São Paulo and Recife branches concentrated on recruiting and organizing workers. In isolated instances, affiliates supported strikes; sometimes, they developed a minimum program that usually called for enforcement of existing labor legislation. But Vargas distrusted the ANL's leftist leanings and its potential as an opposition force. He first passed the National Security Law, under which police harassed the organization. When this treatment only served to radicalize some members, he outlawed the ANL in 1935. Communists then turned to conspiracy, leading an abortive uprising that same year. In neither case did workers rally massively to their cause. But Vargas used the uprisings as an excuse to purge Communists and progressives in general from the labor movement.[36]

Two years later, not wishing to give up power, Vargas led a coup in order to avoid elections. This left him supreme and ushered in the Estado Novo ("new state"), which lasted until 1945. During this time, Vargas ruled in a personalistic, authoritarian manner, skillfully playing off interest groups against each other. On the labor front, the Estado Novo Constitution of 1937 (many of its labor articles taken from Mussolini's labor code) and the Consolidation of Labor Law promulgated on May 1, 1943, carefully regulated all working-class organizations and tightened government control over them.

The Constitution and the consolidation law clearly delineated Vargas's ideas on labor's corporative role in Brazilian society. Article 514 of the law listed the duties of unions: "to collaborate with the public authorities in the development of social solidarity; to maintain legal aid services for their members; and to promote conciliation in labor disputes." In line with his philosophy, strikes and lockouts became illegal as "antisocial and harmful to labor and capital, and incompatible with the highest interests of national production." These codifications also created a system of local, regional, and national labor courts to settle disputes. The courts' decisions bound both parties, and government-appointed judges presided over them.[37]

The Ministry of Labor retained vast control over unions through a series of mechanisms, the most effective of which were the power of intervention and the ability to legitimize or cancel union elections. Union funds derived from a union tax (*imposto sindical*) amounting to one day's pay collected annually from workers whether they belonged to a union or not. The ministry received all monies, which it then transferred to special union accounts in the national bank. The ministry controlled the flow of funds because any large withdrawal needed its express approval. Furthermore, the *imposto* could be used only for legal purposes such as social services; thus, after 1937, it could not serve as a strike fund.

Social legislation continued to expand during the Estado Novo. By 1943, laws guaranteed Sunday rest, paid vacations, a minimum salary, severance pay, an eight-hour day, and medical services. A social security system provided accident and old-age compensation, retirement funds, and housing loans. Workers also received low-cost food at work. The government extended benefits to non-unionized workers and created a series of schools to train skilled workers and apprentices.

Between 1930 and 1943, Vargas achieved his major goals in the labor sector. First, he prevented any significant unrest during the economic crisis. Second, he built a whole system of state controls and almost eliminated progressive elements within the movement. The Labor Ministry and its agents could manipulate labor organizations through intervention, nonrecognition, and control over finances. A constantly expanding bureaucracy within the ministry and social security apparatus provided jobs used to co-opt labor leaders. Ministry influence extended least in the older, more established unions in leading industrial centers. However, the government had formed many of the newer unions in smaller urban centers. Members of these unions had either little or no previous organizational experience and so were easily susceptible to official control. By 1945, perhaps 300,000 to 400,000 workers belonged to a union, and the number of unions increased from 589 in 1935 to 872 in 1945. Lastly, Vargas successfully pushed industrialization and eased the process of capital accumulation through wage policies and state services.[38]

Structures developed after 1930 shaped labor's future course. Recent rural immigrants and newly founded unions predominated within the labor movement. These workers possessed no tradition of struggle or even significant collective work experience. Accustomed to agrarian paternalism, they slipped easily into a hierarchical system dominated by state bureaucrats. Often they overwhelmed workers with union experience by sheer numbers. The purging of progressive leaders further prevented radicalization. Without a vanguard element, newly incorporated workers could not immediately acquire a sense of solidarity or class. For them, unions functioned only as dispensaries of social services, not as vehicles for class struggle. Newcomers thought their well-being depended totally upon state agencies. Moreover, these workers thought they had improved their situation and thus remained temporarily satisfied. In one sense, they had actually done so; under existing laws, migrants received social and economic benefits unheard of in the countryside. In turn, union officials quickly learned that approval from the ministry or from the appropriate government agents, rather than rank-and-file support, won benefits; conversely, they learned that opposition to government wishes led to their removal and that violations of the labor code brought only repression. Thus most workers and officials preferred to stay within the limits set by the state.

On a larger scale, political divisions within the working class hampered action. Communists, Catholics, independent leftists, and reformists all competed for movement leadership.[39] The working class remained fragmented along several lines. Legislation after 1930 applied only to urban labor; rural conditions remained much the same as they had been before 1930. That circumstance reflected Vargas's desire not to antagonize the agrarian elites and the fact that superexploitation of rural labor eventually generated, through the export-import process, funds for industrial development. Divisions also split the urban working class. A growing layer of skilled and semiskilled persons received higher wages than other workers. Those getting benefits under the law became increasingly separated from the marginal millions who crowded around mushrooming cities. Furthermore, organized workers developed no viable means of co-ordinating activities. The law expressly prohibited inter-industry confederations, and the Estado Novo banned all political parties.

Under these conditions, real wages for skilled, unskilled, and white-collar workers declined almost steadily after 1930. Before 1943, few signs of workers' discontent appeared despite the fact that Vargas called for even greater sacrifices in wartime. One decree limited job mobility in order to ensure uninterrupted production in vital industries; another lengthened the legal workday to ten hours. In addition, employers systematically violated existing labor legislation. In São Paulo, for example, child labor still prevailed in some industries during the 1940s.[40]

Wartime accelerated Brazil's chronic inflation, and signs of growing unrest began to appear, finally erupting in a wave of strikes. Worse yet for Vargas, opposition groups began to mobilize and call for a return to democratic constitutional rule. In 1943, he responded by raising the minimum wage and promising to loosen controls over unions. He now tolerated some labor activity, hoping to calm workers and give the impression that he backed their demands. In 1944, for example, the government failed to move against strikes by Santos stevedores, Rio bus drivers, bank employees throughout the country, and São Paulo metalworkers. Their victories encouraged others and showed that action could improve their situation.[41]

Elections had been scheduled for 1946, but many thought that Vargas intended not to hold them. In 1945, he initiated a series of moves designed to strengthen his labor support, thereby heightening his enemies' suspicions. He legalized the Communist Party and granted amnesty to political prisoners, including Luis Carlos Prestes, the party's leader. In return, Communists organized workers in support of Vargas; but at the same time, they built their own following. They created the Movimento Unificador dos Trabalhadores (MUT), which called for a national labor confederation and trade-union freedoms. It held a national congress that was attended by 300 labor leaders from thirteen states. During this period, the party urged its followers to stay within the legal framework. It thus ironically called upon the state to sponsor a confederation that in theory would work to destroy the state.[42]

In a more threatening move, Vargas created the Partido Trabalhista Brasileiro (PTB) by ordering the Labor Ministry and other state agencies to mobilize workers. The party grew rapidly and held mass rallies calling for Vargas to remain in office. The "We want Vargas" movement, supported by increasing numbers of workers and backed by the PTB and the Communists, soon prompted a military coup that removed Vargas from office. True to the populist pattern, Vargas never called for workers' support during the crisis.

The Second Vargas Period, 1945–1954

The forced retirement of Vargas brought General Eurico Dutra to the presidency (1946–1950), along with a new constitution. The constitution retained virtually all labor legislation passed since 1930. It legitimized strikes in theory but so restricted their legality that it effectively eliminated them as a means by which workers could better their position. It thus kept the spirit of labor policy after 1930 by maintaining control over labor through government agencies.

Times, however, had changed. The Dutra government faced continued worker unrest. The Communists rapidly gained adherents, and the party represented the best-organized political grouping on the left. Its analysis appealed to workers pinched by inflation and now awakening to the possibility of an independent working-class movement. Its leader, Prestes, enjoyed national prestige, and it benefited from the fact that the Soviet Union had fought with the Allied forces against fascism. In 1945, the party polled 9 percent of the vote and elected representatives to both houses of the National Congress. Through the Brazilian workers' confederation (a body that had not received legal recognition), it gained a following in several important unions, among them stevedores and metalworkers. The Communists still called for mobilization within the legal system and dedicated efforts toward electoral politics, rather than just toward organizing workers, but even these moves threatened Dutra. He outlawed the party in 1947, directly intervening in 143 unions and interfering in numerous others to oust Communists and progressives. The government's desire to attract foreign investment and the emerging Cold War provided a background for his actions.[43]

The PTB, which polled 10 percent of the vote in 1945, competed with the Communists for the workers' allegiance. After Dutra banned the Communist Party, the PTB rapidly gained ground. Its analysis differed from that of the Communists, reflecting Vargas's influence. It followed a reformist, class-collaborationist line, espousing an economic nationalism based on industrialization. However, it avoided discussing the world capitalist system and imperialism and saw no ultimate contradiction between domestic industrialization and foreign investment.

As the 1950 elections approached, Vargas emerged as the strongest candidate. The PTB backed him, as did many Communists, although the Communist Party never endorsed his candidacy. Several factors accounted for Vargas's popular support and his electoral victory. The Dutra government had forcefully repressed the rising tide of illegal strikes after 1946 and had refused to raise the minimum salary despite rampant inflation. Almost any alternative that promised even a mildly friendly attitude toward labor seemed better than the forces behind Dutra. Vargas's ouster in 1945 occurred after he had loosened state controls over labor. Thus it appeared that this policy caused his downfall, which enhanced his prolabor image. Vargas consciously cultivated that image by reminding workers of his labor legislation and recalling the "good old days" of his rule. He promised more concessions if elected and linked his election, workers' welfare, and a quickened pace of industrial development to the nationalistic cause. Many of those recently incorporated into the labor force had experienced a limited social mobility during the Vargas period, and so his campaign promises appeared rooted in reality. Lastly, the 1946 Constitution broadened suffrage, allowing the mass of urban workers to influence significantly the electoral process for the first time.

Vargas's second term in office (1950–1954) exhibited the characteristics of a populist regime. He appealed directly to workers on nationalist grounds. He continued to control labor through the PTB and the state apparatus. He failed, however, to encourage the PTB's expansion and openly discouraged militant labor actions. When pressed by his enemies in 1953–1954, he moved to bolster his labor support, but always within legal structures. At no time did he fail to oppose, let alone foster, the development of an independent working-class movement, nor did he call on workers to defend the regime. Instead, he played a conciliatory role, offering concessions to both his enemies and his backers.

When Vargas resumed power, the workers' pent-up demands threatened to erupt in widespread unrest. Real wages had continued to fall during Dutra's term and by 1949 had shrunk more than 10 percent of their level a decade earlier. Most workers still lived in misery. A 1951 survey, for example, called 61 percent of the houses in São Paulo uninhabitable and 80 percent of them substandard. Vargas immediately headed off protest by declaring a boost in the minimum wage, the first since 1943. Because the vast majority of workers earned only the minimum wage or less, the increase affected almost all workers.[44]

After 1952, Vargas's rhetoric openly stressed the strength of workers as a class. In 1940, he had addressed workers in these terms: "It is necessary that the proletariat participate in all public activities as an indispensable element for social collaboration. . . . It has always been my desire to solve the problems of the relations of labor versus capital, to unite, harmonize, and strengthen all elements of those two powerful forces of social progress." But in 1954, he said: "With your votes you can not only defend your interest, but you can influence the very destiny of the nation. As citizens your views will bear weight at the polls. As a class, you can make your ballots the decisive numerical force. You constitute the majority. Today you are with the government. Tomorrow you will be the government."[45]

State coercion of labor eased somewhat. In turn, rank-and-file militancy increased. In 1953, the Communists began co-operating with the PTB, siding with what they called the "national and progressive bourgeoisie" against imperialism. Strike activity surged. To meet this challenge, Vargas appointed as minister of labor João Goulart, a long-time ally who was then head of the PTB. Goulart inaugurated a softer line toward illegal labor actions; at times, he even encouraged labor and supported militant strikes. Workers gained more concessions, and Goulart built a following among union officials. This burst of activity occurred mostly within prescribed limits, and workers put forth mostly economic demands. One study calculated that in 1951–1952, the majority of all strikes sought only higher pay or payment of back salaries. Significant sectors among the working class, however, mobilized independently. Corrupt leaders could no longer consistently check rank-and-file demands, and in some cases workers succeeded in electing to union posts candidates not approved by the ministry. In 1953, for example, five major São Paulo unions co-ordinated a general strike and won major concessions. Their victory heightened labor militancy and proved to workers that they did not need state approval to act.[46]

Opposition to Vargas soon arose within the local bourgeoisie linked to foreign investment. The United States also looked increasingly askance at Vargas's nationalist plans, such as the creation of a state petroleum monopoly that would shut out U.S. energy companies. His lax attitude toward increased working-class mobilization only intensified U.S. fears. The United States showed its displeasure by denying loans to Brazil and by official urgings that the government create a better investment climate. Vargas's toleration of the Communists played a part in the U.S. stand, as did his raising real wages. Matters came to a head in 1954. That January, with Vargas's approval, Goulart called for a 100 percent increase in the minimum wage to erase the impact of inflation since 1952. Capitalists, the military, and middle groups protested. A number of high-ranking military officers issued a manifesto against the increase, ostensibly aimed at Goulart but indirectly attacking the president. This sealed Goulart's fate, and Vargas dismissed him. Attacked from the right, Vargas sought labor support while appeasing his opponents. On May 1, he announced his intention to authorize the increase. At the same time, he passed a stricter national security provision and extended the military agreement between the United States and Brazil, deepening U.S. influence over that branch of state.[47]

These measures proved inadequate. Critics now openly feared that Vargas intended to establish a "syndicalist Republic," and some compared him with Perón. Labor indeed represented a considerable force. The number of unions had grown from 872 in 1945 to 1,075 in 1950 and then to 1,300 in 1955. Approximately 1 million persons representing about 30 percent of the urban labor force belonged to an organization.[48] Despite his rhetoric, there is no evidence that Vargas intended to give workers any real power. He consistently defended the bourgeois state and allowed labor almost no autonomy. He never extended labor legislation to cover rural workers or seriously entertained the idea of significant income redistribution. When the military demanded his resignation, Vargas did not call on workers to defend his cause, despite indications that he might have mobilized support through a general strike. Instead, he bowed to his enemies within the ruling class and exited dramatically by committing suicide.

The Radical Populist Period, 1961–1964

The Perón and Vargas eras represent classical populist periods, but populism has many faces. The presidency of João Goulart in Brazil (1961–1964) typifies another variant: radical populism. The main differences between the two are that in radical populism the locus of power moves leftward and the government is less capable of controlling the forces within its coalition, including labor.[49] Goulart, for example, was constantly forced leftward *within* the limits of populist politics. As Brazilian society became polarized, he became trapped between opposing forces and was ultimately overthrown. The failure of progressives to prevent the 1964 fascist coup stemmed directly from years of populist control, which hampered the formation of an independent mass or working-class movement. True to populist form, Goulart refused to mobilize workers in defense of his government and sought to contain the crisis by steering a center course.

The death of Vargas ushered in an interim government that responded to the fears raised during Vargas's last years by cracking down on labor. The crackdown helped elect Juscelino Kubitschek and his vice-president, the ubiquitous Goulart, in 1956. Their tenure, which lasted through 1960, brought a series of contradictory maneuverings as the government tried to appease the local bourgeoisie and the imperialists while maintaining popular support. The contradiction sharpened after 1961 and only played itself out in the 1964 coup. Kubitschek tried to avoid class antagonisms and satisfy both national and foreign capital. His economic policy oscillated between inflationary spending and austerity programs. Sometimes, the government encouraged limited labor demands; at other times, it repressed labor activity. Real wages reflected this ambivalence, temporarily surging upward only to fall behind. All during that time, Goulart worked to cultivate his following among labor leaders, often personally intervening in labor disputes and favoring demands he considered within the government's capacity to grant. Unionization continued to grow. By 1960, perhaps 40 percent of all industrial workers belonged to an organization, and the number of unions in 1957 totaled over 1,500.[50]

The brief presidency of Jânio Quadros in 1961 served only to confuse the situation further. Quadros resigned shortly after taking office. That left Goulart, the vice-president, the legal successor. Conservative opposition permitted Goulart's accession only after it passed a constitutional amendment that clipped executive power. Goulart, backed by an increasingly militant left, forced a plebiscite on the issue, which restored full presidential power in early 1963. From that time, the battle lines became clearer: a rapidly growing and ever more radical political movement on the left; Goulart in the center; and gathering forces on the right led by the military, church elements, and sectors of the bourgeoisie close to foreign capital.

The impending crisis reflected deep contradictions that had been brewing within Brazilian society since 1930. After World War II, foreign investment had grown, rising on an annual average from $200 million during the period from 1946 to 1950 to $350 million in the period from 1951 to 1955 and to $750 million during the period from 1956 to 1960. The influx of capital spurred industrialization, but foreigners monopolized entire sectors of the economy, squeezing domestic capital into minority positions within the more dynamic sectors or driving it into less profitable ones. As a result, the local bourgeoisie divided into those taking a nationalist position in favor of limiting foreign input and those dependent upon international capital. The latter forces abandoned their fleeting alliance with the working class forged under Vargas because their interests and those of most of the working class steadily diverged. More immediately, when foreign investment faltered in 1960, a recession followed. The dependent local bourgeoisie called for measures to renew the flow of funds from abroad. Progressive forces, however, demanded basic structural reforms, including nationalization and restrictions on foreign investment. Kubitschek's ambivalent policy had avoided facing the contradiction, but Goulart no longer had that option.[51]

After 1955, new actors emerged who threatened to change Brazilian politics. A series of radical populists (some of them revolutionary socialists) threatened to outflank established populists from the left. Men like Leonel Brizola from Rio Grande do Sul and Miguel Arraes of Pernambuco won resounding electoral victories by campaigning on progressive platforms. In office, they, unlike most populists, made good on many campaign promises. Arraes used his position as governor to support a sugar workers' strike that eventually triumphed. Brizola mobilized provincial forces against the conservatives in the civilian-military crisis of 1961 and then molded a leftist bloc in the National Congress that represented progressive elements at the national level. Their presence served as an example of what politicians could actually do for workers and exposed populist rhetoric as empty platitudes.[52]

Mobilization in the countryside after 1955 also proved significant. Communists had organized rural workers in the 1930s and 1940s but had failed to build permanent organizations because of state and local repression. In 1955, rural activity resumed, at first in the form of peasant leagues, many of them under the influence of Francisco Juliâo, a young politician from the northeast. These organizations spread throughout the region, eventually incorporating as many as 250,000 persons. Their success led other political groups into the arena. Soon Communists, left- and right-wing Catholics, and a number of diverse leftist groups all actively campaigned in the countryside.

Progressive forces had long demanded land reform, and Goulart had included it among his political promises. When alien or potentially competing groups mobilized in rural areas, Goulart moved to strengthen his own position and head off the opposition. In March 1963, he promulgated the Statute of the Rural Worker, which extended most existing labor legislation to agricultural workers. Once legalized, rural organization grew rapidly, but the government now took a hand in it through a special agency. In November, a national rural confederation, Confederação Nacional dos Trabalhadores na Agricultura (CONTAG), formed under government sponsorship but also backed by Communists, left-wing Catholics, and the PTB. Its founding congress attracted twenty-nine federations from nineteen states representing 743 rural organizations. After that, the number of legal rural unions skyrocketed, reaching 270 in 1963 and 1,300 in 1964.[53]

Through these efforts, Goulart hoped to shore up his position by procuring rural support of a government-controlled rural movement, much as Vargas had done with urban labor thirty years before. At the same time, he raised the possibility of extending the vote to illiterates (most rural dwellers fell into this category). If he championed the cause of rural workers, government agencies could ensure that they would cast their ballots for him. By 1964, however, rural mobilization remained more a potential than a real force, despite the fact that over 500,000 persons belonged to some kind of organization.[54] Ideological splits between those contending for workers' allegiance prevented any co-ordination of rural activity. Most rural organizations failed to develop local leadership, and students or activists with urban backgrounds often occupied key posts. Ten years could not overcome centuries of oppression and repression by landlords and the government. Furthermore, probably one-third of all rural entities took mildly reformist positions. That segment, led by reactionary Catholics, taught that rural justice did not include basic changes in property relationships. In 1964, the military, often aided by these same conservatives, easily dismantled most rural groups.[55]

While these events were unfolding in the countryside, urban labor also took the offensive. After 1956, labor slowly recovered traditions of struggle lost during the 1930s. Gradually, new leaders arose, many of them within the PTB, but some representing other tendencies. Constant inflation and the failure of politicians to deliver on promises showed workers that they must defend themselves.[56] A heightened awareness about the sources of Brazil's real problems played an important role in the process. As in other Latin American countries after 1959, students and radicalized petit bourgeois intellectuals, many influenced by the example of the Cuban Revolution, helped raise consciousness by providing and disseminating anti-imperialist analyses that complemented the workers' day-to-day experience. These forces on the left, while continuing to voice economic demands, called for a basic restructuring of Brazilian society. They pinpointed imperialism as the principal enemy, followed by the Brazilian bourgeoisie, which obeyed the dictates of international capitalism. Goulart's systematic refusal to view national problems in these terms alienated his support on the left.

The principal lessons for workers, however, lay not in theory but in practice. Strikes multiplied throughout Brazil during the late 1950s. In São Paulo, 964 strikes occurred during 1959, resulting in the loss of 2.3 million person hours; in 1960, 3.3 million hours were lost. Workers co-ordinated their actions, beginning with a pact in 1956 among several São Paulo unions. Skilled workers led this surge, reflecting rising militancy among those previously contented with a relatively privileged position within the working class. After 1961, labor intensified its drive, and at least 169 major strikes occurred between 1961 and Goulart's fall.[57]

Unity still eluded the movement, but attempts to build greater solidarity persisted. The Third National Labor Congress represented a step in that direction. However, U.S.-backed, procapitalist union officials sabotaged the meeting by first objecting to the seating of leftist delegations and then withdrawing from the congress.[58] In 1962, elements from the PTB and the Communist Party formed the Comando Geral dos Trabalhadores (CGT). Goulart temporarily encouraged this illegal body because he hoped to use it for his own purposes. In July 1962, CGT unions threatened a general strike with Goulart's approval in order to prevent the inauguration of a conservative cabinet. When the conservatives resigned, the CGT refused to cancel the action, even though the president urged it to do so. Two months later, they called another strike, again against Goulart's wishes. By this time, even those labor leaders still dependent upon the government were finding it difficult to defy rank-and-file demands.

Radicalization among workers continued, and Goulart's ability to control labor declined steadily. He now reacted to workers' demands instead of calling the tune. Individual labor leaders accumulated some real power within the system, aided briefly by Almino Afonso, who occupied the Labor Ministry during 1963. Goulart acted predictably against the threat. He dismissed Afonso and then, in the middle of 1963, broke with the CGT. The organization then went over to the opposition, joining the leftist bloc headed by Brizola. Goulart now tried to create his own labor confederation, but it failed. His inability to meet labor demands lost him popular backing, but his failure to check worker unrest also earned the enmity of conservatives. Circumstances dictated that he choose sides, but he did not.[59]

Why did workers fail to react against the April 1964 right-wing military coup? The answer lies in labor's continued weakness. Despite rising militancy since the 1950s, ideological splits rent the workers' ranks. Conservative Catholic groups as well as U.S.-supported reformists fought for the allegiance of white- and blue-collar workers and actively undermined all other organizing efforts. Goulart struggled to placate labor groups in order to keep their demands within the limits of populist politics. He also repressed those organizations he could not manipulate in an attempt to maintain control over the movement. In some instances, the Communists supported Goulart based on their belief in the peaceful conquest of power through class alliances, thus sometimes splitting with the militant forces within labor's ranks that opposed the government. However, these groups also remained divided and unable to co-ordinate their activities.

Furthermore, many labor leaders sought only personal power. They mobilized workers behind immediate issues, even confronting Goulart as a means of winning rank-and-file support, but they did not plan for long-range struggle. Ultimately, the locus of their strength lay within political circles. Their success or failure depended more on the president and the elites, in this case primarily the military, than on the power of their unions. Although strikes spread spontaneously once they began, their inception and results depended on the union bureaucracy's political perception of the situation and on the level of repression unleashed by the military or local and state governments.

Under these conditions, little factory-level organizing or ideological education took place among workers. Although political rather than economic demands formed a part of the programs set forth by labor after 1960, economic demands still constituted the primary motive for labor activity. Strikes most often succeeded when real wages lagged furthest behind inflation. Labor did not come anywhere near its organizing potential. For example, in greater São Paulo, a bastion of militancy, only 13 percent of the workers in metals, electricity, and textiles belonged to unions. Lastly, despite the CGT, little national coordination existed. Urban and rural movements functioned independently. Radicalized sectors throughout Brazilian society operated largely without institutionalized links. No revolutionary party formed to bring together peasants, urban workers, students, radicalized petit bourgeoisie, and those elements within the armed forces (mostly noncommissioned officers) who favored basic reforms.[60]

The end came for Goulart after he had increased the minimum wage in early 1964 in response to a wave of strikes. Almost simultaneously, he announced a new reform program nationalizing privately owned oil refineries, imposing rent control, expropriating some unproductive lands, and stabilizing prices. He then asked the National Congress for a constitutional amendment allowing illiterates to vote. These moves came too late to gather left support and proved too much for the ruling class. Encouraged by the United States, the Brazilian armed forces acted in April to oust Goulart and install a right-wing dictatorship.[61]

POPULISMS COMPARED

Three sets of variables appear crucial to the course of Latin American populisms: first, the international dimension, which includes the world economy and the attitudes of imperialist governments toward populist regimes; second, the historical configurations that determine the shape and nature of domestic ruling classes and labor movements; and third, the immediate historical events surrounding the rise of populists. Despite the importance of national events and historical patterns, however, striking similarities emerge to support the hypothesis that a Latin American populism exists.

Populist governments and leaders operated within traditional capitalist frameworks. Although some of their policies might be considered radical within that context, none seriously altered basic socioeconomic relationships. Perón's income redistribution efforts, like those of Vargas or Goulart on a lesser scale, represented a temporary policy designed to gain support among the working class. The expansion of social services and the extension of state powers also merely echoed measures adopted by other countries in response to the Depression. No populist leader acted to change basic property relationships or to alter class power positions. With the exception of Goulart, they refused, for example, to touch the agrarian sector; and when Goulart threatened to do so, he was quickly overthrown.

Populist politicians tried to maintain tight control over their followings, repressing opposition groups and allowing supporters little or no autonomy. They particularly feared the development of an independent working-class movement. Only during a brief moment under Goulart did workers or their representatives occupy key national posts from which they could build a separate power base. Instead, government agencies, often staffed by union bureaucrats, held power over labor. Co-optation also occurred in the form of expanded social services, fringe benefits, and labor legislation, but always granted by the state, never won by workers through their own organization and struggle. Those who attempted to act without government approval suffered repression.

Finally, populist rhetoric outpaced performance. Glorification of the working class or calls for social justice served to enhance the image of populist leaders and governments, but reality fell short of promises. Nevertheless, many workers actually bettered their living standards, which gave populist politicians a basis for their claims. But economic and social benefits flowed only when sufficient surplus existed both to continue redistribution and to assure domestic and foreign capitalists sufficient return on their investments. When the economic climate clouded over, the working class and the peasantry suffered reductions in both types of benefits.

International factors greatly influenced populism. Its roots lay in the Depression, during which the ruling class in dependent areas momentarily gained an opportunity for self-aggrandizement. Subsequent attempts at internally financed industrialization changed relationships between government and labor. Sooner or later, the ruling class had to tackle the problem of organizing labor because it needed a disciplined and orderly work force and because it had to find the way to incorporate workers into the national economy and the urban population. Populism provided one means to accomplish these ends. Populist politicians sought working-class support. At the same time, they used their control over organized labor to smooth the social dislocations caused by industrialization. Thus populism served as a channel for modern capitalist development. Temporary cross-class alliances were formed that included sectors of the bourgeoisie and unionized members of the working class. These lasted until the 1950s, when changes within the world economy caused local bourgeoisies to ally with international capital. Foreign investment penetrated the modern and dynamic sectors of the economy, using the labor force that classical populism had organized and disciplined. That process doomed populist coalitions. Imperialist governments bought off, bought out, or economically ruined those sectors of the bourgeoisie within those coalitions. At the same time, they demanded an end to nationalist policies and even greater control over the working class.

The imperialist offensive against populist regimes used economic pressures, curtailing vital exports to Argentina and cutting off loans to Brazil, for example. It encouraged domestic antipopulist groups such as the military in Brazil. And it supported pro-capitalist elements within local labor movements such as the anti-Peronist COASI or reformist unions at Brazil's Third Labor Congress (see Chapter 6). In the end, these efforts helped topple populist regimes. New governments quickly abandoned populist policies. Workers' real wages fell, as did social services. In Brazil, real wages declined almost 10 percent within two years of Vargas's death; and by 1974, the minimum wage in Brazil had lost 44 percent of its 1964 purchasing power. In Argentina, wages matched or passed their 1955 level (already reduced from 1950) only once in the following decade.[62]

The successful attack on working-class living standards underscores the point that without government protection, workers could not preserve even limited gains. This fact stemmed from populism's tactic of preventing independent working-class mobilization. Co-opted labor leaders had no interest in educating the rank and file, and they collaborated fully with the government in preventing autonomous movements. Furthermore, at least in the 1930s, most workers did not have the necessary experience in unions or politics to counter pressures from above. Those who tried generally met repression.

Long- and short-range historical factors also influenced populist periods. Vargas built a labor movement because none existed in 1930 that could be used for his purposes. As a result, he maintained greater control over labor than Perón could in Argentina. Vargas did not need labor's political support until 1945, when he was first seriously challenged by his enemies. Goulart, on the other hand, inherited a labor movement already conditioned by populist politics, which may help to account for the fact that his traditional populist policies failed to control labor. In Argentina, the 1930s unfolded differently. There, a potentially strong labor movement existed; consequently, after 1930, the government forcefully repressed labor in order to implement its economic plans. The repression created the conditions for Perón's populist successes. But he had to incorporate workers into a political party, distribute greater benefits, and bring a larger percentage of workers into his coalition and into labor organizations because the level of organization and struggle was far above that found in Brazil.

The classical populist period still influences Argentine labor. The bureaucracy's strength derives from hierarchical structures erected after 1943. The predominantly electoral strategy advocated even by Peronism's more progressive sectors indicates that pre-1955 events still condition working-class politics. On the other hand, the massive labor mobilization between 1943 and 1955 assured the continued existence of a viable labor movement. In Argentina, the struggle is over control of the labor movement, whereas in Brazil it revolves around the establishment of organized labor as a permanent institution. In Brazil, the Vargas period paved the way for Goulart and radical populism. In Argentina, the Perón years sowed the seeds for continued labor action after 1955. Thus the legacy of populism appears contradictory. On one hand, it greatly aided continued state control over labor by unfriendly regimes; on the other, it brought a series of important organizing steps that have enabled workers to continue their struggles.

Historical differences also shaped post-populist periods. The Brazilian military crushed all workers' opposition after 1964. Only after 1967 did the first signs of a revitalized working-class movement appear. In Argentina, the civilian and military regimes that followed Perón proved incapable of destroying existing union structures, and they could not eradicate Peronism from the ranks of labor. A deteriorating economic situation, constant repression, and the contrast with the years before 1955 served to keep Peronism alive among workers. Although the union bureaucracy on several occasions indicated its willingness to ally itself with non-Peronist regimes, it did not succeed in bending the rank and file to its wishes. After 1966, a class-oriented (*clasista*) left developed inside the labor movement. It advanced the thesis that labor should organize and act independently. The ruling class opened the way for Perón's return and third presidency in 1973 partly in response to this leftward drift. Perón and his current wife, Isabelita, who succeeded him in office after his death in July 1974, pursued typically populist policies. They quickly moved to quash the growing left wing inside the Peronist movement. On the labor front, they supported the traditional bureaucracy against all militancy. The deteriorating economic situation and constant right-wing and imperialist pressures, however, doomed the third Peronist experiment to failure. Opposition groups on the left soon countered the government's conservative bent with increased activity. In turn, the government escalated its offensive, unleashing a full-scale terror campaign against the left. Gradually the country drifted into an undeclared civil war. Finally, the right-wing military once again took matters into its own hands and toppled the regime of Isabelita Perón in March 1976. The new military rulers immediately instituted dictatorial rule and initiated an all-out offensive against the left and progressive elements within the labor movement. Since that time, Argentina's internal strife continues unabated.[63]

NOTES

[1] Quote from Theotonio Dos Santos, "Brazil: The Origins of a Crisis," in *Latin America: The Struggle with Dependency and Beyond,* Ronald H. Chilcote and Joel C. Edelstein, eds. (Cambridge, Mass., 1974), p. 432; Kenneth Paul Erickson, "Populism and Political Control of the Working Class in Brazil," in *Ideology and Social Change in Latin America,* Juan E. Corradi, June Nash, and Hobart A. Spalding, Jr., eds. (New York, 1977), pp. 200–236, discusses populism in general and its Latin American variant.

[2] The original manuscript included the Chilean Popular Front period as a case example, but considerations of length dictated its removal. Populist regimes now in power, for example, would include Michael Manley's government in Jamaica and the Burnham government in Guyana.

[3] Celso Furtado, *Economic Development of Latin America* (Cambridge, Eng., 1970), pp. 39–42.

4 A first general statement on this appeared in Kenneth Paul Erickson, Patrick V. Peppe, and Hobart A. Spalding, Jr., "Research on the Urban Working Class and Organized Labor in Argentina, Brazil, and Chile: What Is Left to Be Done?" *Latin American Research Review* 9, no. 2 (Summer 1974): 122–124.

5 Furtado, *Economic Development of Latin America*, p. 86; the continuities of U.S. policy in David Green, *The Containment of Latin America: A History of the Myths and Realities of the Good Neighbor Policy* (Chicago, 1971).

6 On U.S. capitalism and foreign policy, including "safe investment climates," see North American Congress on Latin America (hereafter NACLA), *Yanqui Dollar: The Contribution of U.S. Private Investment to Underdevelopment in Latin America* (New York and Berkeley, Calif., 1971), pp. 1–64, and especially p. 18.

7 On Argentina in general, see Juan E. Corradi, "Argentina," in *Latin America: The Struggle with Dependency and Beyond*, Chilcote and Edelstein, eds., pp. 305–407; and James R. Scobie, *Argentina: A City and a Nation*, 2d ed. (New York, 1971).

8 Corradi, "Argentina," pp. 337–347; Oficina de Estudios para la Colaboración Económica Internacional (hereafter OECEI), *Argentina económica y financiera* (Buenos Aires, 1966), table 123, p. 170; general political developments in Alberto Ciria, *Parties and Power in Modern Argentina* (Albany, N.Y., 1974).

9 OECEI, *Argentina económica y financiera*, p. 170; Samuel L. Baily, *Labor, Nationalism, and Politics in Argentina* (New Brunswick, N.J., 1967), p. 81 and chap. 3 for labor developments in the 1930s.

10 See Raquel Meléndez and Néstor Monteagudo, *Historia del movimiento obrero* (Buenos Aires, 1971), chap. 3; and Alberto J. Plá, "La crisis social: De la restauración oligárquica a la Argentina de masas," in Alberto Ciria et al., *La década infame* (Buenos Aires, 1969), pp. 87–100.

11 Among others, see Jacinto Oddone, *Gremialismo proletario argentino* (Buenos Aires, 1949), pp. 397–415.

12 On the Communists in this period, see Celia Durruty, *Clase obrera y peronismo* (Córdoba, 1969), and especially pp. 57–60 on construction workers.

13 Miguel Murmis and Juan Carlos Portantiero, *Estudios sobre los orígenes del peronismo/1* (Buenos Aires, 1971), p. 77.

14 OECEI, *Argentina económica y financiera*, pp. 171–174; Murmis and Portantiero, *Estudios sobre los orígenes del peronismo*, pp. 88–89.

15 Carlos Fayt, *La naturaleza del peronismo* (Buenos Aires, 1967), p. 88; and data from F. Peña Guzmán, "The Development of Argentinian Social Formation (16th Century–1955): Dependence, Industrialization, and the Labour Movement" (M.A. thesis, Social Sciences, Institute of Social Studies, The Hague, 1974), pp. 68–69.

202 ORGANIZED LABOR IN LATIN AMERICA

[16] A good account of events between 1943 and 1946 is in Félix Luna, *El 45: Crónica de un año decisivo* (Buenos Aires, 1969).

[17] See Baily, *Labor, Nationalism, and Politics in Argentina*, chap. 4.

[18] Luna, *El 45*, p. 268.

[19] Roberto Carri, *Sindicatos y poder en la Argentina* (Buenos Aires, 1967), pp. 28–30 on this law.

[20] On Perón, labor, and the 17th of October, see Luna, *El 45*, chap. 3; Hugo Gambini, *El 17 de Octubre de 1945* (Buenos Aires, 1969); Luis Monzalvo, *Testigo de la primera hora del Peronismo* (Buenos Aires, 1974), memoirs of a railroad union man who participated in these events; and especially Juan Carlos Torre, "La CGT y el 17 de Octubre de 1945," *Todo es Historia*, no. 107 (March 1976).

[21] On the Labor Party, see the views of its Vice-President in Walter Beveraggi Allende, *El Partido Laborista, el fracaso de Perón y el problema argentino* (Buenos Aires, 1956); and its program in Fayt, *La naturaleza del peronismo*, pp. 121–130.

[22] The Blue Book is United States Government Memorandum: *Consultation Among the American Republics with Respect to the Argentine Situation* (Washington, D.C., 1946), and Perón's answer in Tte. Gral. Juan D. Perón, *Azul y Blanco* (Buenos Aires, 1946); on these events, see Baily, *Labor, Nationalism, and Politics in Argentina*, pp. 90–95; and Beveraggi Allende, *El Partido Laborista*, chaps. 5–8; on the Labor Party's weakness, see Walter Little, "Party and State in Peronist Argentina," *Hispanic American Historical Review* 53, no. 4 (November 1973): 646–649.

[23] On this period and its political and economic formations, see Eldon Kenworthy, "The Formation of the Peronist Coalition" (Ph.D. diss., Political Science, Yale University, 1970); and David Rock, "The Survival and Restoration of Peronism," in *Argentina in the Twentieth Century*, David Rock, ed. (Pittsburgh, 1975), pp. 179–221.

[24] Data from OECEI, *Argentina económica y financiera*, p. 170; Víctor Testa, "Crecimiento 1935–1946 y estancamiento 1947–1963 de la producción industrial argentina," *Fichas de investigación económica y social* 1, no. 1 (April 1964): 6; Jorge M. Katz, *Production Functions: Foreign Investment and Growth: A Study Based on the Argentine Manufacturing Sector, 1946–1961* (Amsterdam–London, 1969), p. 107; Corradi, "Argentina," pp. 367–370; Rock, "Survival and Restoration of Peronism," pp. 184–187.

[25] In addition to the general works already cited, see two anti-Peronist period pieces: Robert J. Alexander, *The Perón Era* (New York, 1951); and George Blankston, *Perón's Argentina* (Chicago, 1953); a summary about labor in Santiago Senén González, *Breve historia del sindicalismo argentino* (Buenos Aires, 1974), chaps. 2–8; also on the controversy around who supported Perón in 1946 and after: Gino Germani, "El

surgimiento del peronismo: El rol de los obreros y de los migrantes internos," *Desarrollo Económico* 13, no. 51 (October–December 1973): 435–488; Eldon Kenworthy ,"Interpretaciones ortodoxas y revisionistas del apoyo inicial del peronismo," *Desarrollo Económico* 14, no. 56 (January–March 1975): 750–764, and Tulio Halperín Donghi, "Algunas observaciones sobre Germani, el surgimiento del peronismo y los migrantes internos," ibid., pp. 766–781; Kenworthy and Halperín Donghi argue against the thesis that recent migrants formed the basis for Perón's support and seem to have the best of the matter.

26 Quotes from Argentine Republic, Ministry of Education and Culture, *Peronist Doctrine* (Buenos Aires, n.d.), pp. 55, 56, and the Rights of Workers, pp. 335–339.

27 Quoted in Jorge Fodor, "Perón's Policies for Agricultural Exports, 1946–1948: Dogmatism or Commonsense?" in *Argentina in the Twentieth Century*, Rock, ed., pp. 159–160, and for Perón's economic policies in general; on the U.S., see Green, *Containment of Latin America*; on economic growth and foreign penetration, see Eduardo F. Jorge, *Industria y concentración económica* (Buenos Aires, 1971), chaps. 3–4; and Mónica Peralta Ramos, *Etapas de acumulación y alianzas de clases en la Argentina* (Buenos Aires, 1972).

28 See Fodor, "Perón's Policies for Agricultural Exports"; Corradi, "Argentina," pp. 365–374; Carlos F. Díaz Alejandro, *Essays on the Economic History of the Argentine Republic* (New Haven, 1970), which contains useful data but a conservative interpretation, chaps. 2, 3, 7.

29 OECEI, *Argentina económica y financiera*, p. 91; Dardo Cúneo, *El desencuentro argentino (1930–1955)* (Buenos Aires, 1965), p. 124.

30 A first step toward a more realistic evaluation of Evita is Nancy Caro Hollander, "Si Evita viviera . . . ," *Latin American Perspectives* 1, no. 3 (Fall 1974): 42–57, and on women from the Peronist period to the present, "Women Workers and the Class Struggle: The Case of Argentina," *Latin American Perspectives* 4, nos. 1 and 2 (Winter and Spring 1977): 180–193.

31 On U.S. labor in Argentina, see Serafino Romualdi, *Presidents and Peons* (New York, 1967), pp. 49–63, 140–156; on labor in general, Baily, *Labor, Nationalism, and Politics in Argentina*, chaps. 6–7; Rock, "The Survival and Restoration of Peronism," pp. 192–194; Cúneo, *El desencuentro argentino*, pp. 138–139.

32 This section relies on Timothy F. Harding, "A Political History of Organized Labor in Brazil" (Ph.D. diss., Hispanic American Studies, Stanford University, 1973), probably the best single work on Brazilian labor history. Information not footnoted comes from this source; political events with a conservative interpretation in Thomas E. Skidmore, *Politics in Brazil, 1930–1964* (New York, 1967); Vargas's program in

J. F. W. Dulles, *Vargas of Brazil: A Political Biography* (Austin,, Tex., 1967), p. 55; on labor and 1930, see Paulo Sérgio Pinheiro, *Política e trabalho no Brasil: Dos anos vinte a 1930* (Rio de Janeiro, 1975).

33 Legislation in Hirosê Pimpão, *Getúlio Vargas e o direito social trabalhista* (Rio de Janeiro, 1942); and J. V. Freitas Marcondes, "Social Legislation in Brazil," in *Brazil: Portrait of Half a Continent*, T. Lynn Smith and Alexander Marchant, eds. (New York, 1951), pp. 385–391.

34 Number of unions in 1935 from Kenneth Paul Erickson, "Labor in the Political Process in Brazil: Corporatism in a Modernizing Nation" (Ph.D. diss., Political Science, Columbia University, 1970), Table B-3, p. 48; geographic distribution in Harding, "Political History of Organized Labor in Brazil," p. 90.

35 Robert J. Alexander, *Communism in Latin America* (New Brunswick, N.J., 1957), p. 110.

36 Robert M. Levine, *The Vargas Regime: The Critical Years, 1934–1938* (New York, 1970), pp. 58–80, 100–124.

37 Quote on strikes in Dulles, *Vargas of Brazil*, p .177. Erickson, "Labor in the Political Process in Brazil," is the best discussion of legal controls over labor; see especially pp. 46–61.

38 George Wythe, *Brazil: An Expanding Economy* (New York, 1949), p. 239; Kenneth Paul Erickson, *The Brazilian Corporative State and Working Class Politics* (Berkeley, Calif., 1977), chap. 3.

39 On Catholics, Howard J. Wiarda, *The Brazilian Catholic Labor Movement* (Amherst, Mass., 1969), pp. 14–17.

40 On wages and hours, see *The Development of Brazil: Report of the Joint Brazil–United States Economic Development Commission* (Washington, D.C., 1954), pp. 37–38; on the war period, Warren Dean, *The Industrialization of São Paulo, 1880–1945* (Austin, Tex., 1969), pp. 225–226; wages 1930–1938 in Levine, *Vargas Regime*, p. 25; wages also in Octavio Ianni, *Estado e planejamento económico no Brasil, 1930–1970* (Rio de Janeiro, 1971), p. 41, Table 1; Dulles, *Vargas of Brazil*, pp. 245, 247.

41 Timothy F. Harding, "The Politics of Labor and Dependency in Brazil—An Historical Approach," *International Socialist Review* 33, no. 7 (July–August 1973): 13.

42 On the 1943–1945 period, see Francisco Weffort, "Origems do sindicalismo populista no Brasil (a conjuntura de após-guerra)," *Estudos*, no. 4 (April–June 1973): 67–105; on strikes, Dulles, *Vargas of Brazil*, p. 264.

43 On the Communists, see Ronald H. Chilcote, *The Brazilian Communist Party: Conflict and Consensus, 1922–1970* (New York, 1974), pp. 53–57.

44 Richard M. Morse, *From Community to Metropolis* (Gainesville, Fla., 1958), p. 215; Ianni, *Estado e planejamento no Brasil*, p. 100.

45 Octavio Ianni, *Crisis in Brazil* (New York, 1970), p. 90; and Skidmore, *Politics in Brazil*, p. 134.

46 Leôncio Martins Rodrigues, *Conflito industrial e sindicalismo no Brasil* (São Paulo, 1966), pp. 53–54.

47 Ruy Mauro Marini, *Subdesarrollo y revolución* (Mexico City, 1969), p. 33.

48 Harding, "Politics of Labor and Dependency in Brazil," pp. 39–41.

49 Erickson, "Populism and Political Control of the Working Class in Brazil," introduces the notion of radical populism; my interpretation differs slightly from his. His article presents a careful analysis of labor-government relations in this period.

50 Harding, "Politics of Labor and Dependency in Brazil," p. 41.

51 Miguel Arraes, *Brazil: The People and the Power* (Harmondsworth, Eng., 1972), pp. 66–67; on foreign control, see Dos Santos, "Brazil: The Origins of a Crisis," and his classic study, "Foreign Investment and the Large Enterprise in Latin America: The Brazilian Case," in *Latin America: Reform or Revolution?* James Petras and Maurice Zeitlin, eds. (Greenwich, Conn., 1968), pp. 431–453.

52 See, for example, Arraes, *Brazil: The People and the Power.*

53 A plethora of works examine rural labor. A sampling includes Robert E. Price, "Rural Unionization in Brazil" (Research Paper No. 14, University of Wisconsin Land Tenure Center, 1964); Clodomir Moraes, "Peasant Leagues in Brazil," in *Agrarian Problems and Peasant Movements in Latin America,* Rodolfo Stavenhagen, ed. (Garden City, N.Y., 1970), pp. 453–501; Joseph A. Page, *The Revolution That Never Was* (New York, 1972), on the Northeast; Emanuel de Kadt, *Catholic Radicals in Brazil* (London–New York, 1970), on the radical Catholic Movimento de Educação de Base and progressive Catholic efforts in the countryside; Chilcote, *Brazilian Communist Party,* pp. 16, 152, 160–172, on Communist organizing; several translations of Julião's writings are also available.

54 Chilcote, *Brazilian Communist Party,* p. 163 n.72.

55 Timothy F. Harding, "Labor Challenge to Dictatorship," *Brazilian Information Bulletin,* no. 13 (Spring 1974): 2.

56 See, for example, the survey data in Michael Lowy and Sarah Chucid, "Opinoes e atitudes de líderes sindicais metalúrgicos," *Revista Brasileira de Estudos Políticos,* no. 13 (January 1962): 132–169.

57 Harding, "Politics of Labor and Dependency in Brazil," p. 408, on strike data; Chilcote, *Brazilian Communist Party,* p. 169, on 1961–1964.

58 Timothy F. Harding, "Implications of Brazil's Third Labor Congress," *Hispanic American Report* 13 (October 1960): 567–572; on the U.S. and Brazilian labor as well as the economy, see Kenneth Paul Erickson and Patrick V. Peppe, "Dependent Capitalist Development, U.S. Foreign Policy, and Repression of the Working Class in Chile and Brazil," *Latin American Perspectives* 3, no. 1 (Winter 1976): 19–44.

[59] Specifics on Afonso's tenure in office and the nature of this increased power are in Erickson, "Populism and Political Control of the Working Class in Brazil."

[60] An excellent analysis of labor under Goulart is Kenneth Paul Erickson, "Political Strikes in Brazil, 1960–1964: Strengths and Weaknesses of Organized Labor" (*Occasional Papers* No. 17, New York University, Ibero-American Language and Area Center, 1975), pp. 1–33; on labor in this period and after the coup, see Angela Mendes de Almeida and Michael Lowy, "Union Structure and Labor Organizations in Contemporary Brazil," *Latin American Perspectives* 3, no. 1 (Winter 1976): 98–119.

[61] Authors like Skidmore have asserted that the United States played virtually no role in the coup that overthrew Goulart in 1964, claiming that only the "Jacobin left and the Communists" dared make such claims. The *Washington Post*, December 20, 1976, published documents showing that the "United States was prepared, if needed, to support militarily the Brazilian armed forces' ouster" of Goulart in a plan known as "Operation Brother Sam." Documents further show that U.S. Ambassador Lincoln Gordon, who still denies any U.S. complicity, was assigned to order a U.S. naval task force then assembled off the Brazilian coast to act or not at his discretion. See Skidmore, *Politics in Brazil*, Appendix, "The United States Role in João Goulart's Fall," pp. 322–330.

[62] Erickson, "Populism and Political Control of the Working Class in Brazil," Table 1, pp. 96–97; *Latin American Newsletter*, May 9, 1975, p. 4.

[63] See Almeida and Lowy, "Union Structure and Labor Organizations in Contemporary Brazil"; Juan E. Corradi, "Argentina and Peronism: Fragments of the Puzzle," *Latin American Perspectives* 1, no. 4 (Fall 1974): 3–20; and NACLA, *Argentina in the Hour of the Furnaces* (New York and Berkeley, Calif., 1975). On repression of labor as well as other groups within Argentine society, see Latin American Studies Association, Sub-Committee on Academic Freedom and Human Rights in Argentina of the Committee on Academic Freedom and Human Rights, *Report*, and documentary supplement, "Argentina de hoy: Un régimen de terror, informe sobre la represión desde julio de 1973 hasta diciembre de 1974," available from the LASA Secretariat; and on recent events, Donald C. Hodges, *Argentina, 1943–1976: The National Revolution and Resistance* (Albuquerque, N.M., 1976), chaps. 4, 5, and Epilogue.

5

LABOR AND REVOLUTION:
BOLIVIA AND CUBA

In Bolivia and Cuba, workers broke the co-optive–repressive mold implanted during the first decades of the twentieth century. In each country, sectors within the labor movement backed a revolution when new forces swept reactionary governments from power. But the long-range results differed. In Cuba, a revolution fundamentally changed the socioeconomic system; in Bolivia, despite temporary advances, counterrevolutionary forces captured power and reinstituted the co-optive–repressive syndrome. How did revolutionary situations develop in Cuba and Bolivia, and why did revolution succeed in one country and fail in the other? Four major determinants affected the situation: the collective historical experience of the working class; the immediate characteristics of each upheaval; the strategy adopted by the working-class and revolutionary organizations; and the international dimension, including outside intervention.

The Cuban working class possessed a long history of militant struggle that helped revolutionaries to mobilize workers. In Bolivia, miners in particular had engaged in protracted class warfare, but most other working-class sectors lacked experience. Both revolutions shared an anti-imperialist and anti–ruling-class bias. In Bolivia, the triumph in 1952 of the Movimiento Nacional Revolucionario (MNR) represented the ascendancy of bourgeois-democratic elements. Its main current desired reform of the system but not a true revolution. It hewed to a nationalist, developmentalist policy along capitalist lines that included substantial state participation and an attempt to incorporate new groups into national life. In Cuba, the 26th of July Movement, along with its allies, which triumphed in 1959, sought far-reaching changes. It aimed to free Cuba from foreign domination, not just loosen the strings of control, as did the MNR. Ultimately, it sought to create a socialist society in Cuba by ending capitalist modes of production and relationships. The revolutionary wing of the Revolution won out over those who did not wish the society totally restructured.

In Bolivia, those aspiring to revolutionary change lost out to reformists. In retrospect, it appears that the Bolivian movement missed opportunities that might have produced different results. Workers, spearheaded by miners, for a time formed the most powerful armed group within the country. However, they allowed an increasingly unfriendly government to rebuild the nation's armed forces and strengthen peasant militias committed to the status quo. They also failed to organize other workers and remained relatively isolated. An active political party might have provided a vehicle capable of realizing revolutionary goals, but none was formed. Thus the reformist nature of the MNR and the lack of independent working-class organization prevented a successful revolution.

In Cuba, the 26th of July Movement operated as a political force that brought together those anti-imperialist elements committed to social change. It allied with reformists but did not give them a dominant place within the Revolution. Once in power, it took decisive steps to neutralize the military by arming the people and politicizing the population. At the same time, it rapidly broadened working-class participation.

External factors played an important role in these upheavals. Before their revolutions, both countries lay firmly in the grip of U.S. imperialism. U.S. investment dominated whole sectors of each economy. As single-product export economies—sugar for Cuba, tin for Bolivia—they depended upon U.S.-controlled markets for sales and imported anywhere from 65 to 85 percent of all goods from the United States.[1] As a result, the U.S. State Department quickly became involved in the internal affairs of both nations, but its responses varied. In Bolivia, it maneuvered gradually to undermine the Revolution and assure predominance of pro-U.S. conservative elements concentrated in the armed forces. In Cuba, it aided traditional pro-U.S. groups to head off the 26th of July Movement. When this failed, it moved forcefully by instituting economic sanctions and supporting counterrevolutionary forces, culminating in the ill-fated Bay of Pigs invasion of 1962.

LABOR AND REVOLUTION: BOLIVIA, 1932–1964

Most observers mark 1952, the year MNR took power, as a watershed in Bolivian history. Viewed from labor's perspective, however, this periodization appears inadequate. The revolutionary era divides into three segments: from the outbreak in 1932 of the Chaco War between Bolivia and Paraguay to 1946, during which time labor emerged as a contender for national power and bourgeois politicians attempted to co-opt the movement; from 1946 to 1954, the years of labor's ascendancy and greatest influence; and from 1956 to 1964, the period marked by labor's shift to the opposition, renewed government repression, and Bolivia's return to the U.S. orbit.

Before discussing labor, a word on the Bolivian economy is necessary. Tin forms the nation's economic base, until very recently accounting for about 90 percent of exports and a similar percentage of foreign exchange earnings needed to buy imports. As a result, the international price of tin and the availability of foreign markets has vitally affected the country. The tin industry grew rapidly after 1920. Three men, the so-called Tin Barons, controlled the industry.* They operated their companies essentially as foreign enterprises, at times forging close links with U.S. capital, and they maximized profits regardless of the impact on Bolivia. From the 1920s until nationalization in 1952, these magnates steadily decapitalized their holdings. Profits generated by Bolivian workers and natural resources flowed abroad instead of being reinvested at home. No national bourgeoisie arose to challenge their position, and the middle groups remained a small, powerless force in the cities.[2]

Reliance on tin also shaped Bolivia's working class. The total labor force numbered around 50,000, with tin miners constituting

---

* Carlos Aramayo, Mauricio Hochschild, and Simón Patiño.

the largest group. They controlled the key sector of the economy, and as in other countries, this allowed them to exercise an inordinate influence on national life. As a result, much of Bolivian labor history revolves around the miners. Light industry, transport, and commerce employed workers; but even as of 1950, only 9.3 percent of the economically active population counted as a modern proletariat. The vast majority resided in rural areas, where perhaps two-thirds toiled on large estates in conditions closely resembling serfdom.[3]

A Revolutionary Labor Movement Forms, 1932–1946

The Depression and the Chaco War paved the way for change. The economic cataclysm caused a 60 percent plunge in world tin prices. Between 1929 and 1933, Bolivian exports fell 70 percent, causing severe economic dislocation.[4] The Chaco War undermined the prestige of the army and of almost all national political leaders. Fought for a variety of reasons, including national pride, control of oil reserves supposedly located in the disputed territory, an outlet to the sea, and as a means to combat the Depression at home, the conflict proved increasingly unpopular as it dragged on without resolution. It particularly affected the working class and the peasantry, who did not identify with the idea of national honor in a country that cared little for them. Nor did it matter to them whether the government gained control over land that foreign oil concessionaires would then exploit. These two groups, however, supplied the almost 80,000 corpses that dotted the battlefields, and they suffered most from the rampant inflation caused by the Depression and the war.

At this time, the labor movement provided the only channel for working-class discontent. The movement had revitalized during the relative economic prosperity of the late 1920s. Socialists, anarcho-syndicalists, and Communists all vied for ascendancy. In the early 1930s, anarchosyndicalists and Communists actively organized miners, urban workers pressed for the right to organize, and existing organizations expanded.[5]

The presidency of Daniel Salamanca (1931–1934) and the war

curtailed organized labor's revival. Salamanca, like others who rose to power on the heels of the Depression, pursued policies openly hostile to labor. The war brought continued violence against workers. Many labor organizations opposed the conflict as an imperialist venture between ruling classes and even counseled workers not to fight. They continued to agitate for economic improvements. Salamanca responded by outlawing any union threatening a strike. He jailed some labor leaders and sent others to the front. That offensive forced many militants into exile and drove almost all working-class organizations underground. But opposition to the unpopular conflict enhanced labor's national prestige.[6]

The vacuum in national leadership after the end of the war in 1935 opened new possibilities, and several political parties emerged. They almost unanimously agreed on the need to modernize Bolivia, including gaining a broader political consensus, which meant consulting labor. But they disagreed on the means to achieve their goals. Against this background, the military viewed increased labor and popular unrest during 1935 and 1936 with disquiet. Finally, a typographers' strike, soon supported by anarchosyndicalists and Communists, led to a military coup. The coup ushered in a period of "military socialism" that lasted until 1939. During that period, a series of multiclass coalition governments under the influence of European corporatist ideas sought to incorporate labor into the national political arena under carefully controlled supervision. To do this, they granted some of labor's demands by creating a Ministry of Labor headed by a former union official. In addition, they passed a mandatory unionization law and formed the Permanent National Assembly of Union Organizations to unify the movement and administer and institutionalize new legislation. The social security system was also expanded.

The more militant working-class groups resisted co-optation. At the 1936 First National Workers' Congress, Communists broke away to form a separate confederation. Anarchosyndicalists declared their opposition to the participation of political parties in the labor movement. Both effectively blocked efforts to muster workers' support for an official political party.[7]

In 1937, the government tried a new labor policy. It promulgated a labor code patterned after the Chilean code of the 1920s (see page 77). The Código Busch (named after the president, Colonel Germán Busch) formally inaugurated Bolivia's co-optive–repressive period. The state now assumed a mediating role between labor and capital. It defined labor's legal rights and took over social functions as they applied to workers. The code guaranteed basic rights for the first time, although it covered only urban workers. Its 122 articles included the right to strike and organize, the closed shop, collective and binding contracts, job protection, paid vacations, women's and children's protective measures, expanded pensions, better work conditions, and measures against the grossest forms of exploitation by employers. It outlined formal procedures for settling labor disputes but gave the state power to decide between contestants. The government also could legally recognize unions or not and declare strikes outside the law. In short, the code echoed legislation passed in other Latin American nations, providing a basis for what Bolivia's rulers hoped would be the development of a state-controlled labor movement.[8]

The growth of political parties proved vital to future labor developments. Two organizations, the Partido Izquierdista Revolucionario (PIR) and the Partido Obrero Revolucionario (POR), were formed on the revolutionary left. They hoped to mobilize the working class to seize state power and transform Bolivia into a socialist state. The MNR, on the other hand, occupied a moderate position, wishing only to incorporate workers into a modernized capitalist state. All three parties spread their message among workers and sought to gain influence within the labor movement, carrying on an ideological battle that continued well into the 1960s.

The PIR took a Communist position. It held that Bolivia must pass through stages of capitalist development before a revolutionary situation could emerge. Especially after 1946, it usually allied with what it called "progressive bourgeois" governments or movements, which would advance this process. The PIR worked to build a class-based vanguard party in which organized labor would be one segment. Railroad workers and teachers constituted its principal labor backing, although it had also gained some following among miners before 1946.

The POR, founded in 1934, grew rapidly after 1940. Its analysis differed from the PIR's, although it shared an anti-imperialist and class focus. The POR held that labor should not be subordinated to a political party. It sought to build an autonomous working-class movement whose goal would be a revolutionary workers' government. Every PORist had to join a union, and the party maintained a highly organized and disciplined structure.

The MNR, in contrast, saw the country's problems in developmentalist terms, denying class interpretations. It thought that national capitalism under a government representing all sectors could remedy the economic situation. Direct foreign investment should be curtailed and, if necessary, eliminated in order to allow for the country's free development. True to its elite (and rightist) origins, the MNR at first disdained popular support. When that approach failed to build a strong viable organization, it recruited among all dissatisfied sectors, including workers.[9]

Labor made significant strides and waged important struggles between 1936 and 1945. Several groups of white- and blue-collar workers either formed unions and national organizations or strengthened and revitalized existing ones. In 1939, a dissident faction of POR sponsored a national miners' congress and founded the first industry-wide organization in that sector. Although government repression soon doomed the organization, its formation served as a precedent for future action, and many militants gained valuable organizing experience from it.[10]

The most important working-class action occurred during 1942 at the Patiño mining complex of Catavi, where about 10,000 persons labored in the galleries and above ground. The outbreak of World War II had increased the demand for tin, particularly after the Japanese occupation disrupted supplies from Malaya. In response to U.S. appeals, the government accepted voluntary controls on tin prices and guaranteed delivery at artificially low prices, costing the country millions of dollars in foreign exchange. A steady inflation marked these years. The cost of living rose 16 times between 1931 and 1943, but mine wages advanced only 8.5 times. The economic squeeze, combined with the miners' gradual politicization, soon led to discontent. In 1942, Catavi workers petitioned the company for wage increases and improvements in job and living conditions. Management refused to bargain, claiming that it did not recognize the union. The government, urged on by the United States, backed this position. It cited Bolivia's commitments to produce tin at agreed prices. When the workers defiantly struck, it sent troops, who massacred miners and their families. Official sources claimed that 40 persons lost their lives, but independent observers placed the toll at closer to 400.[11]

The Catavi disaster had national repercussions. Its memory has served as a rallying cry for miners ever since. And the MNR turned the incident into a national scandal when the government tried to suppress knowledge of it. MNR members strongly criticized the government in Congress. Open defense of the miners forged the first important links between the MNR and the miners. The MNR investigating committee that visited the mines shortly thereafter solidified the contacts. The discredit heaped upon the government led indirectly to its overthrow in 1943 by the MNR in alliance with a nationalist, military faction known as RADEPA (Razón de Patria). The new government also proved short-lived. In 1946, conservative military elements once again seized control, instituting yet another repressive, pro-U.S. regime.

The MNR-RADEPA coup of 1943, however, initiated a period during which labor could organize more freely. It also brought new legislation sponsored by the MNR, which wanted to increase its influence among the working class as part of its effort to build a popular, mass party. In 1944, the *fuero sindical* (labor bill of rights) became law. This protected union officials and members from layoffs, transfers, and firings, thus depriving employers of one important tactic used to prevent organization. It also guaranteed and eased conditions under which workers could unionize. The MNR combined its legislative campaign with an organizing drive. In 1944, a miners' convention met and formed a national federation, the Federación Sindical de Trabajadores Mineros de Bolivia (FSTMB). The MNR used its position in the government to exclude militant delegations and held a majority at the gathering. The federation's reformist economic demands for more pay, minimum wages, and social legislation reflected that fact. It failed to mention labor's political role or basic socioeconomic reforms. At that point, the MNR had succeeded in attracting the support of workers and orienting the country's most important labor organization toward its own political position.[12]

After the FSTMB's inauguration, political parties of all persuasions increased their efforts to influence workers. The PIR attacked the MNR–RADEPA government as fascist-oriented. Two years later, however, the PIR firmly allied with the conservatives and became closely identified with their repressive policies toward the working class, especially the miners. As a result, PIR influence within the labor movement dwindled. The POR, however, worked assiduously to cultivate a constituency among miners. It gradually won a substantial following and showed increasing strength at miners' conventions in 1945 and 1946. During the 1946 meeting, the FSTMB, under growing and decisive POR influence, attacked the government. It called for an independent working-class movement free of traditional politics and denounced the MNR as unresponsive to workers' demands because it placed the interests of the party before those of the working class.[13]

The FSTMB Extraordinary Congress, held in Pulacayo in November 1946 in response to the conservative coup, marked a high point in Bolivian working-class history. PORists, although not a majority, set the gathering's tone. The congress approved the militant Thesis of Pulacayo, one of the most revolutionary documents ever endorsed by a Latin American working-class organization. It stated that even in underdeveloped Bolivia the proletariat constituted the revolutionary class, and it named miners as the most advanced and combative sector. It defended the concept of permanent revolution, holding that in backward countries, the democratic-bourgeois revolution against feudal conditions and the socialist revolution against capitalism would follow one upon the other in a continuous process. Therefore, workers must prepare for both, not for one at a time. It stressed the anti-imperialist struggle by linking national conditions to international capitalism and the Bolivian struggle directly to working-class internationalism, specifically noting the importance of solidarity between Bolivian and North American workers.

The Thesis also discussed worker and parliamentary politics. It condemned class collaborationism, arguing for class struggle led by the proletariat in conjunction with peasants, artisans, and some sectors of the petit bourgeoisie. It counseled against workers' participation in nonrevolutionary governments and opposed popular fronts as put forth by the Communist Party and pacts or compromises with other classes. It held parliamentary politics to be secondary during times of workers' ascendancy but necessary to provide a revolutionary forum when the movement stagnated. It therefore called for a Miners' Parliamentary Bloc as an immediate tactic. Finally, it stressed that workers, peasants, and progressive petit bourgeois elements should act together but organize independently.

The Thesis also presented a number of immediate demands that, although subordinate to class struggle, formed an important part of the revolutionary process. It asked for a basic real minimum wage, a forty-four-hour work week (thirty-six hours for women and children), with jobs apportioned among the labor force in times of unemployment, and guaranteed collective contracts. It advised workers to arm themselves to prevent future massacres and to prepare for future struggles.

What accounts for the miners' radicalization? Better organization allowed ideas to reach more workers. The recently formed revolutionary parties provided fresh analyses. The analyses mutually reinforced each other to heighten the workers' awareness of the need for independent organization. Objective living and working conditions accelerated the process, as did government repression to protect foreign interests. More immediately, the economic cycle turned down in 1946, and those affected willingly adopted a militant program, particularly after the conservatives seized power. Lastly, the PIR and to a lesser degree the MNR fell into temporary disrepute with some segments of the working class for their collaboration with bourgeois military governments. The Thesis took a more radical position than that held by most rank-and-file miners, but it still expressed the aspirations of a major portion of the group. Most important, it served as a guide for future action.[14]

Labor and the Revolution, 1946–1956

The ideological crest reached in 1946 inaugurated a period for miners and labor in general to test theory against practice. A six-year struggle culminated in 1952 with the triumph of the Bolivian Revolution. This event, in turn, initiated a half decade of crucial importance for labor and the working class. In 1952, a true working-class revolution seemed possible; by 1956, it no longer did. In 1946, however, the panorama still looked bleak. The military, which overthrew the MNR–RADEPA government, called elections, which a conservative won. The new government returned to traditional policies, attacking previous labor gains and attempting to crush all opposition.

The mines naturally became a focal point in the struggle between the government and the working class. One major clash occurred in 1947 in the Patiño mines. There, after a series of strikes, lock-outs, threats, and futile negotiations, the miners occupied a number of mines in accordance with the Thesis. The government sent an investigatory commission; its report documented the atrocious existing conditions but solved nothing. The authorities finally forced an end to the strike. Under the guise of protecting workers from "a small group of foreign agitators" who supposedly manipulated them through the unions, it froze all union funds and jailed a number of leaders. But turmoil in the camps continued. The government then declared a state of siege. Safely protected now by the army, the company fired 7,000 workers. It next rehired those deemed "safe," excluding all activists. This "white massacre" (so named to distinguish it from "red massacres," which involved workers' deaths) failed to stem the miners' drive. The FSTMB's Fourth Congress publicly endorsed the Thesis. However, it modified that position in secret deliberations, counseling a need for better preparation in strike situations and warning against needless confrontation with superior forces. It thus tacitly admitted that a revolutionary situation did not yet exist.[15]

Working-class agitation continued. A mass movement again shook the Catavi complex in 1949, leading once more to a massacre in which government troops killed over 800 people. As the counterattack against labor intensified, working-class activity moved underground, and growing numbers of antigovernment leaders went into exile. By 1950, the government felt secure enough to freeze wages and outlaw strikes. Constant repression, however, served to underscore the need for unity among opposition groups. The MNR effectively used that sentiment to increase its ranks. By endorsing armed tactics, it projected a revolutionary image that attracted those desiring fundamental changes, including many leftists. Slowly, an alliance formed between revolutionary working-class organizations and the MNR. In 1949, workers aided an unsuccessful MNR uprising. A strike in 1950 against the spiraling cost of living turned into a revolutionary general strike. The government reacted with widespread violence, including the air force bombing of a La Paz workers' district, which resulted in numerous casualties. The escalating conflict made it clear to workers that they must establish a friendly regime or else be slowly crushed.[16]

The conservatives grew more and more isolated. Their indiscriminate use of force, gross mismanagement of public funds, and a deteriorating economic situation alienated significant numbers within the middle groups and even members of the armed services who came to realize that some change was unavoidable. Finally, the government called elections in 1951. It allowed MNR candidates to run, hoping to manipulate the vote in its own favor. Contrary to expectations, the tactic failed; the government had misjudged the depth of public sentiment against it. The military, however, voided the election results by decree, an act which further discredited the regime. Finally, in April 1952, the MNR, now supported by national police and dissatisfied army officers, successfully bid for power. Dynamite-wielding FSTMB members and other groups of armed workers joined the movement, actively fighting at mining centers, at railheads, and in the streets of La Paz. The Bolivian National Revolution had come to power.

The MNR was no longer a political party in the traditional

sense; rather, it had become a multiclass coalition unified around a national directorate. As such, it housed several tendencies. Frustrated middle and upper-middle sectors composed the right wing. They backed the MNR only for the purpose of capturing high-level positions within the government and feared any real redistribution of wealth; they consistently opposed working-class aspirations. Nationalist-reformists occupied the center. They did not espouse revolution but hoped to transform Bolivia through a loosening of foreign controls and a modified capitalism that would preserve private property while increasing state participation in the economy. Labor, headed by the FSTMB and its allies, formed the left. It backed a revolutionary program which proposed that only a socialist system could solve the country's ills. The center held a balance within the coalition and at first managed to keep the MNR united by playing one wing against the other. But inevitably, it had to choose sides. At that time, consistent with reformist politics and its class position, it opposed the left. Thus, after 1954, the MNR gradually split.

To the MNR's left stood the POR. It maintained a considerable following among miners and other working-class groups. Two tendencies vied for supremacy within the POR. A hard-line faction argued strict adherence to the Thesis, which meant noncollaboration with the MNR. A majority "realist" position postulated that the proletariat alone did not yet have sufficient power to accomplish a revolution. Workers, therefore, had to ally with the MNR and push it as far and fast as possible to the left. Realists thought that this strategy would work because the MNR needed labor support to stay in power. In turn, labor could ill afford the enmity of the country's strongest political force.[17]

Within a short period, largely at labor's insistence, the Revolution took seven major steps: It decreed universal suffrage; nationalized most tin mines and created a state mining corporation, Corporación Minera de Bolivia (COMIBOL), to administer them; implemented workers' control (*control obrero*) in COMIBOL mines, giving workers veto power over major decisions; created the Central Obrera Boliviana (COB), a national labor confederation; instituted an agrarian reform program in peasant areas; disbanded the reactionary armed forces; and initiated a "co-government," or coalition rule, allowing workers and peasants to choose some government officials, such as the minister of mines.[18]

At this juncture, organized labor occupied a strong position. It had successfully pushed the Revolution leftward and seemingly laid a basis for further advances. Miners, for example, made up about half of the 50,000-to-70,000-member armed people's militia, the country's only military force. Furthermore, the government remained committed to change and to an at least mildly anti-imperialist position. Most important, the government needed workers' support.[19]

Control over the COB lay at the heart of MNR strategy. At the time, workers provided the only assurance of continued MNR rule. In 1953, for example, the confederation successfully mobilized its forces against an attempted coup. By consulting the COB on all issues, the government gained legitimacy; but to keep its power, the government needed control over that body. In addition, MNR representatives within the confederation could check the left and prevent it from radicalizing the Revolution. Tensions between labor and government, however, existed from the first. Nationalization, for example, raised an immediate dispute. A miners' commission had originally framed nationalization proposals that included workers' control but provided no indemnification to former owners. The MNR, under pressure from the United States, which temporarily withheld recognition, opposed the no-indemnity proposition and pressured the miners into dropping the demand in return for other gains, such as worker control. At first, COMIBOL functioned reasonably smoothly. The FSTMB elected two of its seven directors. At the local level, workers' delegates exercised veto power over decisions in each mine and served in advisory capacities on technical questions and matters related to workers. Later, the state petroleum agency (YPFB) instituted a similar plan.[20]

From 1952 on, the MNR actively maneuvered to win labor support. The government granted wage increases, expanded the social security system, and ordered extra pay for workers with families. It also improved job conditions. In the mines, which received special attention, it reinstated workers who had been fired since 1946, opened stores that sold goods below retail prices, instituted special bonuses, and announced an ambitious housing program.

The MNR took more direct steps to win control over labor in order to prevent the left wing from gaining strength and to check the influence of revolutionary forces outside the coalition. This procedure involved the use of co-optation and force through government agencies. In unions not under its control, it formed caucuses to oppose the leftists. In extreme cases, it even banned radicals from union elections, although the rank and file sometimes ignored the government and elected whom they pleased. In many cases, however, the ability to hand out patronage posts, a judicious placing of funds, and the occasional use of forceful intervention assured that the center within the MNR increasingly controlled organized labor. In less than a year after the Revolution, the government moved to capture PORist unions; through the same mechanisms, it succeeded, for example, in ousting that tendency from the Cochabamba workers' federation.

Developments inside the COB illustrate the gradual deterioration of left strength in the face of the government's actions. The confederation incorporated various tendencies and aided the drive to unionize workers. Soon after the Revolution, workers in most urban sectors had either re-formed unions destroyed during the repression or organized for the first time. Most of these new COB members responded to influence of the center within the MNR. The confederation's first congress in 1954 revealed internal divisions between left and center. Miners formed the largest single representation, but the body failed to accept the miners' proposal to endorse the Thesis. Instead, under MNR pressure, it adopted a position calling for a mixed economic system; and in consonance with MNR reformism, it outlined only immediate economic and social goals.[21]

The COB administered the workers' share of co-government. In theory, it exercised a veto over official decisions, and the government consulted it on all important measures. It also nominated candidates to fill ministerial posts such as labor, transport, and mines and petroleum. However, the COB increasingly became an extension of the MNR and less and less an independent working-class organization. MNR labor leaders dominated its administrative posts and functioned as government bureaucrats rather than as legitimate working-class representatives. Similar problems arose in the FSTMB and in the mines. There, too, a co-opted MNR bureaucracy gradually replaced revolutionary militants and workers' control turned into a defensive watchdog function rather than a partnership of equals in which workers joined in managing the industry. The MNR's national leadership encouraged the process, aiding pliable union officials against militant rank-and-file demands and doling out just enough concessions to prevent widespread workers' discontent. At times, it purposefully violated agreements with workers in order to absorb their energies in rectifying the situation and prevent them from organizing for the purpose of formulating new demands.[22]

At the same time, the MNR cultivated the peasants' allegiance to counter organized labor. The 1953 agrarian reform extended land ownership, and the MNR made sure that those receiving land knew who had passed the law. By again using government agencies, it monopolized the process of organizing rural unions, occasionally using force against the efforts of the PIR, POR, and FSTMB to recruit peasants. Once assured of control over the peasant movement, it beefed up peasant militias, which later predictably defended the MNR position against critics on the left.[23]

The Revolution Turns Right: Labor in Opposition After 1956

Working-class elements within the Revolution accomplished much after 1952. However, the gradual erosion of their power by the center led to a shift in the balance of power. In 1956, the inevitable clash between labor and conservatives occurred. Tension continued, and gradually the working class was forced on the defensive. In 1964, the military returned to power, and subsequent governments have, with few exceptions, followed antilabor policies.

Continuing economic problems led to conflict between workers and the government. Inflation skyrocketed and, despite repeated wage increases, real wages declined almost 40 percent between 1952 and 1955. A new economic policy became imperative. Under threat of an end to U.S. aid, which would have provoked an immediate economic collapse, the government accepted the Stabilization Plan drawn up by the International Monetary Fund. It agreed to combat inflation by freezing wages, lifting import controls, abolishing special mine stores, and implementing measures to increase workers' productivity. Labor, especially the miners, opposed the plan. They said that it tied Bolivia closer to imperialist powers by greatly increasing the foreign debt and that loosening import restrictions would flood the market with foreign goods and smother national industry. They also objected to the fact that the plan blamed miners for the rising costs of tin production and advised a cut in personnel along with other measures that would effectively end workers' control.[24]

The COB's second congress met the issue head on. Government supporters endorsed the stabilization; the left and left-center argued against it and specifically censured the MNR and the United States for imposing hardships on the working class. The POR went further, pushing for the formation of an independent worker-peasant movement free of MNR and government influence. In a close vote, the COB approved the left-center position and called a general strike to prevent the plan's implementation. At that point, the MNR's labor strategy began to pay dividends. Following a presidential appeal and all-out pressure by government officials, labor's ranks split into progovernment and antigovernment camps, and the strike failed. The stabilization plan proceeded as scheduled, producing exactly the consequences foreseen by the left.[25]

The initiative now rested with the right and center, which quickly followed up their victory. After 1956, labor suffered a steady stream of defeats. Bureaucrats increasingly occupied government posts once reserved for representatives of the working class. Dependent upon the MNR and not beholden to a labor constituency, these people usually opposed militant labor demands. In 1959, for example, the Labor Ministry ruled in favor of employers in a textile strike, marking the first time since 1952 that the ministry had openly sided with management. Strikers received harsh treatment even when merely protesting falling purchasing power or noncompliance with social legislation. In 1961, the government adopted yet another foreign stabilization plan under which it promised increased worker productivity in return for loans. When labor again demonstrated against these measures, the government denounced the move as a "Communist plot" and detained or exiled many labor leaders.[26]

One by one, labor's hard-won gains disappeared. By 1965, the government had rescinded workers' control in the mines, the *fuero sindical,* and what remained of co-government. That same year, the military government, which had taken power in 1964, abolished all existing unions and the COB. It ruled that they must reorganize along apolitical lines, and it prohibited members of political parties from holding union offices. Miners resisted this decree by electing militants anyway, but many noncomplying unions were forced underground.[27]

Labor did not acquiesce quietly to all these measures. Numerous strikes and several general strikes shook the country, but the workers' power to paralyze the economy had dwindled. The military, rebuilt with massive U.S. assistance, now had sufficient firepower to deal quickly with mine occupations. The injection of loans and aid from the United States gave the government some economic leeway to withstand temporary disruptions in exports. Furthermore, the government did not hesitate to call on peasant militias to repress worker agitation under the guise that "Communists" controlled the labor movement and that if successful they would take away peasant properties. After 1964, mass labor action met violence. Between 1964 and 1969, for example, six major confrontations between the army and miners took place. In 1965, the army occupied the mining camps after extensive bombing by air force planes. Only during the brief regime of Juan José Torres (October 1970–August 1971) did labor get a respite from constant harassment, but it could not regroup sufficiently to defend his populist government from the conservative coup that followed.[28]

Despite this situation, many organized groups maintained a revolutionary outlook. In 1962, the COB supported the Cuban Revolution and endorsed the creation of an independent union movement. Several labor groups declared solidarity with guerrilla columns operating after 1967, and in 1970 the FSTMB approved a revolutionary socialist position. In the face of continued repression, workers in many sectors have maintained their organizations as focal points for future working-class action.[29]

Conclusion

Why did labor's position deteriorate rapidly after 1952? For one thing, the most militant and revolutionary workers operated from positions of both strength and weakness. Miners controlled the key economic sector and carried arms (i.e., dynamite) as a normal part of their work. Yet, they remained geographically isolated from other working-class centers. Thus, opposing forces could surround them and confine their action to the mines and immediate zones. Mining camps also provided convenient targets for air force bombers and fighter planes. Furthermore, labor revolutionaries faced severe obstacles. Continual repression took a steady toll of militants over the years. Many workers found it easier to accept the status quo than to place their jobs and lives in jeopardy. Finally, the center and right within the MNR, supported after 1954 by the United States and other imperialist forces, effectively used a combination of co-optation and repression to deflect workers from a revolutionary path. When necessary, the government granted immediate economic and legal gains to neutralize the left and win working-class support. When these measures led to economic difficulties, it instituted austerity programs "to save the country," calling those who opposed such schemes traitors. Lucrative pay-offs in terms of union and government positions and graft not only created a malleable bureaucratic group within the ranks of labor but also sowed profound distrust of all leaders among workers. As one observer noted, the only persons trusted by miners are those who demonstrably refused to sell out, the dead ones.[30]

Working-class revolutionaries committed a series of tactical errors. In 1952, the miners failed to consolidate their position by immediately extending their support to other working-class groups and peasants. Instead, even when they represented the most powerful armed force within the country, they left the task of organizing to others. POR's realist position aided this process by channeling energies away from building an independent worker-peasant alliance.

The MNR used its superior resources to split the working class and peasants into antagonistic blocs. Peasants became defenders of the MNR because the MNR organized them and because it took full credit for agrarian reforms. However, the failure to organize and politicize peasants proved less serious than the fact that the revolutionary forces allowed the army to rebuild. They did not push labor's advantageous position; instead, they stood aside while U.S. advisers and $8 million in direct U.S. military aid resurrected the armed forces. By the 1960s, the army had become the most powerful institution in the land and one dedicated to turning back the clock on the Revolution and restoring Bolivia's dependent status.[31]

Workers faced two enemies: the reactionary forces, including imperialism; and the bourgeois democratic forces inside the revolution. Perhaps the combination could not be overcome. Nor does the blame totally fall on the shoulders of labor. A student of Bolivian labor summed the situation up this way: "The proletariat's failure to seize power in Bolivia is directly linked to the inability of revolutionary parties to guide and direct revolutionary unions. In Bolivia the trade unions replaced the parties."[32] Thus revolutionaries failed to build the coalition spelled out in the Thesis of Pulacayo, and that failure may have cost them the opportunity to make a successful revolution.

LABOR AND REVOLUTION: CUBA, 1935–1961

The Revolution that triumphed in Cuba on January 1, 1959, has remained in power, inaugurating Latin America's first society dedicated to building socialism. The working class played an important role in events prior to 1959 and formed a key pillar of support for the Revolution after that date. The following analysis concentrates on labor's role between 1935 and 1961, particularly in the period after 1952. In one way, this distorts reality, for almost every sector of Cuban society took part in the drama: students, peasants, traditional politicians, women, urban middle sectors, religious groups, and even elements from the upper class and the armed forces. In that sense, the Revolution represented a true popular uprising against sixty years of dependency, oppression, and misgovernment. Labor occupied center stage in this historical progression only at certain points, such as 1933; and working-class support for the Revolution proved most vital after the anti-Batista forces seized power. However, the 1950s could not have unfolded as they did without widespread working-class and labor participation.

The Co-optive–Repressive Period: The Batista Years, 1935–1944, and the Auténticos, 1944–1952

The 1935 general strike discussed in Chapter 2 marked the final outburst of working-class activity in the period begun by mass struggle against Machado. A co-optive–repressive period in Cuban labor history followed, during which the state strengthened and formalized the systems first utilized by Grau San Martín in 1933.

Although other men formally occupied the presidency, Batista emerged from the 1933 crisis as Cuba's real ruler. He harbored corporatist ideas that included a greater state role within the economy and the organization of interest groups into formal blocs. He would serve as power broker between these groups and thus maintain control. Concurrently, his command over the armed forces would prevent any violent upheavals. The traditional parties and the Auténticos, on the other hand, wished for a return to constitutional rule under which they could hope to occupy government positions. The conservatives, once the threat of social revolution subsided, increasingly opposed Batista. They wanted less government intervention and disliked having to depend upon a person whom they considered an upstart. The Auténticos still hoped to implement their reform program developed prior to 1933.[33]

Having secured relative social stability through a harsh crackdown on labor and working-class organizations, in the late 1930s Batista sought to gain working-class support. Gradually, an understanding or tacit alliance emerged between Batista and the Communists. In return for labor peace, he legalized the party, allowed it to use the media freely, and restored its right to organize. Strategic considerations influenced the rapprochement: Batista gained important mass backing, and the Communists won the opportunity to explain their position and to recruit openly. The alliance also fit into Communist popular front strategy, which expressly approved alliances with bourgeois governments committed to the world struggle against fascism. Batista, who followed U.S. foreign policy lines, qualified on those grounds.

The Communist Party moved to rebuild the labor movement and increase its influence. Early in 1939, after a series of local and provincial elections, some 1,500 delegates representing 576 unions met and founded a new central labor organization, the Confederación de Trabajadores de Cuba (CTC). Later that same year, representatives from 78 sugar workers' unions formed the Federación Nacional de Trabajadores Azucareros (FNTA), which replaced the moribund SNOIA.[34]

Organized labor grew rapidly in both size and strength. In 1938, before the CTC's founding, just over 200,000 workers belonged to unions. By 1939, the CTC alone boasted a membership over 200,000, and the figure swelled to almost 350,000 two years later. The FNTA also expanded, claiming over 100,000 members in 1941. In all, an estimated one-third to one-half of the total permanent work force belonged to some labor organization, although the degree of unionization varied by sector. The level of organization was particularly high among workers in the sugar, tobacco, transport, textile, and manufacturing sectors. Other groups, such as coffee workers, remained without formal means to express their demands. Among union members, some 19 percent regularly paid CTC dues, and 47 percent contributed to their locals. This low level of financial commitment stemmed from the extreme poverty of most workers and from the fact that, as recently organized workers, many still did not see the value in supporting their unions. About three-fourths of the unionized workers belonged to the CTC, which was organized primarily along industrial lines. It also included local and provincial federations.[35]

The Comisión Obrera of the Partido Revolucionario Cubano (Auténtico), headed by Eusebio Mujal and representing Grau's followers, vied with independent unions and Communists for leadership of the expanding labor movement. Communists controlled the most important unions and federations, including those of sugar, tobacco, and transport workers, and the provincial federations of Oriente and Las Villas. The Auténticos held important minority positions inside the sugar and maritime unions, and they controlled the restaurant workers' union. The maritime trades, public employees, and electrical workers remained independent. Most provincial federations, including the important Havana one, remained divided among these three ideological tendencies.[36]

During this period, Batista strengthened the two-pronged policy of co-optation and repression initiated by Grau and continued by Mendieta (see Chapter 2). A 1940 constitutional convention produced a new national charter that culminated Batista's move toward "constitutional rule." He had convoked the convention only after consolidating his own position and making sure that he would become president in the elections that would follow. The document granted basic rights but delegated substantial power to the state and preserved private property. The twenty-seven articles treating labor reinforced extensive government controls while also providing extended social security benefits for select workers and increased pay in some urban trades. After his election, Batista officially recognized the CTC. He also granted it permission for a radio station and freedom of its own press.[37]

When Batista called elections for 1944, two coalitions vied for office: the Auténticos, backing Grau; and Batista's forces, which included the Partido Socialista Popular (PSP), the Communist political party formed in 1943. Communist influence on the Batista government became a campaign issue, and Grau ran on the slogan "no continuismo, no comunismo" ("no re-election, no

Communism"). The combined votes of the anti-Batista groups, mainly the Auténticos and the Conservatives, proved enough to elect Grau president, and Batista did not dare overturn the result.

Grau's victory heartened Auténtico labor leaders, who perceived an opportunity to oust their Communist rivals from the CTC. Tensions between the two groups had previously come to the boiling point. In 1942, Mujal had forced an open split when the Communists won the majority of elective offices within the confederation. The Auténticos' withdrawal, however, proved short-lived when they realized that nonparticipation only cost them support among workers convinced of the need for labor unity against fascism. At that time, the government had backed the CTC and the Communists, but now an Auténtico government held power. When Mujal and his followers began moving against them, the Communists, led by Lázaro Peña, the CTC secretary-general since 1940, threatened a general strike vote. Grau could ill afford to alienate the Communists, whose following amounted to 25 to 33 percent of all unionized workers and who had their strongest base among sugar workers. To do so risked labor unrest that might give Batista the excuse to rouse the military against him. He therefore compromised under the guise of continuing the labor peace that prevailed during the war. An agreement at the CTC's 1944 congress gave Communists and Auténticos an equal number of posts on the Executive Committee, and independents held the balance. Peña also continued as secretary-general.[38]

Internal tensions, however, continued. Matters finally came to a head at the confederation's 1947 congress. The Auténticos, joined by a substantial bloc of independent unions, charged the Communists with manipulating union elections in order to pack the meeting. Anti-Communist Labor Minister Carlos Prío Socarrás intervened by naming an "impartial" investigating committee. The Communists refused to recognize the committee and held their own congress. The Auténticos and independents responded by withholding dues and staging a rump congress. The CTC had split.[39]

These maneuvers did not take place in a vacuum. Grau now felt reasonably secure in office, and he had helped the Auténticos to gain strength within the labor movement by using government agencies in their favor. More important, as the Cold War gathered momentum, the United States pressured Grau to eradicate Communist influence in all sectors of Cuban society. It therefore followed logically that Prío legalized the Auténtico–independent CTC over its Communist rival. In response, the latter called a general strike, but the government effectively crushed the action by arresting 115 labor leaders and encouraging employers to fire all participants. The bus companies alone, for example, dismissed over 500 workers. This defeat signaled the end for the Communist-backed CTC. Mujal and the Auténticos now controlled the only existing confederation.[40]

In 1948, Prío assumed the presidency. That event signaled yet greater pressures on Communist unions and party members within non-Communist organizations. Unions that failed to affiliate with the Auténtico–independent CTC could not sign legal collective contracts, thus opening the way for employers to impose their own conditions on the workers. Therefore, many unions, even those in which Communists held a majority, gradually drifted back into the official CTC in order to protect the rank and file. The Communist leadership thus placed the interests of the workers first, even if it meant loss of control within an organization. Still, despite these setbacks, they retained a considerable following, and their principled stand won them trust among workers. An estimate in 1950 put Communist strength at a maximum of 10 percent of all unions, with perhaps 25 percent of union membership.[41]

Gradually, the Auténticos forced the independents within the CTC on the defensive. In 1948, they elected Mujal secretary-general. From that time until the triumph of the Revolution, Mujal and his cronies occupied key confederation positions and collaborated with whatever government held power. As one observer said, "The present CTC (Auténtico) leaders draw their strength from the Government. They are the government's lobby with the labor movement, rather than the workers' representatives before the government."[42] That posture, however, was to cost them dearly in the future.

The Revolutionary Struggle: The Second Batista Dictatorship, 1952–1958

At the end of Prío's term in 1952, Batista again seized power when it became apparent that he would not win the forthcoming elections. He ruled dictatorially for two years before carefully orchestrated elections inaugurated a "constitutional" term. His return threatened the Auténtico labor bosses with the loss of their preferred position in government circles. They immediately called a general strike to topple the new regime. When that move failed, the CTC quickly arrived at an accommodation with Batista. In return for continued government backing, Mujal and his associates agreed to see that labor maintained an apolitical stance. They justified their action by claiming that it represented the only way to preserve gains already made by the workers.[43]

No longer in need of Communist support, and having learned the importance of taking cues from the U.S. Cold War policies, Batista continued the anti-Communist campaign begun by the Auténticos. One law, passed in 1954, prohibited Communists or those with Communist sympathies from working in public-service industries; another created a special government agency designed to ferret out Communists. Batista also outlawed the PSP and ruled that any person employed in private or public industry participating in an illegal strike could be fired with loss of all social security benefits. In turn, the CTC received favorable rulings or official blessings for its activities. For example, increased powers to intervene in member unions allowed the national leadership to hand-pick local officers. The government also usually sided with CTC affiliates when strikes sought only narrow economic goals.[44]

Two groups of workers benefited from Batista's "pro-labor" policies: a thin stratum centered in Havana and other large urban centers and the highly skilled sugar mill workers. These groups represented at most 22 percent of the total industrial labor force. In terms of Cuban society, they earned more and lived comparatively better than most workers and therefore thought that they had a real stake in the existing system.[45]

The vast majority of workers, however, remained outside the

privileged group, along with those on the margin of the economic mainstream. Half the total labor force, for example, earned a living as agricultural laborers, in small-scale industries, or in the service sector. This mass, by and large, enjoyed no union representation, little (if any) job security, and minimal legal protection. In 1945, over 52 percent of the agrarian labor force worked less than four months a year, a figure that varied only slightly thereafter. Ten years later, a survey concluded that almost one-third of the labor force remained permanently underemployed, meaning that by the late 1950s some 600,000 Cubans could not earn a satisfactory livelihood.

Cuba boasted the third-highest per capita income in Latin America, but income distribution remained unequal. The average Cuban family in 1952–1953 spent over 55 percent of its income on food because of the high cost of foodstuffs, many of them imported because sugar cane occupied most of the arable land. In cities, rents took 33 percent of family income. Over half the population had no electricity; a third remained illiterate. Rural dwellers suffered disproportionately. Most houses in the country-side lacked running water and indoor sanitation facilities. Three of four rural children did not attend school. Those who could pay for it received reasonable health care. But 95 percent of rural children suffered from internal parasites, and tuberculosis was a major problem. Small farmers paid as much as 30 percent of their income for land, whereas 1.5 percent of the landowners controlled 46 percent of the nation's surface.[46]

Even inside the ranks of the CTC and organized labor, vast inequalities existed. As CTC boss and a national senator, Mujal's income reportedly totaled over $280,000 annually.[47] The opulence displayed by Mujal and other corrupt leaders led workers to resent the forced collection of 1 percent of their salary (checkoff dues) decreed by Batista as part of his deal with CTC leaders. Such disparities aided the Communist Party to survive and maintain its strength within the movement. Although many of its most dedicated leaders had been killed during the repression of the late 1940s and early 1950s, it still remained the second-most-powerful tendency within the labor movement and the best-organized among the anti-Mujalist forces. It stressed the vital necessity for working-class unity and the anti-imperialist nature of the struggle. It continuously strove to bring all sectors of the working class into a single revolutionary movement. Communists, unlike other groups inside the labor movement, placed special emphasis upon recruitment among oppressed minorities. For example, Blacks made up a significant proportion of, and held many key posts in, Communist-oriented unions. That policy helped to combat the racist attitudes that divided the working class.[48] By stressing anti-imperialism, Communists clearly identified a major source of the Cuban people's oppression and placed their struggle in a wider context by linking national developments to similar battles waged by oppressed peoples throughout the world.

The Revolution against Batista, however, initially developed from an amalgam of non-Communist forces, mostly urban professionals and students. After the ill-fated attack on the Moncada military barracks in 1953, the 26th of July Movement (named for the date of the attack) had begun planning its struggle against the government and slowly building a clandestine network. It also forged links with the multitude of other revolutionary groups that existed inside and outside Cuba. Several long-range historical forces worked to the advantage of the 26th of July Movement. A small, white Hispanic elite monopolized key posts throughout Cuban society; many persons, especially students, found upward mobility blocked and turned to radical solutions. Left revolutionary politics also represented one of the few arenas in which minority groups received equal treatment.

Since 1868, the people's anti-imperialist consciousness had grown. The War of Independence and U.S. interventions under the hated Platt Amendment of 1902 further raised this consciousness. Batista's close relations with the United States during his dictatorship demonstrated the nature of Cuba's dependent relationship with its northern neighbor. After 1898, U.S. investment grew rapidly, and North American companies dominated the sugar, banking, and public-utility sectors. Curtailed during the 1930s by the Great Depression, U.S. capital again poured into Cuba after World War II. By 1957, U.S. direct investment reached $850 million, and indirect investment totaled another $211 million. Cuban workers waged some of their most bitter struggles against foreign companies such as American Sugar Refining, Bethlehem Steel, the Cuban Consolidated Railroads, Havana Electric Company (an American Light and Foreign Power subsidiary), Sinclair Oil, United Fruit, and Woolworths. These struggles further heightened anti-imperialist consciousness among the working class.[49]

The anti-Batista movement of the 1950s benefited from another historical phenomenon. Since 1868, when Cubans first rebelled against Spain, violent struggle had been a constant in Cuban history. Thus, violence earned a kind of legitimacy. The revolutionary movement did not have to overcome social opposition to armed struggle, and the use of assassination or bombs merely constituted another commonly used tactic.

In December 1956, a new phase in the fight against Batista began with the opening of the first guerrilla action. From that time, rebel columns operated first in the Sierra Maestra and later in other areas despite Batista's efforts to crush them. This type of warfare kept the fight limited at first, but slowly, the 26th of July Movement attracted widespread peasant support and enlarged the territory under its control. Many writers have highlighted the rural struggle, but urban developments proved just as important. The urban network helped support and supply the guerrillas in the hills and carried out its own actions. Nor did the movement's leadership neglect the urban working class. Their first manifesto, issued in August 1955, called for the "reestablishment of all workers' gains taken away by the dictatorship; the right of workers to broad participation in the profits of all large industrial, commercial, and mining enterprises, which should be paid in addition to salaries or wages at given intervals during the year."[50]

The movement's Program Manifesto dedicated an entire section to labor, chastising particularly "leaders who had submitted to official banditry," and the Sierra Maestra Manifesto of July 1957 called for the "democratization of labor politics, promoting free elements in all unions and industrial federations." By 1957, an extensive urban revolutionary underground existed, organized and co-ordinated mainly by Frank País from Santiago. Groups from the

26th of July Movement, Catholics, Auténticos, students' organizations (principally the Directorio Revolucionario), and eventually, Communists all participated in this phase of the war.[51]

Despite the Mujalists' promise of labor peace, working-class unrest marked the 1950s. In 1955, sugar workers defied the CTC and struck over the government's slashing of year-end bonuses. Batista at first softened his stand, but the workers persisted. Now fearing a mass movement, he agreed to the workers' demands, but later he reneged on his promises and moved forcefully against strikers. The CTC's support for Batista in this conflict led dissidents to call a congress aimed at establishing an independent federation. The move failed, however, because of government repression, which the CTC applauded. In 1957, this time aided by guerrilla forces, sugar workers again called a short strike. The Mujalists denounced it as Marxist-led and urged workers not to join.[52]

Almost from the beginning, the 26th of July leadership accepted the premise that a revolutionary general strike supported by armed action could topple the regime. Marxist theory confirmed that position, and the revolutionaries saw its direct antecedent in the events of 1933. Accordingly, the movement prepared for such an action. In 1957, País brought together the Frente Obrero Nacional (FON) as a national co-ordinating body and clearinghouse for provincial and municipal organizations. These groups maintained maximum autonomy so that they could speak directly for the interests of local workers. Despite these efforts, however, the revolutionaries still lacked a mass following within the unions and few trained cadres existed. Their organization had developed primarily outside the organized labor movement and had not yet time to build a base there. Batista's police and the CTC constantly watched all persons suspected of opposing their rule, and the surveillance hampered recruitment. Many of the older workers distrusted the young revolutionaries. Workers who received benefits through affiliation in CTC unions hesitated to risk them. In addition, the Communists remained apart at this point, seeing the 26th of July Movement as an "adventurist" effort. Finally, Batista still retained some support among workers who remembered that he had brought them some improvements through legislation. Yet, even in 1957, Mujal admitted that opposition existed among a dozen of Cuba's most important unions. The problem for the revolutionaries remained how to effectively mobilize the discontent.[53]

In August 1957, a spontaneous work stoppage following the assassination of País almost totally paralyzed Santiago and other cities, although it gained little following in Havana. This unexpected event confirmed the 26th of July Movement's belief that a general strike could succeed. The revolutionary organizations then prepared for a strike as part of an armed urban uprising and rural offensive during April 1958. Hasty preparations and the failure to build solid organizational bases within many important unions led some elements to pull out, and even the most dedicated revolutionaries expressed doubts on the chances for success. The leadership, nevertheless, decided to press ahead.

The rebel radio and media openly announced the forthcoming strike. In reply, the labor bureaucrats denounced it and clearly stated their position: "People who treat labor well deserve well of labor, and President Batista has done more for labor than any other president Cuba ever had."[54] A lack of co-ordination among underground elements and labor, violent government reaction, and an unwillingness on the part of many workers to participate allowed Batista to crush the movement almost before it started, but in scattered areas workers closed down factories and even occupied whole towns. The strike's failure and the decimation of urban cadre led to a change in tactics. The movement abandoned the idea of an immediate general strike and concentrated on rural warfare.[55]

As the spring advanced and the guerrillas began to make substantial headway, Batista girded for an all-out offensive against them. At that point, developments within the labor movement began to favor the revolutionaries. Batista had declared a state of national emergency, suspending all constitutional guarantees. In the face of continuing urban attacks and guerrilla gains in the countryside, Batista now unleashed indiscriminate terror against all unfriendly forces. For the first time, this included the Communists, because, he claimed, the movement against him was a "Moscow-oriented plot." This development and the conviction that the 26th of July forces could win led increasing numbers of Communists to support the Revolution. In late spring, the 26th of July forces and the PSP signed a unity pact, and the PSP swung its labor support behind the Revolution. Cells grew in almost all unions, and the urban support network expanded noticeably. In zones under guerrilla control, organizers extended contacts with workers. In the sugar mills, PSP and FON co-ordinators moved to oust Mujalist influence and to form a separate organization. In November, 500 delegates met to co-ordinate activities, and the next month a congress pledged support for the Revolution. Sugar workers also responded to the call to burn cane in order to weaken Batista's economic position.

Several national labor caucuses met during the latter half of 1958, working toward greater unity among the diverse anti-Batista forces. In October the FON expanded to incorporate new elements, becoming the United National Workers' Front, headed by the 26th of July labor leader David Salvador. As 1958 drew to a close, a new set of unions emerged whose sympathies lay with the goals set by the 26th of July Movement. When the Revolution triumphed, on January 1, 1959, Mujal and his accomplices quickly followed Batista into exile, leaving the task of restructuring the labor movement to these newly formed organizations.[56]

The Early Revolutionary Period, 1959–1961

The Revolution faced a host of problems. The anti-Batista forces did not form a coherent movement with an organized mass base; rather, they were divergent elements, each fighting for its own program. Large segments of the population, although against Batista and the status quo, stayed outside the revolutionary process, as did vast numbers who took neither side. A massive task of political education loomed. Furthermore, bourgeois institutions needed fundamental restructuring before a transition to socialism could proceed, and existing traditional political groups represented a threat to the Revolution's stability.

Much also hinged on the United States, only ninety miles away. During Batista's last days, the U.S. State Department, although outwardly neutral, began maneuvering to bring to power those favorable to U.S. interests and to prevent Fidel Castro from leading the Revolution. Within two years after this failed, the United States had moved firmly against the Revolution, breaking diplomatic relations with Cuba, instituting an economic blockade, and supporting an invasion by exiles at the Bay of Pigs. Yet, the Revolution maintained and consolidated power inside key institutions, including labor; armed the people to defend their gains; and secured much-needed support from the European Socialist bloc and numerous Third World countries.

The Revolution immediately concerned itself with organized labor as the largest mass institution. The 26th of July forces took over the CTC and ousted the Mujalists. Laws 21 and 22 of January 1959 dealt directly with labor; the former abolished the despised 1 percent obligatory contribution, and the latter suspended all union officials holding office on December 31 and named provisional committees to head the CTC and its affiliates until elections could be called. The CTC committee incorporated several ideological tendencies, including two Catholic leaders, and designated David Salvador as interim secretary-general. Subsequent laws protected agricultural workers who supported the Revolution from reprisals by owners, prohibited companies from dismissing workers for economic reasons, and raised minimum salaries and wages. Two additional acts vested the Labor Ministry with the power to intervene in unions and authorized it to solve labor disputes and fix salary levels.[57]

After elections, in which the 26th of July slates won control over twenty-nine out of thirty-three federations, the CTC congress met in November 1959. Although the delegates agreed to expel the top Mujalists, divisions arose between those committed to socialism and those who wished to maintain previous structures. Many 26th of July labor people favored the latter course, and they united with second-level Mujalist officials and the few remaining Auténticos to exclude Communists from important positions. An intense debate followed, marked by the intervention of numerous Revolutionary leaders. Finally, a compromise emerged giving leadership posts to those who were pro-Revolutionary but neither Communists nor anti-Communists.[58]

New laws consolidated and unified the growing labor structure, enabling the Ministry of Labor to work more closely with unions. Law 969 and subsequent acts formally vested the ministry with powers of intervention in disputes and increased its input into the rapidly expanding social security system. The constitutional reform of 1960 reaffirmed these measures.

Political tensions within the labor movement, however, persisted. Some labor leaders still saw themselves as part of a separate pressure group inside Cuban society. In 1959, Salvador called for a blanket 20 percent wage increase. That same year, sugar workers threatened to strike for higher wages. This move could have disrupted the nation's fragile economy. Fidel Castro personally requested that sugar workers not strike, saying that Cuban society was no longer composed of capitalists and workers divided into antagonistic blocs and that the economy now produced for the benefit of all the people. His plea proved successful, and workers called off the strike. Gradually, pro-socialist forces gained ground, particularly at the grass roots level. As a result, local union elections constantly replaced former leaders with Communists or 26th of July people who had union experience and who enjoyed the trust of fellow workers from previous struggles.[59]

The Revolutionary government continued to encourage unionization. Union membership soon passed 1 million, and the CTC housed 1,542 unions, representing approximately 60 percent of the total labor force.[60] This influx of new unions broadened and democratized the labor movement by eroding the power of elite unions that remained bastions of more traditional elements within the labor movement through 1960 and 1961. Centralization also continued. Local unions in each branch of economic activity formed the basis for national federations. These federations, reduced to twenty-five in number, united member organizations of the CTC, now called CTC–Revolucionario. Local unions also organized on a geographic basis. All entities in a particular administrative district or province met in regional conferences and maintained regional co-ordinating offices. This structure allowed unions to deal with problems on two levels: At confederation meetings, they discussed national matters; at provincial gatherings, they treated local subjects.[61]

The government also initiated measures to improve the lives of the working class. Official programs virtually eliminated unemployment by encouraging people to enter the work force and by creating 500,000 jobs. Other acts expanded social security benefits, improved working conditions, and made a host of free social services available, including day care, education, recreational facilities, and health care. The Revolutionary leadership began a massive housing program and reduced rents to a maximum of 10 percent of a worker's salary.[62] Such accomplishments, in conjunction with the rise in real salaries and reductions of prices of basic goods, concretely demonstrated to increasing numbers of rank-and-file workers the desirability of building socialism.

Growing worker support for the Revolution manifested itself in several ways. Outside Cuba, Mujal and his followers set up the CTC-in-Exile, which joined with other exile groups to conspire against the Revolution. The Cuban Democratic Revolutionary Labor Front formed the trade-union sector of the Cuban Liberation Committee, which was dedicated to the overthrow of the Cuban government. Working closely with U.S. agencies, an unknown number of its members infiltrated Cuba just before the Bay of Pigs invasion in order to lead a massive workers' uprising against the Revolution. It failed to materialize, and their plans proved as unsuccessful as the U.S.-supported exiles' invasion. In fact, large numbers of workers rallied to defend their Revolution. Armed worker militias formed in response to the call for mobilization against the invasion, and in factories and fields throughout the island, workers stood guard against sabotage.[63]

The CTC's Eleventh Congress, in November 1961, reflected the changes that had taken place within the working class and within Cuban society. Workers elected their own representatives to the gathering. Two million persons—95 percent of those eligible—cast secret ballots in these elections, which returned an overwhelming pro-socialist majority. By this time, almost all those dissenting from the Revolutionary mainstream had either left the country or ceased to take part in union politics because they could not get support from fellow workers. The CTC, however, did not confine itself to mere rhetoric about the transformation of Cuban society; it actively participated in the process. It first formally renounced the right to strike, recognizing that strikes are self-destructive in a society in which all members share equally as producers and consumers. Furthermore, since appropriate mechanisms existed to deal with workers' grievances at the factory, local, provincial, and national levels, problems arising either from national production decisions or from daily work situations could be peacefully solved.

The CTC congress also recognized that increased production constituted the central problem facing the Revolution in its struggle against underdevelopment and imperialism. It therefore decided that workers should continue to donate 4 percent of their salaries to the state (a decision originally taken in 1960) in order to speed the process of industrialization and to raise productivity. Labor also increased its role in national planning, and *consejos técnicos* (technical councils) ensured workers a greater voice in decisions at the plant level, including production norms.[64]

Thus, by the end of 1961, organized labor had become integrated into the Revolutionary process. From that time, workers increasingly made basic decisions affecting their lives and played a growing role in deciding the future course of Cuba's transition to socialism.[65]

CONCLUSION

What conclusions can be drawn about labor and revolution? In other words, why did the Cuban Revolution triumph and the Bolivian Revolution fail? Several variables in the Cuban experience stand out. Urban and rural workers shared a tradition of militant labor struggle reaching back more than twenty-five years; the individual and collective experience gained after 1925 prepared the working class for the 1950s.[66] In Bolivia, only a relatively small group, the miners, had accrued similar experience. In situations where such a tradition is lacking, organizing may consume vital energies and leave the movement temporarily vulnerable to hostile forces. Similarly, the failure to mobilize in all sectors can isolate vanguard groups and prevent them from pressing their demands.

The two cases also demonstrate the importance of neutralizing reactionary institutions. The Cuban revolutionaries broadened their base as far and as fast as possible. They checkmated bourgeois power groups by arming peasants, students, and workers and by placing loyal officers in key army posts. They thus turned the Revolution into a popular mass movement, a process that deepened rapidly as the working class reaped concrete advantages and gained more voice in decisions affecting its daily life and future. Pockets of resistance formed among elite groups of workers, who, along with other privileged sectors of Cuban society, had to surrender their favored position. The leadership, however, never allowed those elements to gain the upper hand. Within the ranks of labor, free elections and the formation of new unions soon ousted or isolated those wishing to preserve the old system.

In Bolivia, different patterns emerged. The revolutionary elements within the MNR never held a majority position, nor did they press their advantage in 1952 when they held real power through a practical monopoly on armed force. Instead, they allowed reformists to take the initiative in organizing peasants and other workers and stood by while the armed forces regrouped and rearmed. The failure to push forward revolutionary changes also allowed the MNR to co-opt some segments of the labor movement and eventually to repress militancy.

External forces played a vital role in Cuba and Bolivia. Foreign ownership and control of national resources, finances, and external markets and foreign intervention after each revolution proved to be key factors. Foreign presence aided in mobilizing workers against conservative regimes, but foreign countermeasures quickly followed. The 26th of July Movement saw clearly that only a total break with the United States could make Cuba an independent and sovereign state. It understood the consequences of such a break: U.S. hostility and isolation from capitalist markets, technology, and financing. On the other hand, the leadership also knew that only a socialist society could create true equality among all sectors of Cuban society. Therefore, it willingly accepted the costs of breaking free from the United States and world capitalism. In Bolivia, the mainstream of the Revolution wished only to modify existing conditions. It believed that national capitalist development could solve the country's problems. As a result, it combated anti-capitalist forces and maintained links with the United States and world capitalism. The United States moved against both countries. In Bolivia, it undermined the MNR by using economic pressures, forcing it first to the center, then to the right, and finally destroying it by supporting conservative military men after 1964. In Cuba, the United States hoped at first to pre-empt the Revolution; it then tried economic sanctions and finally resorted to military force. These measures, however, failed, partly because friendly outside powers materially supported the Revolution. The Cuban experience suggests that any revolutionary movement within the capitalist world must prepare to defend itself by armed force against internal and external aggression. Events in Chile between 1970 and 1973 support this conclusion. It also underscores the importance of aid between socialist countries and the necessity for all socialists to practice international proletarian solidarity.[67]

Finally, events in Cuba and in Bolivia indicate that all sectors of the working class and peasantry must participate actively in a revolutionary movement. Unions or organized labor need a wider framework within which to operate. Some central body must co-ordinate working-class actions with those of the rest of society. In Bolivia, the unions stood almost alone and eventually lost the Revolution they tried to make. In Cuba, the 26th of July Movement functioned as a vanguard revolutionary party by bringing all groups together at the national level both during and after the Revolution's coming to power.

NOTES

1 On internal developments and U.S. influence, see Chaps. 1 and 2 of this book; Steven S. Volk, "Class, Union, Party: The Development of a Revolutionary Union Movement in Bolivia (1905–1952), Part 1," *Science and Society* 29, no. 1 (Spring 1975): 26–43; and Robert F. Smith, *The United States and Cuba: Business and Diplomacy, 1917–1960* (New York, 1960).

2 William Lee Lofstrom, *Attitudes of an Industrial Pressure Group in Latin America: The Asociación de Industriales Mineros de Bolivia, 1925–1935* (Diss. Series No. 9, Cornell University Latin American Studies Program, 1968), contains data on the early development of mining and activities of the Tin Barons; see also Steven S. Volk, "The Rise of Organized Labor in the Mines, the Federación Sindical de Trabajadores Mineros de Bolivia, 1944–1952" (M.A. thesis, History, Columbia University, 1971). In 1950 prices, capital in 1928 equaled $160 million; in 1950, $161.2 million.

3 Herbert S. Klein, *Parties and Political Change in Bolivia, 1880–1952* (Cambridge, Eng., 1969), pp. 161–167; Volk, "Class, Union, Party: Part 1," p. 32.

4 Steven S. Volk, "Tin and Imperialism," in North American Congress on Latin America (hereafter NACLA), *Latin America and Empire Report* 8, no. 2 (Feb. 1974): 12.

5 See Klein, *Parties and Political Change in Bolivia*, chaps. 5 and 6; and on labor, Guillermo Lora, *Historia del movimiento obrero boliviano, 1923–1933* (La Paz–Cochabamba, 1970).

6 Klein, *Parties and Political Change in Bolivia*, chap. 5; Guillermo Lora, *La revolución boliviana* (La Paz, 1963), p. 61; Jaime Ponce G., "El sindicalismo boliviano: Resumen histórico y perspectivas actuales," *Desarrollo Económico* 9, no. 3 (April–June 1969): 13, 23–24; Volk, "Rise of Organized Labor in the Mines," p. 16.

7 Klein, *Parties and Political Change in Bolivia*, chap. 9, esp. pp. 312–313.

8 Ibid., chap. 8.

9 On these parties, see Robert J. Alexander, *Trotskyism in Latin America* (Stanford, Calif., 1973), pp. 112, 115–117; Klein, *Parties and Political Change in Bolivia*, pp. 341, 351; James Malloy, *Bolivia: The Unfinished Revolution* (Pittsburgh, 1970), chaps. 6–7; Volk, "Rise of Organized Labor in the Mines," pp. 26–28.

10 Alexander, *Trotskyism in Latin America*, pp. 113–114.

11 Inflation and wages in Raúl Federico Abadie-Aicardi, *Económia y sociedad de Bolivia en el siglo XX* (Montevideo, 1966), p. 105; on the

massacre and worker conditions, see Remberto Capriles R. and Gastón Arduez Eguía, *El problema social en Bolivia: condiciones de vida y de trabajo* (La Paz, 1941); International Labour Office, *Labour Problems in Bolivia: Report of the Joint Bolivian–United States Labour Commission* (Montreal, 1943); and Martin J. Kyne, *Informe al Congreso de Organizaciones Industriales sobre las condiciones del trabajo en Bolivia* (La Paz, 1944), esp. pp. 29–36, a dissenting view from the Commission mentioned in the previous title; on the U.S. and tin, Steven S. Volk, "Class, Union, Party: The Development of a Revolutionary Movement in Bolivia (1905–1952), Part 2: From the Chaco War to 1952," *Science and Society* 29, no. 2 (Summer 1975): 186–187; and Henry W. Berger, "Union Diplomacy: American Labor's Foreign Policy in Latin America, 1932–1955" (Ph. D. diss., History, University of Wisconsin, 1968), pp. 215–217; the latter note that several of Secretary of State Cordell Hull's team of advisers had direct links to Patiño interests.

12 June Nash, "Industrial Conflict in the Andes, the Bolivian Tin Miners" (unpublished MS), p. 11; Ponce, "El sindicalismo boliviano," p. 15; Volk, "Rise of Organized Labor in the Mines," chap. 3, and "Class, Union, Party: Part 2," p. 189.

13 Volk, "Rise of Organized Labor in the Mines," p. 44.

14 Original in Guillermo Lora, ed., *Documentos políticos de Bolivia* (La Paz, 1970), pp. 361–390; an edited English version is Hobart A. Spalding, Jr., and Steve Volk, eds., "The Thesis of Pulacayo," in NACLA, *Latin America and Empire Report* 8, no. 2 (February 1974): 19–23.

15 Nash, "Industrial Conflict in the Andes," pp. 13–15; Volk, "Rise of Organized Labor in the Mines," pp. 87–88, 92–93.

16 Details in Guillermo Lora, *La burocracia sindical y la masacre de Siglo XX* (La Paz, 1963); Alexander, *Trotskyism in Latin America*, p. 123; Klein, *Parties and Political Change in Bolivia*, pp. 383–401; Ponce, "El sindicalismo boliviano," pp. 17–18; and Volk, "Rise of Organized Labor in the Mines," chap. 7.

17 Analysis of these parties in Alexander, *Trotskyism in Latin America*, p. 124, and *The Bolivian National Revolution* (Washington, D.C., 1965), pp. 52–55; Malloy, *Bolivia: The Unfinished Revolution*, chap. 7; Volk, "Rise of Organized Labor in the Mines," p. 91.

18 Alexander, *Bolivian National Revolution*, p. 135; and Steven S. Volk, "Bolivia: The War Goes On," in NACLA, *Latin America and Empire Report* 8, no. 2 (February 1974): 3.

19 John H. Magill, Jr., "Labor Unions and Political Socialization in Bolivia" (Ph.D. diss., Political Science, University of Wisconsin, 1972), p. 49, subsequently published as *Labor Unions and Political Socialization: A Case Study of Bolivian Workers* (New York, 1974).

20 Alexander, *Bolivian National Revolution*, pp. 19, 25–26, 132, and

Trotskyism in Latin America, pp. 103–104; June Nash, "Workers' Participation in Nationalized Mines of Bolivia, 1952–1972" (unpublished MS), pp. 6–7; Malloy, *Bolivia: The Unfinished Revolution*, pp. 177–178.

21 Alexander, *Bolivian National Revolution*, pp. 123–124, 128; Jaime Ponce G., Thomas J. Shanley, Antonio J. Cisneros, *Breve historia del sindicalismo boliviano y legislación social vigente* (La Paz, 1968), pp. 63–66, 71–72; Ponce, "El sindicalismo boliviano," pp. 21–22.

22 Alexander, *Trotskyism in Latin America*, pp. 133–134; Malloy, *Bolivia: The Unfinished Revolution*, pp. 186–187; Nash, "Workers' Participation in Nationalized Mines," pp. 7–8.

23 Alexander, *Bolivian National Revolution*, pp. 60–61, and *Trotskyism in Latin America*, p. 138; Agustín Barcelli S., *Medio siglo de luchas sindicales revolucionarias en Bolivia, 1905–1955* (La Paz, 1966), pp. 289–291; on peasants generally, Dwight B. Heath, Charles J. Erasmus, Hans G. Buechler, *Land Reform and Social Revolution in Bolivia* (New York, 1969); Malloy, *Bolivia: The Unfinished Revolution*, chap. 10 and pp. 232–237, 265; and Cornelius Zondag, *The Bolivian Economy, 1952–1965* (New York, 1966), p. 29.

24 Economic data for this period in Barcelli, *Medio siglo de luchas*, pp. 298–306; James W. Wilkie, *The Bolivian Revolution and U.S. Aid Since 1952* (Los Angeles, 1969); and Zondag, *Bolivian Economy*, pp. 56, 59–62. George Jackson Eder, *Inflation and Development in Latin America: A Case History of Inflation and Stabilization in Bolivia* (Ann Arbor, Mich., 1968), is an explanation and defense of the plan by its designer.

25 Amado Canelas O., *Radiografía de la alianza para el atraso* (La Paz, 1963); June Nash, "Dependency and the Failure of Feedback: The Case of Bolivian Mining Communities" (unpublished MS), p. 6; Malloy, *Bolivia: The Unfinished Revolution*, pp. 238, 298–301; Ponce, "El sindicalismo boliviano," 24–26; Magill, "Labor Unions and Political Socialization in Bolivia," pp. 55–58.

26 Malloy, *Bolivia: The Unfinished Revolution*, pp. 298–299; Volk, "Bolivia: The War Goes On," p. 6; Magill, "Labor Unions and Political Socialization in Bolivia," pp. 61–65.

27 Alexander, *Bolivian National Revolution*, p. 130, cites attempts to set up an anti-MNR and pro-U.S. labor movement in 1950–1951; Erasmo Barrios Villa, *Historia sindical de Bolivia* (Oruro, 1966), p. 156; Eder, *Inflation and Development in Latin America*, pp. 52–54; Nash, "Industrial Conflict in the Andes," pp. 23, 25; Ponce, *Breve historia del sindicalismo boliviano*, pp. 91–92; Magill, "Labor Unions and Political Socialization in Brazil," pp. 61–65.

28 On U.S. aid, see Cole Blasier, "The United States and the Revolution," in *Beyond the Revolution: Bolivia Since 1952*, James Malloy and Richard S. Thorn, eds. (Pittsburgh, 1971), pp. 53–109; Donna Katzin, "Alliance for Power: U.S. Aid to Bolivia Under Banzer," in NACLA, *Latin*

America and Empire Report 8, no. 2 (February 1974): 29; Wilkie, *Bolivian Revolution and U.S. Aid*, pp. 12, 14.

[29] On events from the 1960s to present, see June Nash, "Worker Consciousness and Union Organization: The Problem of Ideology and Practice in the Bolivian Mines," in *Ideology and Social Change in Latin America*, Juan Corradi, June Nash, and Hobart A. Spalding, Jr., eds. (New York, 1977), pp. 116–141; Ponce, "El sindicalismo boliviano," pp. 26–29; Ponce, *Breve historia del sindicalismo boliviano*, pp. 86, 111–114; Volk, "Bolivia: The War Goes On," p. 7; *Documentos del movimiento obrero: De la tesis de Pulacayo al manifiesto de la COB de 1965* (La Paz, 1969) contains texts of declarations endorsed by worker gatherings; analysis of recent events in René Zavaleta Mercado, "Bolivia: Military Nationalism and the Popular Assembly," *New Left Review* 77 (January–February 1973): 63–80, and "Movimiento obrero y ciencia social," *Historia y sociedad, segunda época*, no. 3 (Autumn 1974): 3–35.

[30] Nash, "Industrial Conflict in the Andes," p. 2, calculates that miners could hold out at most a month if besieged in the camps; Magill, "Labor Unions and Political Socialization in Bolivia," p. 59; Nash, "Dependency and the Failure of Feedback," p. 17, on leaders.

[31] Katzin, "Alliance for Power," p. 29.

[32] Volk, "Class, Union, Party: Part 2," pp. 197–198.

[33] On Batista's new policies, see William Appleman Williams, "Historiography and Revolution: The Case of Cuba, *Studies on the Left* 3, no. 3 (1963): 84–85; for a somewhat favorable review of Batista, see Irwin F. Gellman, *Roosevelt and Batista: Good Neighbor Diplomacy in Cuba, 1933–1945* (Albuquerque, N.M., 1973). Portions of this section appeared in "The Workers' Struggle: 1850–1961," *Cuba Review* 4, no. 1 (July 1974): 3–10, 31.

[34] Grupo Cubano de Investigaciones Económicas, *Estudio sobre Cuba* (Miami, Fla., 1963), p. 727; Charles A. Page, "The Development of Organized Labor in Cuba" (Ph.D. diss., Latin American Studies, University of California at Los Angeles, 1952), pp. 87–89; Evelio Tellería, *Los congresos obreros en Cuba* (Havana, 1973), pp. 277–318.

[35] Grupo Cubano, *Estudio sobre Cuba*, p. 726; José Morera, *IV Congreso Nacional de la CTC* (Havana, 1945), pp. 6–7, 16; Page, "Development of Organized Labor in Cuba," pp. 91, 95, 97, 100.

[36] Tellería, *Los congresos obreros en Cuba*, pp. 331–333; Office of Strategic Services, Research and Analysis Branch (R and A No. 3076.1), "The Political Significance and Influence of the Labor Movement in Latin America: A Preliminary Survey: Cuba," (MS, Sept. 18, 1945), contains a detailed analysis of each tendency within the labor movement. It can be found in the National Archives.

[37] Grupo Cubano, *Estudio sobre Cuba*, pp. 737–753.

[38] Jorge García Montes and Antonio Alonso Avila, *Historia del Partido*

Comunista de Cuba (Miami, 1970), pp. 324–326; Mario Riera Hernández, *Historial obrero cubano, 1574–1965* (Miami, 1965), p. 130; Grupo Cubano, *Estudio sobre Cuba*, p. 1182; James O'Connor, *The Origins of Socialism in Cuba* (Ithaca, N.Y., 1970), pp. 180–181; Page, "Development of Organized Labor in Cuba," p. 179.

39 Page, "Development of Organized Labor in Cuba," p. 122; Ramón Ruíz, *Cuba: The Making of a Revolution* (Amherst, Mass., 1968), p. 132.

40 O'Connor, *Origins of Socialism in Cuba*, p. 180; Page, "Development of Organized Labor in Cuba," p. 128.

41 Page, "Development of Organized Labor in Cuba," pp. 160–161.

42 Ibid., p. 223.

43 Montes and Avila, *Historia del Partido Comunista de Cuba*, p. 440; Riera Hernández, *Historial obrero cubano*, p. 147.

44 Grupo Cubano, *Estudio sobre Cuba*, p. 1185; Riera Hernández, *Historial obrero cubano*, p. 148.

45 Wyatt MacGaffey and Clifford R. Barnett, *Cuba—Its People, Its Society, Its Culture* (New Haven, Conn., 1962), pp. 139, 144–145; O'Connor, *Origins of Socialism in Cuba*, pp. 183–184.

46 Above data from Grupo Cubano, *Estudio sobre Cuba*, pp. 810, 814; MacGaffey and Barnett, *Cuba*, p. 41; Fidel Castro, Speech at the General Assembly of the United Nations, New York, Sept. 26, 1960, in *Fidel Castro Speaks*, Martin Kenner and James Petras, eds. (New York, 1961), pp. 6–7. For the links between the July 26th Movement and the socioeconomic situation, Fidel Castro, *History Will Absolve Me: The Moncada Trial Defense Speech, Santiago de Cuba, October 16th, 1953* (London, 1968).

47 Ralph Lee Woodward, Jr., "Union Labor and Communism: Cuba," *Caribbean Studies* 3, no. 3 (October 1963): 24.

48 On minorities and especially Blacks in Communist organizations, see MacGaffey and Barnett, *Cuba*, p. 51; Lowry Nelson, *Rural Cuba* (Minneapolis, 1950), p. 158; and David Booth, "Cuba, Color and the Revolution," *Science and Society* 40, no. 2 (Summer 1976): 129–172.

49 Smith, *United States and Cuba*, esp. pp. 166–167, for U.S. investment and business pressure on Cuba.

50 Rolando E. Bonachea and Nelson P. Valdés, eds., *Revolutionary Struggle, 1947–1958: Volume 1 of the Selected Works of Fidel Castro* (Cambridge, Mass., 1972), p. 269.

51 Quote from Rolando E. Bonchea and Nelson P. Valdés, eds., *Cuba in Revolution* (Garden City, N.Y., 1972), pp. 123–124; see also their *Revolutionary Struggle*, pp. 30, 346, for information on Castro and the labor movement; on the urban phases, see Ramón Bonachea and Marta San Martín, *The Cuban Insurrection, 1952–1959* (New Brunswick, N.J., 1974).

52 Riera Hernández, *Historial obrero cubano*, p. 150; Hugh Thomas, *Cuba:*

The Pursuit of Freedom (New York, 1971), p. 871; Bonachea and Martín, *Cuban Insurrection*, pp. 57–59.

53 Bonachea and Martín, *Cuban Insurrection*, pp. 142–143; Serafino Romualdi, *Presidents and Peons: Recollections of a Labor Ambassador in Latin America* (New York, 1967), p. 187.

54 Joaquín Ordoqui, *Elementos para la historia del movimiento obrero* (Havana, 1961), p. 38.

55 Woodward, Jr., "Union Labor and Communism," p. 30; Bonachea and Martín, *Cuban Insurrection*, pp. 203–213.

56 Ordoqui, *Elementos para la historia del movimiento obrero*, pp. 39–40; Bonachea and Martín, *Cuban Insurrection*, p. 287; Romualdi, *Presidents and Peons*, p. 195; Bonachea and Valdés, eds., *Revolutionary Struggle*, p. 363, for Fidel on cane burning; Thomas, *Cuba: The Pursuit of Freedom*, p. 972.

57 Grupo Cubano, *Estudio sobre Cuba*, pp. 1451–1454.

58 O'Connor, *Origins of Socialism in Cuba*, pp. 190–192; Tellería, *Los congresos obreros en Cuba*, pp. 430–469.

59 Grupo Cubano, *Estudio sobre Cuba*, pp. 1455–1456; J. P. Morray, *The Second Revolution in Cuba* (New York, 1962), p. 118; Woodward, Jr., Union Labor and Communism," pp. 36–37.

60 Roberto E. Hernández and Carmelo Mesa-Lago, "Labor Organization and Wages," in *Revolutionary Change in Cuba*, Carmelo Mesa-Lago, ed. (Pittsburgh, 1971), p. 215, date these figures from the mid-1960s.

61 Tellería, *Los congresos obreros en Cuba*, pp. 476–479, 484.

62 Job figures from *Hispanic American Report* (December 1961): 983; on urban changes, see Maruja Acosta and Jorge E. Hardoy, *Urban Reform in Revolutionary Cuba* (New Haven, Conn., 1973).

63 Frente Obrero Revolucionario Democrático Cubano, *Exposición sobre la situación del movimiento sindical y los trabajadores cubanos* (Montevideo, 1962), is a typical counterrevolutionary document; Grupo Cubano, *Estudio sobre Cuba*, p. 1461; Riera Hernández, *Historial obrero cubano*, p. 140; on U.S. labor in Cuba, see Ronald Radosh, *American Labor and United States Foreign Policy* (New York, 1969), pp. 375–382; Romualdi, *Presidents and Peons*, p. 225.

64 O'Connor, *Origins of Socialism in Cuba*, p. 195.

65 On subsequent developments, see Marifeli Pérez-Stable, "Whither the Cuban Working Class," *Latin American Perspectives* 2, no. 4 (Supplement 1975): 60–77.

66 These links are explored extensively in Maurice Zeitlin, *Revolutionary Politics and the Cuban Working Class* (Princeton, N.J., 1967).

67 On Cuba's proletarian internationalism, see *Center for Cuban Studies Newsletter* 3, nos. 4–5 (Winter 1976), special issue, "Cuba's Foreign Policy: Proletarian Internationalism."

6

THE IMPERIALIST THRUST

A host of external economic and political factors have affected Latin American labor movements. One of these is a continued interest by U.S. labor leaders flowing from their past and present co-operation with U.S. foreign policy. Almost from its founding, big labor, represented by the American Federation of Labor (AFL) and then the AFL–CIO (the two merged in 1955), collaborated with the U.S. government and the ruling class. Briefly, its leadership has worked under the assumption that capitalism is the best socioeconomic system. It sees labor as just another pressure group that should seek to reform the system in its favor. Unions exist primarily to acquire economic benefits for members through collective bargaining whenever possible, using other tactics only when this recourse fails. A constantly rising material standard for affiliated workers constitutes labor's long-range goal. That standard, in turn, depends upon the strength of the system; thus labor has reason to support the system. Furthermore, big labor has limited its organizing activities, particularly after unionizing the major industrial sectors. It realizes that capitalists concede benefits to these elite workers only if exploitation rates remain high among the working class as a whole. The terms *bread-and-butter* and *business* unionism used to describe AFL and AFL–CIO politics derive from the emphasis on purely economic goals and from the collaboration with business in maintaining the system at home and overseas.

AFL–CIO foreign policy has flowed from its domestic positions. It combats anticapitalist ideologies and aids and encourages procapitalist unions. It attempts to influence existing organizations and to form new ones in the image of U.S.-style unionism. Where interests overlap, it works with U.S. corporations. Divisions between business and the labor bureaucracy in foreign policy, as in internal affairs, stem from tactical questions, not from basic philosophical antagonisms. Labor obtains several advantages from its alliance with business and government: The greater U.S. economic power is abroad, the less likelihood there is that opposing ideologies will make headway. The wider capitalism's sphere of influence, the larger the market for U.S. goods; the vaster the pool of available natural resources and the higher the profits of U.S. companies, the stronger the system at home. Foreign investment generates profits that help to maintain U.S. union salaries and fringe benefits; also, in conjunction with pliant foreign unions, it assures supplies of strategic materials needed by the national economy. Finally, labor hopes that unionization abroad will deter companies from moving plants overseas, which costs a loss of jobs at home.

U.S. labor's impact abroad must be studied within the larger context of U.S. imperialism. As part of the U.S. foreign policy team, labor's role in Latin America (as elsewhere) is highly political. It operates on several levels. It openly uses financial and cultural means to influence Latin American workers. It also participates in less visible activities such as intelligence gathering and often is used to disguise official U.S. involvement. In short, U.S. labor's foreign policy credo is: What is good for the U.S. government abroad (and therefore for U.S. capitalism) is almost always good for U.S. labor, and therefore for labor everywhere.

Viewed from the other side, the problem takes on a different complexion. U.S. labor activity aids in the continued exploitation of Latin American workers and natural resources. As a procapitalist agency, it supports the status quo. At best, it helps a few workers gain greater material rewards, but only at the expense of others. It also undermines the ability of workers freely to determine their own lives. Furthermore, U.S. labor support of imperialism helps drain Latin America of millions of dollars annually, taking away vital capital and resources needed to provide basic services.

Despite some successes, particularly in countries where the labor movement had not developed before World War II, significant failures have also marked U.S. labor's efforts. Substantial numbers of workers remain outside the reach of U.S. labor, which concentrates on controlling workers in modernized sectors. These unorganized masses flow into the mainstream of national life in an ever growing wave. But even among highly skilled workers, the AFL–CIO sales pitch has not always worked. In Chile, for example, workers overwhelmingly backed a Marxist government after 1970. In Argentina, workers have continued to support Peronism and have taken increasingly anti-imperialist stands.

As used here, the term *labor's foreign policy* refers only to policy as formulated by the big-labor bureaucrats who control most unions. Rank-and-file workers have not always supported them. Opposition to their domestic and foreign positions has shown itself from the time the AFL first formed and continues today.[1]

U.S. AND LATIN AMERICAN LABOR: THE YEARS TO 1945

Socialists and anarchists both attempted to form regional organizations early in this century, but the Pan-American Federation of Labor (PAFL) emerged in 1918 as the first full-fledged continental grouping. Samuel Gompers, head of the AFL, had pushed for a joint Mexican-American labor conference and for a hemispheric organization. His efforts bore fruit when delegates from the United States, Mexico, and four Caribbean nations created the PAFL. The founding congress hailed the event as a labor supplement to the Monroe Doctrine, clearly indicating the AFL view that U.S. labor would dominate the organization. PAFL's two leading affiliates, the AFL and the Mexican CROM, both hoped to profit from the body. The Mexicans voiced concern over the treatment U.S. unions showed their countrymen in the United States by either denying them admission or treating them as second-class citizens. They also urged the AFL to press to free workers, especially Mexican nationals, from U.S. jails. Widespread racism, particularly in the Southwest, where most Mexicans and Mexican-Americans worked, prevented the AFL from satisfying the first request because it lacked power of enforcement over its locals. The second point also proved thorny because Gompers had personally encouraged the jailing of radical organizers. For its part, the AFL worried about companies using Mexican strikebreakers, but this concern evoked no response from CROM.[2]

The increasing concentration of domestic industry and its expansion overseas also preoccupied the AFL. It needed strength to counter growing corporate power and to discourage business from moving abroad to capitalize on cheap labor. Support of, and influence over, a hemispheric labor confederation could bolster AFL influence in national affairs and assure it a voice in foreign policy. The AFL's ability to work together with CROM, a pressure group in Mexico, could make the U.S. government less willing to alienate the AFL. Cooperation with Latin American labor also might avoid criticism that the AFL did not support internationalist goals. In addition, friendly relations with CROM buttressed pro-establishment labor forces in Mexico and helped contain militant groups competing with CROM. This process, involving ever closer collaboration with the government and the ruling class, paved the way for increased U.S. investment by helping mold a labor movement that operated within a capitalist framework.

The PAFL held two congresses, one in 1919 and a second in 1924. Neither managed to do more than pass resolutions of mutual support for the labor movements in the less than a dozen nations that had sent delegations. The demand for representation at the Second Pan-American Financial Congress helped Gompers win a seat at the gathering, but he accomplished little there. Gompers's death in 1924 and CROM's fall from favor five years later doomed the PAFL. Projected congresses for 1929 and 1931 never convened, and a final attempt to resurrect the organization in 1938 failed. Several factors prevented the PAFL from becoming a viable entity. Those important Latin American labor organizations that could have lent support espoused far more radical philosophies than either the AFL or CROM. Many of the groups that joined PAFL represented only small, weak, and often precarious organizations. Finally, the AFL's desire to extend its influence and impose U.S. unionism impeded greater co-ordination.[3]

Two short-lived organizations formed in 1929, the anarchist Asociación Continental Americana de Trabajadores and the Communist Confederación Sindical Latinoamericana. The latter developed an anti-imperialist program with special emphasis on organizing both industrial and rural proletariats and claimed 600,000 members from fourteen countries. It also specifically condemned the PAFL as a U.S. imperialist organization.[4] In 1938, yet another regional confederation formed, the Confederación de Trabajadores de América Latina (CTAL). It grew rapidly under the guidance of the Mexican leader Vicente Lombardo Toledano. By 1944, it boasted 3.3 million members in sixteen nations, a considerable achievement in view of labor's weakness in most Latin American countries.

Unlike the PAFL, this organization excluded U.S. participation, although it maintained links with the Congress of Industrial Organizations (CIO), the AFL's more progressive rival. The exclusion rested on CTAL's position that Latin American workers must resolve their own problems and that imperialism prevented continental self-determination. CTAL endorsed class struggle and proletarian internationalism and called on workers to strive for common economic goals and to create democratic and socialist institutions. When war threatened, CTAL modified its immediate demands, urging workers to form an antifascist bloc.

CTAL incorporated various ideologies, but Communist organizations predominated. It held congresses and sponsored regional conferences, convening meetings for petroleum, agricultural and forest, and transport workers. The organization lost impetus after 1945 under capitalism's Cold War counteroffensive. Gradually, repressive domestic anti-Communist regimes either forced most of its affiliates underground or severely crippled them through restrictive legislation. By the late 1950s, the organization existed mostly on paper, and it officially disbanded in 1962.[5]

THE COLD WAR AND IMPERIALISM: AGENCIES AND ORGANIZATIONS

The onset of war reawakened interest in Latin America on the part of U.S. labor and government. In 1941, Nelson Rockefeller, co-ordinator for inter-American affairs heading the Office of Inter-

American Affairs in the State Department, arranged to have the AFL and CIO sponsor and partially fund tours for Latin American labor leaders. The Bureau of Labor Statistics undertook a series of studies on Latin America, and several publications aimed at the area rolled off government presses. In 1943, the first labor attachés arrived in U.S. embassies; four years later, the Labor Department established a permanent international labor office that included Latin America under its jurisdiction.

The AFL, hoping to confront CTAL and establish a dominant position in inter-American labor affairs, proposed a regional entity; but the U.S. government frowned on the plan, fearing that it might inhibit co-operation with the CTAL's antifascist front. In 1945, however, the AFL again called for the formation of a hemispheric labor body, this time with government approval. Two years later, it enlisted a former OSS operative, Serafino Romualdi, as full-time "labor ambassador" to Latin America, a post he occupied until 1965. Romualdi embarked on a continental tour in 1946–1947, marshaling support for the proposed regional confederation. In 1948, a congress met and founded the Confederación Inter-Americana de Trabajadores (CIT) as a rival to the CTAL and to Argentina's Peronist CGT, which the AFL considered fascist. Two years later, CIT became the Organización Regional Inter-Americana de Trabajadores (ORIT).[6]

Fathered by the AFL, ORIT adopted similar ideological positions, although not without some internal dissension. The organization's prime goal is to fight Communism and to promote "democratic trade unionism." It preaches reform within the capitalist system, denying the existence of class antagonisms. Instead, it sees Latin American labor as just another interest group, comparable to the military, the church, or large landowners. As such, labor needs strengthening in order to compete with the others on equal terms. ORIT points to the United States as an example of the rewards that the system can give the working class and organized labor. Labor's goals, aside from fighting Communism, are full employment for members and ever increasing economic benefits. It never examines whether workers can actually achieve equality under capitalism. It also dodges the issue of U.S. imperialism. It argues pragmatically that Latin America must accept the fact that the United States will play a major role on the continent because of its geographic proximity and advanced stage of economic development.[7]

ORIT supports only what it calls democratic unions, even if these depend upon political parties or are government-controlled. It maintains, however, that unions should be nonpolitical, that it endorses no political ideology, and that it does not take part in political acts. Yet, it works closely, for example, with the U.S. State Department. The U.S. embassy in Mexico printed an ORIT publication, and the U.S. Information Agency produced a documentary film praising ORIT. In addition, it took such "nonpolitical" stands as supporting the Bay of Pigs invasion of Cuba, the ouster of Goulart in 1964, and the 1965 U.S. intervention in the Dominican Republic. It also worked closely with the Mujalists in the Cuban CTC before the Revolution and has continued to work with the CTC-in-Exile in its activities against the Cuban government. On the other hand, it has not denounced the current Brazilian and Chilean governments despite the fact that they have severely curtailed all trade-union freedoms. ORIT's criteria for approval or censure solely depend upon a particular government's relationship with the United States.[8]

ORIT's size is hard to estimate. Optimistic observers claim that the organization includes some fifty to fifty-five national labor organizations and approximately 28 to 30 million members. Effective membership, of course, is much lower because Latin American labor groups grossly overestimate their size. ORIT receives funds from a number of known sources and probably from several unknown as well. The AFL-CIO provides over 50 percent of its monies, but it also gets funds from U.S. government agencies and international labor organizations.[9]

ORIT engages in varied activities apart from its regular congresses, at which delegates gather to discuss anti-Communist strategies and general objectives. Education of trade-unionists constitutes one activity. In 1951, it began sponsoring candidates for the trade-union leaders' school at the University of Puerto Rico, a project it continued until the U.S. government took over

several years later. In 1962, it opened a special trade-union institute in Cuernavaca, Mexico, on land donated by the state governor
and declared tax-free. There ORIT runs regular courses, like those
for peasant leaders and women trade-unionists, and seminars such
as the one on peasants and ideology held in 1971. ORIT also
co-operates with several U.S. government agencies. For example,
it set up a special Department of Economic and Social Affairs to
co-ordinate with the Alliance for Progress. In addition, it sponsors
periodic inter-American conferences such as its 1967 seminar on
campesinos or a labor education seminar for seventy Latin American labor experts held in conjunction with UNESCO in 1966.[10]

ORIT is a regional organization, but extraregional entities, such
as the International Trade Secretariats (ITS), also play a role in
Latin America. These are world groupings of national industrial
unions in a particular industry or related group of industries.
During the 1950s, many of these established Latin American
offices. In Peru, no less than five opened branches before 1960.
Most ITS rely heavily on U.S. affiliates for funding, but several
receive substantial financing from private foundations. The State,
County, and Municipal Employees' ITS, the Public Services International, and the International Federation of Journalists, for
example, got grants from the Gotham and Granery Funds, respec-
tively, both proven CIA conduits. The ITS hold Latin American
regional congresses, sponsor educational courses, and provide
support for local members.[11]

A variety of U.S. agencies also maintain considerable interest
in labor matters. The Alliance for Progress provides, among other
things, financial assistance. Its first labor loan, for example, consisted of a $400,000 grant to a Honduran union for housing, which
one source characterized as an outright "reward for anti-Communist zeal to a company controlled union." Universities
contribute, too. Cornell University, for example, has co-operated
through its School of Industrial and Labor Relations by training
Latin American labor leaders and, under a USAID contract, set
up the Department of Labor Relations at the then-conservative
University of Chile.[12]

The AFL–CIO, however, is the most important architect of U.S. labor foreign policy. Recently, it spent some 23 percent of its budget on international affairs each year. It is the largest contributor to ORIT and pumps as much as $2 million annually into a special projects fund to complement the $1 million flowing into its international activities accounts. How this money actually gets spent is known only to the AFL–CIO top brass.[13]

Until recently, the AFL–CIO's most important creation has been the American Institute for Free Labor Development (AIFLD).[14] Inaugurated in 1962 by and under the policy direction of the AFL–CIO, this organization was formed "primarily in response to the threat of Castroite infiltration and eventual control of major labor movements within Latin America." It is dedicated to "strengthening the democratic labor sector in terms of institution building . . . in terms of technical assistance and social projects . . . primarily in the areas of education and training, manpower studies, cooperatives, and housing."[15] Clearly, AIFLD's central functions are to combat noncapitalist influences within the ranks of Latin American labor (it also opposes the Confederación Latino-Americana de Trabajadores [CLAT], formerly the Confederación Latino-americana de Sindicatos Cristianos [CLASC], of Christian Democratic origin) and to strengthen U.S. labor's influence and the U.S. business image in order to develop procapitalist, reformist unions while maintaining Latin America as a field for investment.

Business, government, and labor provide AIFLD's main resources, and they share common goals. As George Meany, chief of the AFL–CIO, said, "We believe in the capitalist system and we are members of the capitalist society. We are dedicated to the preservation of this system, which rewards the workers."[16] This sentiment is totally consonant with the words of AIFLD's expresident and current chairman of the board, J. Peter Grace (head of W. R. Grace, a company with extensive interests in Latin America), that AIFLD must "work toward a common goal in Latin America, namely supporting the democratic form of government, the capitalistic system and general well-being of the individual." AIFLD, he continued, "is an outstanding example of a national consensus effectively at work for the national interest of the United States and for the best interests of the people of Latin America."[17] Just how this works we shall see later.

The U.S. government has provided the bulk of AIFLD's support. Between 1962 and 1967, 89 percent of its funds derived from USAID; labor contributed 6 percent; and business, represented by grants from over seventy corporations, only 5 percent. This means that almost $16 million of government money flowed into AIFLD. Government funding has increased steadily, from 64 percent in 1962 to 92 percent in 1967; by 1971, AIFLD ranked as the fifteenth largest recipient of USAID contracts, with a total of $7.6 million. At times, AIFLD garners support from other sources. Between 1961 and 1963, one writer claims that it received nearly $1 million from CIA conduits.[18] Heavy government funding strengthens AIFLD's position and means that fewer funds are potentially available to other organizations in the labor field, giving it a practical monopoly in areas such as workers' housing.

Big business, private institutions, and labor are amply represented within AIFLD's governing body. Aside from Grace and Meany, executives from Anaconda Copper, Gulf Oil International, Johnson and Johnson International, Merck, Owens-Illinois, and Pan American Airways, and members of the Institute of International Education and the Fund for International Social and Economic Education, both donees of CIA fronts, hold or have held AIFLD positions.[19]

Within its overall plan, AIFLD has two central functions. First, it trains labor leaders, based on the belief that the practice of Latin American unions of forming political ties is undesirable. Training takes place on both regional and local levels. Local seminars lasting one week to three months instruct those attending in history and international activities of the labor movement, organization, structure, finances, collective bargaining, labor legislation, and democracy versus totalitarianism. "The aim of these local seminars, as well as more advanced AIFLD courses, is to give basic trade union education to union members, develop leadership skills, and teach methods of strengthening their unions against totalitarian infiltration and tactics."[20] Selected students move to regional and national classes, and a few ultimately go to the headquarters at Front Royal, Virginia. AIFLD's Centro de Estudios Laborales del Perú, for example, spent about $200,000 annually. Opened in Lima during 1962–1963, the center also ran a branch in Arequipa, giving night courses, short seminars in various provinces, and longer residential programs for the best students from the seminars. In all, 11,800 Peruvians have received AIFLD training, including almost all important labor leaders of the Confederación de Trabajadores del Perú, the country's largest labor confederation and an exponent of AIFLD-style unionism.[21]

AIFLD's *1975 Annual Progress Report* states that 259,876 persons have taken one of its courses. The Front Royal Center has graduated almost 2,000 individuals to date. The composition of the 1972 trainees shows that school's breadth. Of 140 persons receiving degrees (110 men and 30 women), 80 came from Spanish-speaking countries, 20 from Brazil, and another 40 from English-speaking areas.[22] AIFLD sponsors courses in labor economics. This program, first run by Loyola University in New Orleans and then by Georgetown University in Washington, D.C., now works out of Mount Vernon College in the nation's capital and has graduated 145 people. The institute also underwrites periodic hemispheric educational gatherings such as its VII Inter-American Labor Economics Course of the University of Miami Seminar on the Caribbean, hosted by the Center for Advanced International Studies there. On a regional basis, the Central American Institute for Trade Union Studies, founded in 1963, organizes regular programs for regional labor leaders. Lastly, AIFLD publishes books and pamphlets; recent releases consisted of a primer on democracy and a history of the world trade-union movement in Spanish.[23]

AIFLD's second major function involves numerous specific projects. These include education for technical assistance in the field of social service activities; literacy, vocational, and health and sanitation training (all of which include the inevitable democracy versus totalitarianism lectures); so-called Impact Projects, which encompass donations of items such as sewing machines to poorer unions; and just plain union-to-union assistance programs, which may involve a simple gift of office equipment or assistance in a major undertaking.

In Peru, for example, the AIFLD Social Projects Division helps local organizations apply for loans and assists in steering them through appropriate bureaucracies. The Impact Projects Fund and the Co-Operative Advisory Service lend money to consumer co-operatives and credit unions and to worker-run businesses. At least four such projects (a printing firm, a bus line, a sewing co-operative, and a textile factory) have been funded. This type of endeavor is based on the same logic as the type of land reform that distributes small plots to peasants. Workers gain a stake in the system through property ownership and, in theory at least, become its defenders. In underdeveloped areas, where capital for industrial ventures is scarce, it builds small industry, which does not compete with larger national or international companies but in fact often complements them as feeders. It also ties workers to AIFLD or some other U.S. agency financially. AIFLD also instructs labor people in organizing social projects in their communities. Citing the Peruvian case again, community efforts in the mushrooming shantytowns (*barriadas*), a potential hotbed of discontent, receive financial aid through AIFLD-educated residents. That aid serves a dual function: It familiarizes participants with capitalism's way through immediate pay-off, and it counters efforts by members of militant groups to rally support among the poor and marginal groups.[24]

Housing is another major AIFLD area. Projects exist in over a dozen Latin American countries, and AIFLD has spent over $77 million on 18,048 units. Housing funds almost invariably are awarded to staunchly anti-Communist unions facing competition from progressive rivals. In theory, the housing provides individual unions with both an incentive to offer to recruits and a reward to give to faithful members. In actuality, cost factors mean that only middle-level bureaucrats can afford individual units. Nor have plans made in Washington gone according to schedule. In several cases, the projects have stalled; and in others, the end product has been of an inferior quality.

AIFLD also administers the Regional Revolving Loan Fund, underwritten initially by USAID grants for $625 million. This fund totals some $812.4 million and has lent monies in twelve countries for five-year terms at little or no interest. More recently, funds have been channeled into trade-union credit unions as a means of providing loans to union members. The process gives individuals access to credit otherwise unavailable, but it also ties them firmly into consumerist patterns and debts that bind them closer to the system. Funds have also gone to finance vacation centers, a cause that further divides elite, pro-U.S. unions from the bulk of the working class.

Intelligence, according to some sources, is a key AIFLD function. In addition to providing cover for U.S. government operatives, the organization itself serves as an information-gathering arm. The recruitment process for seminars from the local to national levels and applications for housing projects form an ideal means for gathering data on individual unions and their members. A brief glance at official application forms shows the wealth of information they provide. Information is channeled back to Washington, where government agencies other than AIFLD can tap it for their own purposes.[25]

AIFLD works closely with a host of public and private U.S. institutions. A recent high-level meeting in Cuernavaca, Mexico, for country program directors and Washington-based AIFLD officers indicates this relationship. Those present included Arturo Jáuregui, secretary-general of ORIT and an AIFLD director; the head of the government-sponsored Mexican labor confederation CTM; directors of the Asian-American Free Labor Institute and African-American Labor Center, both roughly equivalent to AIFLD in their respective areas; top-level aides from the Alliance for Progress, the Peace Corps, and USAID; the co-ordinator for inter-American affairs for the secretary of state; representatives from the Inter-American Development Bank and Council of the Americas; and the labor studies director at Florida International University in Miami. Delegates from seven ITS also attended.[26]

U.S. Labor Foreign Policy in Action

A growing body of evidence has become available concerning U.S. labor activities abroad and its role in U.S. foreign policy. The brief examples that follow illustrate these operations. In Brazil, for example, Romualdi met with President Dutra in 1947 and with government help established contacts with labor leaders who could be counted on for support against both the Communist Party and the PTB. U.S. labor, however, did not move into Brazil until the late 1950s. From 1956 on, ORIT affiliates created a series of state- and local-level training programs and arranged trips for labor leaders to the United States.

U.S. labor and its allies really swung into action during Goulart's presidency. ORIT, AIFLD, and the U.S. embassy, through its labor attachés, worked hard to support non-Communist and nonradical labor groups and to oppose the left-dominated CGT, the nation's principal progressive labor organization (see Chapter 4). This effort climaxed at the Third National Labor Congress of 1962, at which U.S. labor specialists flown in expressly for the occasion plotted strategy for the so-called democratic trade-union leaders. They convinced this minority bloc to pull out of the gathering and thus undermined attempts to unify labor. The Movimento Democrático Sindical, under its motto "God, private property, and free enterprise," received aid and advice in sponsoring its own meetings and in setting up trade-union courses. In addition, the Instituto Cultural do Trabalho (ICT), AIFLD's local affiliate, and an institute for labor studies partially financed by U.S. business concerns trained labor personnel and disseminated procapitalist and anti-Communist labor publicity. AIFLD moved into the rural Northeast during 1963 in response to growing radical movements there, initiating a series of training and aid programs for reformist labor groups and leaders.

U.S. labor moved against Goulart and progressive labor organizations in other ways, working to neutralize possible support for the government before and during the coup. In 1963, AIFLD trained a special all-Brazilian class in the United States. These activities prompted AIFLD's social projects director to testify in

Congress that "what happened in Brazil on April 1 did not just happen—it was planned—and planned months in advance. Many of the trade union leaders—some of whom were actually trained in our institute—were involved in the revolution and in the overthrow of the Goulart regime."[27] Shortly after the coup, the AFL–CIO inter-American affairs director interviewed the military junta's chief, asking for expanded AFL–CIO activity in Brazil, which soon happened. The ICT stepped up its activities and by the middle of 1973 had trained 28,892 trade-unionists in regional courses and almost 1,000 more in its São Paulo center. AIFLD, in conjunction with private U.S. organizations such as the Co-Operative League of the United States of America and government agencies such as the CIA, continued its rural activities after 1964. It enlarged training and service centers, and by the early 1970s some 24,000 unionists and 3,500 *campesino* leaders had received AIFLD-related training and social projects existed in every state. Because the military now rigidly controls all political and union activity, most rural unions only "hold democratic elections to choose leaders who draw handsome salaries, take courses from AIFLD, and do very little."[28] ITS have also been at work in Brazil. The International Federation of Petroleum and Chemical Workers, for example, was expressly invited to help "clean up" supposedly Communist-infiltrated unions. This task has involved, in part, the distribution of funds to friendly union leaders and paid trips to the United States.[29]

In Chile, a strong working-class movement has backed leftist political parties since the 1930s. Once the Cold War began, U.S. labor worked hard to strengthen non-Communist unions and federations. The effort continued in the 1960s, when ORIT and AIFLD attempted to split the trade-union movement by dividing the left-controlled Central Unica de Trabajadores (CUT), Chile's leading labor central, through peeling off the minority conservative unions. To accomplish that, they urged all entities to join the CUT and paid back dues for those so inclined in order to allow them voting privileges to make their staged walkout more impressive. The maneuver failed, but AIFLD did create the Confederación Nacional de Trabajadores (CNT), a conservative body whose largest affiliate is a Valparaíso-based maritime federation. AIFLD graduates figure prominantly among its leadership and its stated policy, true to U.S.-style unions, is "to cooperate with owners and the directors of big business."

AIFLD education programs grew particularly rapidly after 1970, when a Marxist coalition, the Unidad Popular, won the presidential elections. By that time, about 10,000 persons had graduated from local courses, a figure equivalent to 3 to 4 percent of Chile's total trade-union membership; and from February 1972 to February 1973, the number of Chileans enrolled at Front Royal increased almost 400 percent. Although the CNT made little headway among Chilean workers, U.S.-trained people played key roles in sabotaging the Unidad Popular's plans whenever possible. In the copper mines, where Christian Democrats, Socialists, and Communists all shared a following among the workers, procapitalist unionists tried every possible tactic to prolong conflicts between the workers and the government and had some success. U.S. labor strategy earned its best results among the so-called *gremios* (independent worker-employer associations). Many of the Chilean *gremio* leaders maintained close contact both with right-wing political groups and with the U.S. embassy and U.S. labor. Recurrent strikes by *gremios* in the distribution sector (clearly financed by outside sources) disrupted the economy and helped prepare the way for the fascist coup of 1973 that imposed a brutal military dictatorship.[30]

U.S. organizations played no less a role in the Chilean countryside. By 1967, AIFLD had trained over 3,000 *campesino* leaders. The International Development Foundation (IDF) proved more important. It opened operations in Chile during 1964 as a private foundation, emphasizing peasant organization. Almost single-handedly, it formed the Confederación Nacional Campesina by supplying legal assistance, technical skills, and money to create unions willing to join. This peasant confederation, in contrast with similar groups mobilized by the left, aimed at achieving agrarian reform through establishing small private holdings rather than through any collective or co-operative ventures. When it became known that IDF received funds directly from CIA fronts, the organization retired from Chile, and USAID took over its programs. A number of U.S. sources also supported the Rural Education Institute, a conservative Catholic institution backed by the National Agricultural Society (which represents large landholders) that conducted classes for peasants and peasant leaders. Espousing a violently anti-leftist line, the institute by 1965 succeeded in creating twenty-three education centers in which it trained over 4,000 persons. Naturally, both IDF and USAID quickly became substantial supporters of the institute.[31]

U.S. agencies have also intervened in the Dominican Republic. Before the assassination of the long-time dictator General Rafael Trujillo in 1961, the AFL–CIO already had trained a number of Dominican exiles in both Puerto Rico and New York. They quickly returned to the island and soon formed the Frente de Obreros Unidos para Syndicatos Autónomos (FOUPSA), a coalition of anti-Trujillo groups. Shortly after its founding, the AFL–CIO urged a purge of all "undesirable elements"; when FOUPSA refused, the AFL–CIO even resorted to bribery. It utilized the same tactic during the 1961–1962 general strike, offering FOUPSA's head $30,000 to call off the movement. When this ploy failed, a defamation campaign against FOUPSA officials and the organization, charging that it was really a Communist front, achieved the desired result. FOUPSA split into two factions. One, the Bloque FOUPSA Libre became the Confederación Nacional de Trabajadores Libres (CONATRAL), under AFL–CIO-trained leaders. By 1962, the AFL–CIO and ORIT, both of which used Cuban exiles from Batista days to train Dominicans, almost totally dominated CONATRAL.[32]

CONATRAL's positions reflected U.S. influence. It steadfastly opposed any unification attempts in the Dominican movement, despite contrary statements on the part of its leaders and the AFL–CIO. It opted for bread-and-butter unionism, summed up by the position that "unions exist to obtain benefits for their members—period." That attitude clashed with the political realities of the situation. The Dominican government, like most governments in Latin America, could regulate wages, control strikes, rule over the collective bargaining procedure, and generally manipulate labor for its own purposes. Nevertheless, CONATRAL refused support for the populist Juan Bosch in the presidency, even though he allowed labor relative freedom, advocated profit sharing, and promoted recognition of majority unions as legitimate bargaining agents in each sector rather than using government power to give favored unions that position. CONATRAL justified its actions with the usual declarations of noninvolvement in politics, but its stand really mirrored the fact that the United States disapproved of Bosch.[33]

Bosch's case merits further attention because it sheds light on the workings of imperialism. When Trujillo's regime ended, Bosch emerged as the strongest candidate in the elections, which he duly won. Although U.S. organizations openly voiced their distrust and later did everything to assist the military coup that finally ousted him in 1963, other agencies prepared for the contingency that he would assume power. The International Institute for Labor Studies, headed by the well-known social democrat Norman Thomas, funded the Inter-American Center for Social Studies in the Dominican Republic, which trained most of the technicians and high-level government officials who served under Bosch. Later, it became known that the institute received backing from the J. M. Kaplan Fund, a CIA conduit. Furthermore, the institute's vice-president, a man active in Dominican affairs and exposed as a CIA agent, had overseen the creation of a pro-Bosch peasant federation that mobilized the rural vote. Once Bosch's term began, however, U.S. operatives allowed the federation to disintegrate slowly. This fact, combined with AFL–CIO-fostered divisions in the labor movement, left Bosch without any substantial pillars of organized support and facilitated his overthrow.[34]

Additional actions by CONATRAL and imperialist agencies deserve mention. Shortly before the military coup that ousted Bosch, CONATRAL paid for a full-page advertisement in a local newspaper calling for the military to save the country from Communism, a barely disguised invitation for the action that soon took place. It played no active role in the popular uprising against the Cabral government of April 1965 that led directly to U.S. military intervention. It did, however, praise the invasion, echoing the AFL–CIO, State Department, and ORIT line that the intrusion thwarted Communism and prevented another Cuba. In the 1966 elections, it almost openly supported the reactionary candidate backed by the United States (and the AFL–CIO, ORIT, and the like), even though he took on an antilabor position. These stands by CONATRAL's leadership, which rarely if ever consulted the rank and file before issuing the organization's official statements, cost the organization. After its endorsement of the intervention, several unions resigned, and membership fell from an estimated 100,000 to about 25,000.[35]

AIFLD operated actively in the Dominican Republic. It trained peasant leaders in conjunction with ORIT and the AFL–CIO and initiated several social projects, including a housing development for sugar workers in the town of San Pedro de Macorís. Investment for the scheduled $3 million complex derived 67 percent from the Inter-American Development Bank and 33 percent from an AFL–CIO loan guaranteed by USAID. However, the project soon ran into trouble when AIFLD's hidden conditions came into the open. No competitive bidding for construction contracts had taken place, and AIFLD apparently had awarded them at will. AIFLD had also insisted that only CONATRAL unions work on the complex. And, as in similar projects elsewhere, AIFLD had restricted access to the new housing to CONATRAL members. The illegality of these procedures under Dominican law temporarily forced the project to halt. Finally completed in 1967 through direct AID financing, the complex amounted to 110 units, rather than the 700 to 900 originally promised.[36]

After 1965, CONATRAL remained isolated and unrepresentative despite a massive propaganda campaign to enhance its image. Between 1962 and 1969, AIFLD spent $1.6 million in the country (not counting housing). In the late 1960s, it tried but failed to form a new organization. Then, in 1971, AIFLD created the National Confederation of Dominican Workers to replace the moribund CONATRAL. However, it never prospered because its membership consisted mostly of company unions and tightly controlled progovernment organizations.

As U.S. investment grew, doubling between 1965 and 1975 to nearly $400 million, labor strategy changed. In response to a growing anti-imperialist consciousness among Dominicans, AIFLD reduced its programs. The government-labor apparatus concentrated less on the labor movement and worked more directly with multinational corporations to squash militant working-class activity. The ITS came to play a larger role as AIFLD's activities met increasing criticism from nationalist and anti-imperialist labor elements. Several ITS expanded their activities through funds from U.S. affiliates, which, in turn, received monies from AIFLD. The International Transport Workers' Federation and the Postal, Telegraph, and Telephone International (PTTI) both worked to strengthen reformist unions against existing progressive unions in their respective sectors. The government encouraged these efforts by using force against independent labor organizations and leaders.

Management took matters into its own hands on the properties of the multinationals. At Gulf and Western's La Romana sugar estate, the company hired Cuban exiles and former Trujillo thugs to break the existing union, branding it as Communist. It then formed a company union and forced Dominican workers to join. However, it excluded all Haitian *braceros,* who formed the lowest-paid sector of the work force. Falconbridge Nickel Company used similar tactics, hiring a known CIA operative to oversee the creation of a company union and destroy the existing workers' organization.[37]

U.S. labor activities in Argentina over the past decades provide further insights into the workings of labor foreign policy. The AFL–CIO opposed the Peronist labor movement almost from its origins (see Chapter 4). In 1947, the AFL–CIO formally broke relations with the CGT and threw its support behind COASI, which was composed of non-Peronist and non-Communist unions. It continued to back these so-called democratic trade-unions (the name invariably given to pro-U.S. factions) in opposition to the "fascistic" Peronist unions throughout Perón's terms in office. The AFL–CIO sent several missions to Argentina during this period to investigate charges of state intervention within the labor movement, and it carried on an active propaganda campaign throughout the hemisphere against both the CGT and the Agrupación de

Trabajadores Latino Americanos Sindicalizados (ATLAS), the Peronist continental labor organization.[38]

After Perón's ouster in September 1955, the AFL–CIO maintained its anti-Peronist policy. Within a year of the coup, U.S. labor officials arranged a series of meetings between the government and "democratic" labor leaders to co-ordinate strategy for restructuring the labor movement without the now-outlawed Peronists and combating continued Peronist support within a majority of the unions. But internal factionalism and a deteriorating economic situation prevented the unification of the labor movement.[39]

The AFL–CIO pursued its efforts. During the Frondizi period (May 1958–March 1962), for example, George Meany met with the Argentine president and agreed upon a new plan to reconstitute the CGT, excluding only Communist and hard-line Peronist unions. That strategy also failed. Despite tacit government backing, the "democratic" unions could never muster enough strength to dominate the movement and so reverted to divisionist tactics.[40]

By 1963, it became obvious that only a change in tactics could rebuild the labor movement and still maintain procapitalist unionism. Accordingly, the AFL–CIO tried to split the Peronist ranks, actively courting those right-wing elements that they thought could be won over by material concessions. This new stance resulted from earlier failures but also flowed from events inside the country and the labor movement. Foreign investment, much of it from the United States, surged in the 1960s. Thus, as in other dependent areas, the interests of U.S. business and labor (and therefore the U.S. government) coincided. Both sought an anti-Communist, procapitalist labor movement dedicated to bread-and-butter unionism. Divisions inside the Peronist camp also dictated the new strategy. Gradually, a conciliatory labor bureaucracy emerged within several major unions. These officials saw an opportunity to consolidate their lucrative positions through dealings with national authorities. The constant deterioration of the economic situation after 1955 afforded them the chance to secure their positions by pursuing purely economic goals. At the same time, a number of militant leaders, backed by growing numbers within the rank and file, openly began to link workers' demands to an anti-imperialist, pro-socialist position. U.S. labor's policy change thus came in reaction to the emergence of a militant left-wing labor sector and a growing imperialist penetration of the Argentine economy.[41]

As elsewhere, AIFLD became one major agent of U.S. policy, and its activities in Argentina increased markedly after 1963. The number of grants to leaders rose and for the first time included selected CGT officials. AIFLD also initiated a series of housing projects, including its largest in Latin America. Through 1974, almost half of its housing expenditures went to Argentina. Using monies loaned by a number of private U.S. insurance companies, AIFLD selected four unions from fourteen applicants for the project (in all, it solicited twenty unions), including the elite Light and Power Workers' Union, one of the country's largest and a particular target for U.S. influence because of its right-leaning Peronist leadership. At the same time the Inter-American Development Bank supplied loans for housing projects in the interior, which were also awarded either to anti-Peronist or right-wing Peronist unions. Much of the money earmarked for housing only lined the pockets of union leaders, and the housing units, costing $6,000 to $12,000 each (a substantial sum for any Argentine worker), went mainly to middle-echelon bureaucrats. Given the intelligence-gathering function of housing projects, the emphasis in Argentina, where AIFLD faced a difficult situation, is not surprising. Argentine unions also received seventeen impact projects involving substantial loans.[42]

Strong nationalistic and anti-U.S. sentiment among rank-and-file workers prevented AIFLD from operating as openly in Argentina as it did in other countries. It therefore increasingly combined its programs with those of ITS, a tactic later employed elsewhere when nationalist or progressive elements threatened AIFLD and U.S. labor's position. By 1974, eight ITS (incorporating thirty-two local unions) functioned in Argentina, and the PTTI maintained a subregional office there. These organizations cosponsored seminars with AIFLD, gradually extending their programs into the interior. In all, 2,682 workers from twenty-one unions received training in courses and seminars by 1969.[43]

As class struggle escalated, AIFLD found itself on the defensive. In 1968, it opened an office in Córdoba, a center of the militant, progressive workers' movement and focal point of opposition to the right-wing bureaucrats, mostly located in Buenos Aires. Soon, however, it closed the office and in 1974 shut down its entire Argentine operation under pressure from the nationalist left-wing of the labor movement. To offset these reverses, U.S. labor increasingly relied on the ITS. Education programs have become part of ITS internal structures, although AIFLD graduates conduct the classes. Local unions also give internal education modeled on programs created in Washington, D.C., and Front Royal and taught by AIFLD trainees. Both these changes have lowered the U.S. labor profile. AIFLD and the U.S. embassy, however, still sponsor trips for labor leaders to the United States and bring officials to the United States for training and indoctrination through the Inter-American Labor Economics Program, officially administered by the OAS. AIFLD also has supplied funds for union-related projects, granting five large loans to finance savings and loans institutions for specific unions between 1969 and 1973.[44]

Although the United States and its agents cannot play as decisive a role in Argentina as they can in nations with less mature labor movements, their presence gives procapitalist unions extra resources in their struggle against nationalist and anti-imperialist forces. In smaller countries, this type of aid can have an important impact. In Guatemala, U.S. labor aided the conservative coup that overthrew the progressive regime of Jacobo Arbenz in 1954, and its continued efforts in that country led one observer to say that "US government and representative agencies have successfully dominated much of the organizational framework above the local level" since that time.[45] In Guyana, U.S. efforts helped topple Prime Minister Cheddi Jagan in 1963. There, CIA agents worked as labor people, AIFLD maintained anti-Jagan trade-union leaders on its full-time payroll, and the American Federation of State, Country, and Municipal Employees supplied almost $1 million in strike benefits to anti-Jagan forces through the Public Services International.[46]

U.S. labor has particularly targeted industries or nations considered vital to the U.S. economy. When Ecuador struck oil, U.S. labor programs there greatly expanded. As of 1975, over 10 percent of the entire labor force, including a heavy representation from the oil sector, had received some kind of AIFLD-related education.[47] In Jamaica, similar events occurred in the bauxite industry once the international giants, Alcan Aluminum, Kaiser Aluminum, and Reynolds Metals, moved in. In 1952, the United Steel Workers of America (USWA) aided the foundation and growth of the Jamaican National Workers' Union (NWU) among bauxite workers. By 1954, the NWU, with support from the USWA, had defeated its more progressive rival union and since then has monopolized that sector. Although the Jamaican workers have received some material benefits, the major advantages accrued to the USWA and the companies. The steelworkers assured an orderly supply of bauxite, upon which jobs of aluminum workers in the United States depend. The union has called no strike since the 1950s and has settled all disputes peaceably. The companies gained labor peace and an additional bonus: The union screens out workers who disagree with its philosophy. A survey of corporate executives, for example, found that they viewed the NWU as "a useful social institution serving a police function, which is of value to the company."[48]

In the 1960s and 1970s, three additional groups have received special attention from U.S. labor. Increased demands for agrarian reform and rising sentiment against foreign agribusinesses such as United Brands (formerly United Fruit) have led to emphasis on programs for peasants and agricultural workers. In 1967, 74 rural leaders, including a group representing unions of United Brands' workers, graduated from AIFLD–USAID programs. The 1974 Front Royal course included one semester specifically for banana workers from Central and South America. Women constitute another group recently getting more attention. AIFLD now holds a series of special courses for women at Front Royal and in the field. Because increasing numbers of women join the work force annually, this effort, like the one aimed at rural workers, prepares for the future as well as dealing with the present. Such educational efforts have a multiplier effect that can be important in areas where no solid independent union movement exists. A study by the Central American Labor Studies Institute indicates the importance of outside training in such an area. Of 174 graduates surveyed, 85 had been elected to a union office, 72 organized a new union, 50 percent gave an educational course, and 70 percent handled one or more grievances at their workplace. The survey also noted that 80 percent of the graduates favored the Central American Common Market, which benefits major U.S. corporations far more than it does the people of the countries involved.[49]

Opposition to overt U.S. labor activities inside Latin America has mounted in recent years. It is now also growing in the United States. The rank and file are not consulted on AFL–CIO activities abroad or informed about their intent. For example, one study acknowledged that in response to questions about AIFLD, "no more than two out of fifty labor officials knew even the barest detail about the organization . . . and not a single one of hundreds of union members canvassed had any idea at all of the existence of AIFLD!"[50] But this situation is changing. Recently, workers formed the Union Committee for an All-Labor AIFLD, which seeks to eliminate the influence of government, business, and the CIA from the organization and turn it into one controlled by workers and unions. The Santa Clara County Labor Council recently confronted a high-ranking AIFLD official and condemned its role in Chile. Unionists at the 1975 convention of the Communications Workers of America expressed opposition to U.S. unions engaging in covert activities in Latin America, and other labor gatherings have expressed similar sentiments.[51]

CONCLUSION

External factors have influenced and continue to influence organized labor in Latin America. Among these factors are foreign labor organizations. The AFL forged links between North and

South American workers in the 1910s. From the first, it sought to influence Latin American labor in reformist directions. U.S. labor's interest in Latin America grew proportionately with the increase in U.S. investment. Beginning in the late 1930s, U.S. labor and the U.S. government openly coordinated their efforts to ensure Latin American labor's co-operation in the anti-Axis war effort. After World War II, they worked to prevent the growth of anti-capitalist unions and to build business unionism throughout the continent. Furthermore, U.S. labor bureaucrats actively supported the efforts of U.S. government and business to topple unfriendly regimes in Latin America.

The results of U.S. labor's foreign policy have varied. In some cases, it succeeded in checking the growth of leftist organizations and in building up or forming unions in its own image. In other cases, its policies have shown meager results. U.S. efforts could not contain the rise of an anti-imperialist, socialist consciousness among Cuban workers or curb Peronist influence in the ranks of Argentine labor. Chilean workers voted solidly for a Marxist president in 1970 despite considerable expenditure of funds and energies by U.S. labor and the U.S. government to prevent it. U.S. labor claims to sponsor democratic unions, but its greatest successes in Latin America have come in countries with authoritarian military regimes and its strongest supporters have been tied to conservative political parties and governments.

NOTES

[1] Some of this material appeared in "U.S. and Latin American Labor: The Dynamics of Imperialist Control," *Latin American Perspectives* 3, no. 1 (Winter 1976): 45–69, and in Juan E. Corradi, June Nash, and Hobart A. Spalding, Jr., eds., *Ideology and Social Change in Latin America* (New York, 1977), pp. 55–91.

[2] On early relationships, see James D. Cockcroft, *Intellectual Precursors of the Mexican Revolution, 1900–1913* (Austin, Tex., 1968), pp. 126–127; and Harvey A. Levenstein, *Labor Organization in the United States and Mexico* (Westport, Conn., 1971), chaps. 1, 2, and 6; on PAFL in general, see Sinclair Snow, *The Pan American Federation of Labor* (Durham, N.C., 1964).

3 Levenstein, *Labor Organization in the United States and Mexico*, chaps. 7, 8, and p. 162.

4 Brief reviews in Moisés Poblete Troncoso and Ben G. Burnett, *The Rise of the Latin American Labor Movement* (New Haven, Conn., 1960), p. 133; Juan Arcos, *El sindicalismo en América Latina* (Bogotá, 1964), pp. 13–14; on CSLA, A. Losovsky, *El movimiento sindical latinoamericano (sus virtudes y sus defectos)* (Montevideo, 1929), which is an official report on the founding congress; and F. Pérez Leirós, *El movimiento sindical de América Latina* (Buenos Aires, 1941), p. 50.

5 Pérez Leirós, *El movimiento sindical de América Latina*, pp. 48, 54–62; Vicente Lombardo Toledano, *La Confederación de Trabajadores de América Latina ha concluido su misión histórica* (Mexico City, 1964), pp. 16–35, 134–137; Poblete Troncoso and Burnett, *Rise of the Latin American Labor Movement*, pp. 137–139; Carroll Hawkins, *Two Democratic Labor Leaders in Conflict* (Lexington, Mass., 1973), p. 9.

6 Levenstein, *Labor Organization in the United States and Mexico*, pp. 168, 178–183, 187; and Serafino Romualdi's rich autobiography, *Presidents and Peons: Recollections of a Labor Ambassador in Latin America* (New York, 1967).

7 See Poblete Troncoso and Burnett, *Rise of the Latin American Labor Movement*, pp. 142–146, which includes ORIT's general program; Hawkins, *Two Democratic Labor Leaders in Conflict*, contains the best summary of ORIT's ideology.

8 Levenstein, *Labor Organization in the United States and Mexico*, pp. 220, 227; Hawkins, *Two Democratic Labor Leaders in Conflict*, pp. 50–52; *Hispanic American Report* 15, no. 1 (March 1962): 82.

9 Size estimates from *AIFLD Report* 10, no. 9 (September 1972): 7; and Hawkins, *Two Democratic Labor Leaders in Conflict*, p. 1. Budget estimates from P. Reiser, *L'Organisation Régionale Interamericaine des Travailleurs (ORIT) de la Confederation Internationale des Syndicats Libres (CISL), 1951–61* (Geneva, 1962), pp. 156–157.

10 Information on these and other activities in Hawkins, *Two Democratic Labor Leaders in Conflict*, pp. 23, 117; *Hispanic American Report* 12, no. 7 (September 1960): 468, 491; ibid., 14, no. 9 (December 1961): 944; and Arnold Zack, *Labor Training in Developing Countries* (New York, 1964), pp. 31–32.

11 John P. Windmuller, *American Labor and the International Labor Movement, 1940–1953* (Ithaca, N.Y., 1954), p. 96; on ITS and the CIA, see David Langley, "The Colonization of the International Trade Union Movement," in *Autocracy and Insurgency in Organized Labor*, Burton H. Hall, ed. (New Brunswick, N.J., 1972), pp. 303–306; for Peru, William J. McIntire, "U.S. Labor Policy," in *U.S. Foreign Policy and Peru*, Daniel A. Sharp, ed. (Austin, Tex., 1972), p. 303; a list of ITS and their U.S. affiliates appears in Carl Gershman, *The Foreign Policy*

of American Labor, published under the auspices of The Center for Strategic and International Studies, The Washington Papers series, 3, no. 29, pp. 79–82.

[12] Quote from *Hispanic American Report* 15, no. 8 (October 1962): 702; P. O'Brien, "AID and Trade Union Development" (unpublished MS), p. 5; and Zack, *Labor Training in Developing Countries,* p. 33.

[13] On U.S. labor in Latin America, see Ronald Radosh, *American Labor and United States Foreign Policy* (New York, 1969), chaps. 11–13, and, on AFL leaders, pp. 438–449, also Langley, "Colonization of the International Trade Union Movement," pp. 297–298; financial figures from George Morris, *CIA and American Labor: The Subversion of the AFL–CIO's Foreign Policy* (New York, 1967), p. 79; and Jeffrey Harrod, *Trade Union Foreign Policy: A Study of British and American Trade Union Activities in Jamaica* (Garden City, N.Y., 1972), p. 125.

[14] On AIFLD's origins, see Sidney Lens, "Labor Lieutenants and the Cold War," in *Autocracy and Insurgency in Organized Labor,* Hall, ed., p. 319; Langley, "Colonization of the International Trade Union Movement," p. 301; and *Hispanic American Report* 13, no. 8 (October 1960): 576.

[15] Quoted in U.S. Senate, Committee on Foreign Relations, Subcommittee on American Republics Affairs, *Survey of the Alliance for Progress, Labor Politics and Program,* 90th Congress, 2d Session, July 15, 1968, pp. 9 and 5. This report details AIFLD's actions and organization.

[16] Langley, "Colonization of the International Trade Union Movement," p. 299, quoting Meany on April 2, 1966, talking to a business group composed of Rockefeller interests.

[17] U.S. Senate, *Survey of the Alliance for Progress,* p. 15; on W. R. Grace, AIFLD, and labor, see North American Congress on Latin America (hereafter NACLA), "Amazing Grace: The W. R. Grace Corporation," *Latin America and Empire Report* 10, no. 3 (March 1976): 12–14.

[18] Funding, in U.S. Senate, *Survey of the Alliance for Progress,* p. 11; AID figures from Michael Locker, "AID for the Domestic Economy," in NACLA, *Latin America and Empire Report* 6, no. 2 (February 1972): 20; CIA support from Jim Mellen, "Leaders for Labor—Made in America," in NACLA, *New Chile* (Berkeley, Calif., 1972): 55.

[19] See Susanne Bodenheimer, "The AFL–CIO in Latin America: The Dominican Republic: A Case Study," *Viet Report* (September–October 1967): 19, and *AIFLD Report* 11, no. 5 (May 1973): 5.

[20] Quote from U.S. Senate, *Survey of the Alliance for Progress,* p. 35. Bodenheimer, "AFL–CIO in Latin America," pp. 17–18, observed a course in the Dominican Republic which included eighteen hours on "democracy and totalitarianism," five hours on collective bargaining, and five hours on industrial problems, but nothing on topics like profit sharing, legislation, or social security.

21 William A. Douglas, "U.S. Labor Policy in Peru—Past and Future," in *U.S. Foreign Policy and Peru*, Sharp, ed., p. 320; and McIntire, "U.S. Labor Policy," p. 304.

22 *AIFLD Report* 8, no. 1 (November 1970): 1; ibid. 11, no. 1 (January 1973): 2–3; AIFLD, *Annual Progress Report, 1962–1975*, pp. 1, 3.

23 *AIFLD Report* 10, no. 1 (January 1972): 3; ibid. 10, no. 3 (March 1972): 5–6; ibid. 10, no. 9 (September 1972): 1; ibid. 11, no. 2 (February 1973): 3, 6; ibid. 11, no. 8 (October 1973): 3; AIFLD, *Annual Progress Report*, p. 1.

24 Douglas, "U.S. Labor Policy in Peru," pp. 320–321, 324.

25 Details on projects in U.S. Senate, *Survey of the Alliance for Progress*; Richard K. Lorden, "The American Institute for Free Labor Development in Action," *Brazilian Business* 48, no. 9 (September 1967): 35; and on housing, especially Susanne Bodenheimer, "U.S. Labor's Conservative Role in Latin America," *The Progressive* 31, no. 1967, p. 27; Mellen, "Leaders for Labor," p. 55; fund data in *AIFLD Report* 11, no. 9 (December 1973): 5; and AIFLD, *Annual Progress Report*, pp. 2–4; on intelligence gathering, see, for example, NACLA, *Argentina in the Hour of the Furnaces* (New York and Berkeley, Calif., 1975), pp. 63–64.

26 *AIFLD Report* 10, no. 1 (January 1972): 1–2.

27 Quoted in U.S. Senate, *Survey of the Alliance for Progress*, p. 14; on Brazil in general, see Kenneth Paul Erickson and Patrick V. Peppe, "Dependent Capitalist Development, U.S. Foreign Policy, and Repression of the Working Class in Chile and Brazil," *Latin American Perspectives* 3, no 1 (Winter 1976): 19–44, esp. pp. 36–41.

28 Joseph A. Page, *The Revolution That Never Was* (New York, 1972), p. 232.

29 Timothy F. Harding, "The Political History of Organized Labor in Brazil" (Ph.D. diss., Hispanic American Studies, Stanford University, 1973), pp. 330, 415–416, 425–436, 505, 565–566, 575, 603; trainee figures from *AIFLD Report* 10, no. 5 (March 1972): 5; McIntire, "U.S. Labor Policy," p. 301.

30 Alan Angell, *Politics and the Labour Movement in Chile* (London, 1972), pp. 265–269; Mellen, "Leaders for Labor," pp. 56–58; NACLA, *Latin America and Empire Report* 8, no. 2 (February 1974): 31–32; O'Brien, "AID and Trade Union Development," pp. 8, 10; Fred Hirsch, *An Analysis of our AFL–CIO Role in Latin America* (San Jose, Calif., 1974), pp. 30–42; Erickson and Peppe, "Dependent Capitalist Development," pp. 30–36, note that West German Social Democratic foundations also gave funds for training programs; on labor and the copper mines, see Francisco Zapata S., "The Chilean Labor Movement and Problems of the Transition to Socialism," *Latin American Perspectives* 3, no. 1 (Winter 1976): 85–97; on the Chilean historical process, see NACLA,

"Chile: Recycling the Capitalist Crisis," *Latin America and Empire Report* 10, no. 9 (November 1976) and "Time of Reckoning: The U.S. and Chile," ibid., 10, no. 10 (December 1976).

[31] Angell, *Politics and the Labour Movement in Chile*, pp. 252–258; O'Brien, "AID and Trade Union Development," pp. 5–6, 16–19.

[32] Susanne Bodenheimer, "AFL–CIO in Latin America," pp. 17–18.

[33] Ibid., p. 18; Susanne Jonas, "Trade Union Imperialism in the Dominican Republic," in NACLA, *Latin America and Empire Report* 9, no. 3 (April 1975): 16–18.

[34] Fred Goff and Michael Locker, "The Violence of Domination: U.S. Power and the Dominican Republic," in *Latin American Radicalism*, Irving L. Horowitz, Josué de Castro, and John Gerassi, eds. (New York, 1969), pp. 267–272; Jonas, "Trade Union Imperialism in the Dominican Republic," pp. 26–27.

[35] Bodenheimer, "AFL–CIO in Latin America," pp. 27–28; Hawkins, *Two Democratic Labor Leaders in Conflict*, pp. 52–53.

[36] Bodenheimer, "AFL–CIO in Latin America," pp. 19, 27. On other housing projects, see Bodenheimer, "U.S. Labor's Conservative Role," p. 27; Mellen, "Leaders for Labor," p. 55; Jonas, "Trade Union Imperialism in the Dominican Republic," p. 20.

[37] Jonas, "Trade Union Imperialism in the Dominican Republic," pp. 20–28. On *braceros*, see Arismendi Díaz Santana, "The Role of Haitian Braceros in Dominican Sugar Production," *Latin American Perspectives* 3, no. 1 (Winter 1976): 120–132.

[38] Romualdi, *Presidents and Peons*, pp. 140–153, 156–158; Samuel L. Baily, *Labor, Nationalism, and Politics in Argentina* (New Brunswick, N.J., 1967), pp. 121–122, 149–152; an anti-Peronist view of ATLAS is John Deiner, "Atlas: A Labor Instrument of Argentine Expansion Under Perón" (Ph.D. diss., Political Science, Rutgers University, 1970).

[39] On post-1955 developments, see Raquel Meléndez and Néstor Monteagudo, *Historia del movimiento obrero* (Buenos Aires, 1971), chaps. 5–6; and Santiago Senén González, *El sindicalismo después de Perón* (Buenos Aires, 1971).

[40] Romualdi, *Presidents and Peons*, pp. 159–167.

[41] On imperialist penetration and class alliances in Argentina, see Juan E. Corradi, "Argentina and Peronism: Fragments of the Puzzle," in *Latin American Perspectives* 1, no. 3 (Fall 1974): 3–20; NACLA, "Imperialism in Argentina," in *Argentina in the Hour of the Furnaces* (New York, 1975), pp. 20–41, and "AIFLD Losing Its Grip," in ibid, p. 66.

[42] Romualdi, *Presidents and Peons*, pp. 169–170; NACLA, "AIFLD Losing Its Grip," p. 68.

[43] NACLA, "AIFLD Losing Its Grip," pp. 65–66, 71–72.

[44] Ibid., pp. 68–70.

45 Brian Murphy, "The Stunted Growth of Campesino Organizations," in Richard N. Adams, *Crucifixion by Power* (Austin, Tex., 1970), p. 457.

46 Background material in Ashton Chase, *A History of Trade Unionism in Guyana, 1900 to 1961* (Georgetown, 1968), pp. 206–216; and Colin V. F. Henfry, "Foreign Influence in Guyana: The Struggle for Independence," in *Patterns of Foreign Influence in the Caribbean*, Emmanual de Kadt, ed. (London, 1972), pp. 55–64. Cheddi Jagan, *The West on Trial* (New York, 1972), pp. 226–234, is his version; on CIA, ITS, and AIFLD involvement, see Sidney Lens, "Labor and the CIA," *The Progressive* 31, no. 4 (April 1969): 26; *New York Times*, Feb. 23, 1967; Henfry, "Foreign Influence in Guyana," pp. 65–72; Morris, *CIA and American Labor*, pp. 89–90.

47 On Ecuador, see "Labor: Coming of Age," in NACLA, *Latin America and Empire Report* 9, no. 8 (November 1975): 20–24; on CIA activities in Ecuador and in all Latin America, see the autobiography of an ex-agent, Philip Agee, *Inside the Company: CIA Diary* (Harmondsworth, Eng., 1974).

48 Quote from Harrod, *Trade Union Foreign Policy*, p. 395; see also ibid., pp. 255–290, 312–320; on aluminum companies, see Philip Reno, "Aluminum Profits and Caribbean People," in *Imperialism and Underdevelopment*, Robert Rhodes, ed. (New York, 1970), pp. 79–88.

49 Morris, *CIA and American Labor*, pp. 81–83; Murphy, "Stunted Growth of Campesino Organizations," pp. 459–460, 478; *AIFLD Report* 12, no. 3 (June 1974): 1; ibid. 12, no. 2 (April 1974): 4, on rural workers; also ibid. 10, no. 1 (January 1972): 5; ibid. 11, no. 7 (April 1973): 1; ibid. 12, no. 1 (February 1974): 1, cites two of seven courses for women at Front Royal; and ibid. 13, no. 2 (March 1975): 3, on Central America. On the Common Market, see NACLA, *Guatemala* (Berkeley, Calif., 1975), pp. 86–103.

50 Hirsch, *Analysis of Our AFL–CIO Role in Latin America*, p. 51.

51 See Timothy F. Harding and Hobart A. Spalding, Jr., "The Struggle Sharpens: Workers, Imperialism, and the State in Latin America, Common Themes and New Directions," *Latin American Perspectives* 3, no. 1 (Winter 1976): 6.

POSTSCRIPT

The case studies discussed in this book validate a number of hypotheses concerning the evolution of organized labor in Latin America. The first suggests that common patterns emerge at roughly the same time throughout the continent. Formative, expansive and explosive, and co-optive–repressive periods emerged everywhere. Although national events and socioeconomic factors conditioned the intensity and duration of each, they share marked similarities. The formative period in the countries of the Platine basin, for example, brought a rise of common ideologies among groups of workers occupying key sectors of the economy. Similarly, the populist variant of the co-optive–repressive period displays comparable features in Argentina and Brazil. The imperialist thrust, too, operates within a common range throughout Latin America, although its impact differs from area to area and within individual countries. Even where national events have accelerated or delayed stages, as they have in Mexico or Bolivia, features pertaining to corresponding stages in other nations manifest themselves.

A second hypothesis is that the crucial variables determining organized labor's historical course are the composition of local ruling classes; the nature, composition, and history of the working class; and the direction of the world economy and foreign policy decisions taken in the developed capitalist world. Of these, the international dimension weighs heaviest. Here, too, local configurations produced varied results even within the same period. Furthermore, each period in the sequence is shaped by the preceding one. Thus, for example, the development in the formative period of a strong, militant labor movement in Argentina conditioned events during the expansive and explosive and the co-optive–

repressive periods. The failure to forge a strong movement in Brazil led to a different pattern there both in the 1920s and during the Vargas and Goulart years. Similarly, the historical experience of Cuban workers favorably influenced the course of the Revolution both before and after 1959.

These hypotheses best explain both the similarities and the differences in the historical patterns found throughout Latin America. They may not, however, serve as well in the future. The present globalization of the world economy may change the lines of tension within world capitalism, particularly within backward areas. Since 1945, local bourgeoisies have steadily lost power to the advancing forces of international capital. They have become further integrated into the world system at the cost of their autonomy, although sometimes to their financial gain. As this process continues, the variable represented by the local ruling class will become less important. This trend, in turn, carries other implications. On one hand, the possibility for cross-class alliances between workers and segments of the bourgeoisie will fade. On the other hand, capitalism's primary contradiction, that between the working class and capital, will emerge in clearer perspective. In other words, as tensions between national and international capitalists lessen, those between labor and capital will grow. As this happens, the working class, both in Latin America and in the rest of the world, may assume a leadership role for social revolution that it has so far failed to play.

The presence of contradictory forces makes any evaluation of organized labor in the 1970s difficult. One can argue that organized labor as a pressure group at the national level is losing and will continue to lose power. That analysis stems from the nature of capitalist development in backward economies. Unlike areas of classical capitalist evolution, the relative number of workers entering the industrial work force over time in Latin America has shrunk. Between 1925 and 1960, for example, manufacturing employed less than one-quarter of the increase in the urban work force, or 5 million out of 23 million people. Correspondingly, the tertiary sector (services) has grown rapidly. These figures mean that the percentage of organized workers in the economically active population (now about 15 percent at most) is declining steadily.[1] And it is unlikely to grow substantially in the near future because the tertiary sectors are notoriously hard to organize.

In the countryside, despite the growth of peasant and rural unions, the vast majority remain outside any official structure. As of 1960, for example, 80 million rural dwellers had no organizational representation. This population is also difficult to mobilize, even though its potential for explosive violence is high, as demonstrated by the massive rural movements that shook Latin America in the 1960s.[2]

Nevertheless, trends pointing to the possibility of increasing militancy, even among the best-paid workers, also exist. Dependent capitalist development creates disparities between workers in the industrial sectors and those outside it. It places increasing pressures on industrial workers, too. Capital- and technology-intensive industries create fewer jobs than labor-intensive industry does. The fact that Latin America produces increasingly for and in competition with the world market makes this type of industry the most desirable investment. The number of new job openings, however, are relatively fewer, and new plants threaten even those already employed with obsolescence. Thus even such simple union demands as job security may, in this context, actually lead to conflict. The long- and short-range economic picture may also spur working-class mobilization. The constant drain of money and resources and the need for local capital accumulation leave little surplus for distribution, even among elite workers. Inflation, constantly present in all Latin American countries, steadily erodes salaries and wages, a phenomenon that workers tend not to accept passively.

The real pressures of job security and constantly threatened material standards, in conjunction with the fact that many unionized workers toil in sectors directly or indirectly influenced by external factors, have resulted in demands for structural reforms, not just ameliorations. In many countries, skilled workers have formulated these demands. Mexican railroad and electrical workers, Argentine auto workers, Brazilian metallurgists, and skilled workers in several Chilean industries have all ranked among the most militant labor elements in their respective countries despite attempts by local governments, in concert with imperialist labor agents and agencies, to repress or co-opt them.

The international factor has many sides. The growing presence of transnational corporations serves to heighten anti-imperialist consciousness among workers. It has also given rise to new international consciousness as the working class realizes that national labor organization is increasingly less adequate to combat the transnationals. But the strategy of these corporations is also changing. Investment now flows increasingly through the state, which functions indirectly as a disburser of credit to the private sector and directly as employer. The apparent neutrality of the state disguises foreign control, but profit still returns to imperialist centers through repayments on loans and monies for royalties on patents, licensing, and management contract fees. Thus nationalism, which has played an important role in mobilizing workers against both the foreign and the local ruling classes, is now used to mask and protect foreign penetration of the economy.[3]

At present, organized labor is on the defensive. Reactionary governments, most of them military, rule the majority of Latin American countries, and they pursue policies that are repressive rather than co-optive. Under these circumstances, it is unlikely that the labor movement will soon become a force for radical social change. Nor can this happen, given socioeconomic conditions, without participation by a broad coalition of forces. As the examples of Bolivia, Cuba, and Argentina clearly indicate, labor acting by itself without a solid alliance with other groups and without national political co-ordination, cannot substantially influence events. Groups of elite workers may improve their situations within national economies when their governments pursue co-optive policies, but these will be only small segments of the working class. The fact remains that for both urban and rural Latin Americans the quality of life deteriorates at a rapid pace. The pressures for change build steadily, but the channels for meaningful change are still being cut.

NOTES

1 See Kenneth Paul Erickson and Patrick V. Peppe, "Dependent Capitalist Development, U.S. Foreign Policy, and Repression of the Working Class in Chile and Brazil," *Latin American Perspectives* 3, no. 1 (Winter 1976): 20–28.

2 On Rural Latin America, among others, see Ernest Feder, *The Rape of the Peasantry* (Garden City, N.Y., 1971); Gerrit Huizer, *The Revolutionary Potential of Peasants in Latin America* (Lexington, Mass., 1972); and Rodolfo Stavenhagen, ed., *Agrarian Problems and Peasant Movements in Latin America* (Garden City, N.Y., 1970).

3 On contemporary trends, see Timothy F. Harding and Hobart A. Spalding, Jr., "The Struggle Sharpens: Workers, Imperialism, and the State in Latin America, Common Themes and New Directions," *Latin American Perspectives* 3, no. 1 (Winter 1976): 6; on the state and investment, see Raúl A. Fernández and José F. Ocampo, "The Andean Pact and State Capitalism in Columbia," *Latin American Perspectives* 2, no. 3 (Fall 1975): 19–36.

INDEX